# FIVE FLOORS UP

ALSO BY BRIAN MCDONALD

*Safe Harbor*

*Indian Summer*

*Last Call at Elaine's*

*My Father's Gun*

# FIVE FLOORS UP

### The Heroic Family Story of
### Four Generations in the FDNY

—⁂—

## Brian McDonald

**GRAND CENTRAL**
**PUBLISHING**

NEW YORK  BOSTON

Grand Central Publishing
Hachette Book Group
1290 Avenue of the Americas, New York, NY 10104
grandcentralpublishing.com
twitter.com/grandcentralpub

First Edition: September 2022

Grand Central Publishing is a division of Hachette Book Group, Inc. The Grand Central Publishing name and logo is a trademark of Hachette Book Group, Inc.

The publisher is not responsible for websites (or their content) that are not owned by the publisher.

The Hachette Speakers Bureau provides a wide range of authors for speaking events. To find out more, go to www.hachettespeakersbureau.com or call (866) 376-6591.

Library of Congress Cataloging-in-Publication Data has been applied for.

ISBNs: 978-1-5387-5320-0 (hardcover), 978-1-5387-5319-4 (ebook)

Printed in the United States of America

LSC-C

Printing 1, 2022

*For firefighters*

# Contents

When you have a department whose men and women are expected to be ready at any moment to put their life on the line, to go to the aid of a stranger even when it means that you might put yourself in harm's way, actually in dire peril, I don't think you could pay people to do that job. There has to be something beyond money that makes them do that.

—*William M. Feehan, chief of the department, FDNY, 1991*

I don't think there's any point in being Irish if you don't know that the world is going to break your heart eventually.

—*Daniel Patrick Moynihan, U.S. senator from New York, November 22, 1963*

*Lord, take me where You want me to go;*
*Let me meet who You want me to meet;*
*Tell me what You want me to say; and*
*Keep me out of Your way.*

—*Father Mychal Judge, FDNY chaplain*

# Prologue

On one level, what lies ahead is the story of the modern New York City Fire Department seen through the eyes of the extended Feehan family. From the birth of the motorized FDNY to today's high-tech department, the pages ahead are a chronicle of fires and the men and women who fight them. They also do their best to reveal the social mores, prejudices, and tribal mentality endemic in the department. The FDNY protects itself like a family. Insulates like one. Laughs and grieves like one. It has black sheep, crazy uncles, wise-ass little brothers, precocious sisters (though still not a lot), and a history with enough heroic members to fill Yankee Stadium. We can observe, report, cry, and laugh along with them, but we cannot know fully the bond that binds them. The intimacy firefighters own is forged in fire. It begins perhaps when a recruit enters the academy or when the "proby" sticker comes off the helmet. It is then they become one of them, and everyone else is not. However, away from the firehouse and bunker gear, this is a story of a family recognizable to all of us. At times, the experiences ahead are genuinely heartbreaking. But these pages are also filled with humor, grudges, and enduring love. Like most families, the Feehans and Davans are not perfect. They have their eccentricities, faults, and demons. But they also possess something that today seems in short supply.

In the months after 9/11, the hierarchy of importance in

America was turned upside down. It wasn't fame or fortune that garnered the most admiration, but the courage of firefighters, cops, and other first responders. COVID-19 has rightfully brought the medical community into that exalted group. For periods all too brief in our country, selflessness and a reflexive desire to help others at any price have received the respect they deserve. Still, long before the spotlight shone on them and long after it went back to illuminating the superfluous, firefighter families such as the Feehans and Davans have lived lives of quiet heroism. This is their story.

# FIVE FLOORS UP

# ONE

# Chief Feehan

At another time, on another evening, the gathering at Tara and Brian Davan's might have been a late-summer barbecue. The evening was warm, and the fading summer's air carried the scent of ocean salt. But there was nothing ordinary about this day.

In the backyard, Billy Feehan cupped his hand over one ear with his cell phone pressed to the other as F-16 fighter jets screamed overhead. He and his family had just arrived from Princeton, New Jersey, where they lived. Three police departments—the Princeton Junction, the New Jersey State Troopers, and the NYPD—had formed a relay team to escort them from the leafy town fifty miles south of New York City to his sister and brother-in-law's house in Belle Harbor, New York. It was mid-span on the Verrazano-Narrows Bridge when Billy had his first glimpse of what was left of the World Trade Center. Even from that distance, the enormity of it shocked him. The thick black smoke seemed to reach a mile into the sky.

John Feehan, Billy's brother, and Brian Davan, both firefighters, had just returned home from the Trade Center site still wearing turnout gear. The cement dust that covered them gave their faces a ghostly white appearance, and their eyes were red from the acrid air, exhaustion, and tears. What they had just seen was beyond their understanding. A six-inch shroud of dust covered the remains of the mighty World Trade Center. Brian likened it to walking on the moon. But what he remembers most is not the deadly dust, the moonscape, or even the twisted steel girders. It is the sound of the firefighters' Scott Air-Pak PASS alarms, hundreds of them, buried under a million tons of cement and steel, that he can still hear in his mind today.

On the phone with Billy was Henry McDonald, his father's executive officer, sort of an aide-de-camp. Henry had been the one to call Billy to tell him that his father, Chief William Feehan, had been killed in the attack. Though Henry had retired from the FDNY a few months earlier, there was no one in the fire department who was closer to his dad. Billy wanted to get into the city to see his father's body. Though Manhattan was essentially sealed to traffic, he knew Henry could make it happen.

The Feehan brothers arrived at Bellevue that night around eleven-thirty. A police lieutenant named Jimmy Marron from the 100th Precinct in Rockaway arranged to get them through the police checkpoints. Marron practically grew up with the Feehan children. His dad had come onto the fire department with Chief Feehan and had remained one of his closest friends. A cop in Bellevue led them through a room the size of a gymnasium. A couple dozen doctors and other medical professionals sat at desks waiting for the injured who would never come. Few in the buildings of the World Trade Center survived the attack. The brothers passed a gurney that held the body of a victim. You couldn't even call what they saw remains. Billy was not a firefighter, like his brother, father, and grandfather. He hadn't served in the Army. But it's doubtful any experience could have prepared him for the sight of a body on which a 110-story building had fallen. He turned away and almost lost his nerve.

*Please, God, don't let him look like that,* he thought.

———

The initial relief that his father's body was whole was supplanted by the finality of the moment. Chief Feehan's face, one that had felt the heat of a thousand fires, was white with the dust from the fallen tower. His hands were cut and raw. Someone had told Billy that his father was helping a woman trapped in the rubble from the south tower collapse when the north came down and killed him. That has never been verified, but what we know for certain, from fire department personnel who survived, is that William Feehan's last moments on earth were spent helping the direct recovery effort for firefighters trapped in the Marriott hotel adjacent to the south tower. At least outwardly, and much like his father in that regard, Billy showed little emotion as he looked down at his dad's body. His mind instead went to the things he needed to take care of—the wake and funeral, the phone calls to be returned. There would be time enough for the tears.

———

The day after the attack was no less surreal. Families and friends had begun posting photos of missing loved ones on walls and streetlamps around Manhattan. Rescue workers and firefighters dug through the pile, as they took to calling it. They would continue to do so for months. Though they knew little of the deadly microscopic dust that would kill over a hundred more firefighters and counting, the pile was an ever-shifting active fire scene. Nine hours after the attack, 7 World Trade Center collapsed due to fire and damage it had suffered when the north tower came down. The forty-seven-story building imploded in downtown Manhattan just after five o'clock in the evening, an event that would have shocked and transfixed the city on a normal day, but now seemed insignificant and anticlimactic.

Billy drove to his father's house in Flushing, Queens. He needed some documents, photos, and other personal effects. When he arrived, a reporter was there waiting for him. The press had already obtained his cell phone number, and several reporters had called. He was polite to them, and even answered some of their questions. But when a New Jersey newspaper journalist wanted to know about the last words he had with his father, Billy told her the interview was over. He knew his dad wouldn't want a family conversation dramatized in the press. He silently shook his head to the reporter and walked into the house.

Inside the home in which he grew up, Billy was flooded with memories, some of them painful. For much of his childhood, his mother had been bedridden with physical and emotional ailments. His father, however, was a rock in his and his siblings' lives, attending soccer games, cooking dinner for the family, always there for his children. And he did this while he rose like a rocket to the uppermost echelon of the department. William Feehan had held every rank in the FDNY, including, for a short period, fire commissioner. He is the only person ever to have done so.

In the silence of the empty house, Billy could hear the scampering of squirrels in the eaves of the roof. In the months after his mother's death, friends and family would worry that his father was lonely living in the house by himself.

"I'm not alone," he would say. "I've got my family of squirrels that live in the attic to keep me company."

Billy collected what he needed from his dad's bedroom. The task felt intrusive to him, like a kid pilfering quarters from the top of his father's bureau. It felt like his dad would walk through the door any moment and catch him.

When he learned of the attack and the towers' collapse, he initially believed his father was okay. William was first deputy commissioner at the time, the second-highest rank in the department. They would want him and the senior chiefs somewhere safe, running the response, Billy thought. That comforting belief, however, began to dissolve when call after call to his father's cell phone went directly to voicemail. When he hung up the last time, he knew his father would've been there, right in the middle of everything. For all of his forty-two years of fire service, Chief Feehan ran into burning buildings, not away from them.

When his task at the house was completed, Billy drove to FDNY headquarters in the MetroTech Center, Brooklyn. His father's office, filled now with Chief Feehan's close circle of friends and subordinates, was, as always, immaculate and orderly. Neatly stacked papers and binders sat on his desk next to photos of his grandchildren, including one with a five-year-old Connor, Brian and Tara's son, taken on the deck of a fireboat in New York Harbor. Behind them in the shot, the twin towers of the Trade Center climbed high into the picture-perfect blue sky.

Perhaps it was while he was in his dad's office, where the shelves that surrounded Billy were filled with his father's life and career, that the unanswerable question returned. He needed to do one more thing before the day was over. He turned to Henry in the office.

"I want to see where my dad died," Billy said.

———

Oddly, what struck him first as they approached the site was the office paper. When the Boeing 767s tore into the towers, the impacts had blown out of the buildings a blizzard of copy paper, forms, and documents. The paper swirled and fell like giant snowflakes blanketing the entire area. The shroud covered Trinity Church at the intersection of Wall Street and Broadway. Built before the Revolutionary War, the church, with its grounds and famous graveyard, where Alexander Hamilton is buried, was cloaked in the stationery vestment. As Billy neared the World Trade Center site, what he saw stunned him. Fire department rigs lay scattered and crushed like toys. In all, the collapse of the towers destroyed ninety-eight fire department apparatus and vehicles. The front of Ladder 3 was shorn off, the ladder itself shredded into tangled tentacles. Because the attack came at the change of shifts, the truck "ran heavy," which, in the nomenclature of the department, meant members from both shifts were on it. The company lost eleven members in the collapse. He could see stacks of flattened cars, one on top of the other, assembled that way by huge forklifts. The site itself smoked and burned like a lava pit. Ironworkers had arrived with blowtorches and grapple trucks, and had begun to cut and move mangled twenty-ton pieces of steel girders. Sometimes when the grappler claw pulled an iron beam out of the pile, the oxygen in the air would cause it to burst into flames. Many of the ironworkers at the site had helped build the towers, including Mohawk Indians from Quebec. Slices of the building a dozen stories high stuck out of the mountain of twisted steel and cement. Practically nothing was left from inside the buildings—no desks, no chairs, no computers, no phones, no filing cabinets. Nothing. They'd all been pulverized in the collapse.

And on top of the pile was a scattered army, all with gaunt expressions and vacant eyes. All searching. Firefighters formed bucket lines, digging in vain, wearing boots that seem to melt from the fire that would burn for ninety-nine days. They had to be on guard. Fire plumes blew up through holes as though from an underground volcano. Billy and Henry spoke with a retired fireman and his firefighter son, a proby, who were among the searchers. Both wore bunker gear. They'd been there for twenty-four hours straight, clawing through the mountain of rubble for the proby's older firefighter brother. "This is Chief Feehan's son," Henry said in a way that justified the interruption of the solemn search. "We're trying to get to where his father died."

"Come on," the old fireman said, waving them through an opening in the chunks of cement.

All of the searches would prove futile. Early on, there had been miracles. Ladder 6 from Chinatown, where Chief Feehan spent most of his time as a lieutenant, was one of the few. The company was headed up stairwell B in the north tower and had reached the twenty-seventh floor when the south building collapsed. Captain Jay Jonas would later say he "pulled the plug" on the operation. As his company started back down the staircase, they came upon a fifty-nine-year-old grandmother named Josephine Harris. She'd worked for the Port Authority and had descended from the seventy-third floor and could barely walk. The six men in the ladder company began to help her down the remaining stairs. It was slow going and got more difficult with each step. By the landing on the fourth floor, she said her legs wouldn't move. Josephine was a large woman, and in the narrow stairway it would have impossible to carry her. The firefighters reminded her of her grandchildren, but not even that could help her move. Then a rumble that sounded like the earth was splitting in half came from above. They held on for dear life as a rush of compressed air came from the floors collapsing above.

Seconds later, 106 floors of cement, glass, and steel fell on top of them. Somehow the tumbling steel wedged into a pocket just big enough to hold them. Josephine, the six firefighters from Ladder 6, and several other firefighters with them had no idea what had happened. It would only be later that they realized that had they not stopped for Josephine none of them would be alive. Only sixteen people survived the collapse of the north and south towers. All of them were in stairwell B of the north one.

———

Though he was not an active member of the fire department at the time of the attack, Henry was a firefighter to the cuffs of his turnout pants. His first company was one-fourteen truck, one of the leftovers from the old Brooklyn Fire Department. He made lieutenant and then captain and was put in charge of Ladder 153 in the Sheepshead Bay section of the borough. Later in his career, he became the FDNY's liaison to the Department of City Planning. Mayor David Dinkins appointed Chief Feehan as interim fire commissioner. Henry joined him in headquarters as his top aide. He would stay by the chief's side for the rest of his career. He, like many other retired firefighters, had responded to the recall, the department-wide order that brought over eight thousand active firefighters to the World Trade Center that day. He was on the pile when they found Chief Feehan— he rode in the ambulance that carried Bill Feehan's and Chief of Department Pete Ganci's bodies to the morgue. Bill and Ganci had been running a temporary command center from a loading dock of the Merrill Lynch building on West Street. Because West Street was impassable, filled with iron girders and chunks of the building, he knew the only way they could get to where the command center stood was by going through the partially collapsed Merrill Lynch building. They came out on West Street, some twenty-five feet south of the loading dock. Billy asked Henry if it would be all right for him to have a moment or two alone.

———

Standing on the spot where terrorists murdered his dad, Billy felt nothing for those who killed him. Homicide is the cause of death listed on his father's death certificate, the first issued to a member of the FDNY killed in the attack. There would be anger, plenty. But not at that moment. Instead, he felt strangely comfortable, as though time had stood still and his father's last breath still hung in the air.

Later, Billy would tell people he could have stayed there all night and the night after. At that moment, alone in this shattered and holy place, he'd found the answer to the question that had burned in his mind. His father had died as he would have wanted, wearing his helmet, gear, and a jacket that bore the initials of an organization to which he had long since given his life: the FDNY.

At some point, as he stood in the wreckage, time began to move forward again for Billy. For the rest of America too. Soon Billy's melancholy was replaced with a hollow ache and the growing awareness that he would never have his dad again.

The family held the funeral the following Saturday at St. Mel's in Flushing, the Feehans' parish. Chief Feehan's was the first of three high-profile FDNY funerals that day. Later, Masses would be said for Pete Ganci and Father Mychal Judge, the beloved fire department chaplain. Mayor Rudolph W. Giuliani had proposed to the Feehan family the idea of having the three funerals together at

St. Patrick's Cathedral. The Feehans declined the offer. They knew their father would not have wanted the pomp and attention.

At first, a relatively small group of firefighters gathered to pay their last respects outside the church. In normal times there would have been a sea of firefighters dressed in Class A blues and white gloves for a line-of-duty death. But those members who weren't working were digging through the smoking pile, searching and still holding on to fading hope. The mayor and Fire Commissioner Tom Von Essen spoke at the Mass, one of hundreds they would attend. The commissioner's aide had forgotten to give Von Essen the eulogy he'd written for Bill Feehan. Twenty years later, he still thinks his extemporaneous words that day were inadequate.

As fire officers in white hats and Class A's carried out Bill's coffin draped with an FDNY red-and-white flag, a single violinist played "Ashokan Farewell." Billy had first heard the musician play the tune a few weeks before in the World Trade Center's concourse. He'd come out of the PATH train and was headed toward his office in the Woolworth Building. The sweet sadness of the song reminded him of his dad. He dropped a few bucks in the open violin case and took the violinist's card. Weeks before the attack on the World Trade Center and his father's death, he'd had no reason to hire a violinist. But now, as the melody accompanied his dad's casket into the bright sunshine, the moment seemed fated.

Outside the church, the crowd had grown into the hundreds. The firefighters didn't wear the Class A dress uniforms, but instead bunker gear that was covered in cement dust from the Trade Center. They had come from the pile to pay their respects to a man most of them knew by reputation only. Chief Feehan was a boss, a big boss, and by rank about as far removed from the firehouse as you could get. But even when he held the lofty post of fire commissioner, he insisted on being called "Chief," an homage to the uniform that bound him to the firefighters who now stood in silence and saluted his coffin.

Though a fire service career like no other ended in that bright sunshine, the heroic story of Chief Feehan's firefighter family would continue for two more generations. Just as it had for a generation before.

# TWO

# The Roaring Twenties

On a cold late February morning in 1926, William Patrick Feehan, Chief Feehan's father, walked two blocks from his apartment in Long Island City, Queens, to the Vernon-Jackson subway station. There he hopped on a subway train that took him under the East River one stop to Grand Central Station. The rest of his commute required a two-block walk from the station to East 40th Street and the firehouse that quartered his new fire company, Engine 21. Door-to-door, the trip couldn't have taken him more than fifteen or twenty minutes. To the captain on duty that morning, however, William might as well have come from Schenectady by horse.

"I don't see any mud," the captain said to his brand-new recruit. "Where's the mud?"

William looked nervously back at the fire officer. "I don't know what you mean," he managed to say.

"You come from the country, don't you?" he said. "I thought you'd have mud on your shoes."

Though the captain might have thought he was a hayseed from Queens, William certainly didn't look like a rookie his first morning on the job. He was thirty-four and a bear of a man with a broken nose from an amateur boxing career and a balding head, a physical characteristic of which he was unabashed. One day, later in his career, when he'd gone completely bald, he popped his head up through the sidewalk grate of a building he was inspecting.

"Look what Kreml did to me!" he said to passersby, poking fun at the popular hair tonic of the day.

Why William had waited until nearly middle age to enter a career that would not only define the rest of his life, but those of three generations of Feehan men who followed, is something of a mystery. A family theory exists that the delay might have had something to do with his relationship with his mother. That he was the youngest of ten in an Irish Catholic family goes a long way in supporting that hypothesis. He stayed single and lived at home into his thirties, for the entirety of his mother's life.

Julia Lawlor, William's mom, didn't have an easy go of it. She was born in County Mayo, Ireland, in 1849, and had grown up in the shadow of the Great Famine when nearly a quarter of the Irish population died of starvation. She was married on July 18, 1872, at Saint Abbans in Doonane parish, to William Feehan the elder, an event that did little to make her life any easier. Soon afterward, she found herself pregnant, a condition she would carry for the better part of the next fourteen years. The firstborn, Elizabeth, came in 1873, John Thomas in 1874, Mary in 1875, Dora in 1877, Julia in 1881, and Ellen in 1882 or 1883. Though records are convoluted at best, according to family stories, she also gave birth to other children who died either in childbirth or infancy.

In early July 1883, the Irish Feehans did what one and a half million of their fellow countrymen did in the last half of the nineteenth century: They headed to America for a better life. Apparently, the oldest son, John Thomas, made the crossing in 1882 and sent for the rest. A year later, William Sr., Julia, and the other four surviving children boarded the steamship *City of Paris* with steerage tickets. The crossing, a miserable journey, took an interminable nine days. On July 9, 1883, they arrived at New York at Castle Garden, now called Battery Park. A forerunner to the more famous Ellis Island, the immigration port rotunda was hot, crowded, and smelled awful. One magazine writer of the day described the odor as stifling, a mixture of rancid cheese, onions, and herring, among other things. Though Castle Garden was also much more lenient that its successor—practically no one was sent back or detained, as they were at Ellis Island—it was filled with sharpies, swindlers, and even an employment agency that worked as a front that whisked young women into jobs with bosses who subjected them to sexual assault and abuse. Whatever the Feehans' image of America was beforehand, by the time they made it through Castle Garden, the veneer had peeled off the dream.

They moved into a small apartment at 128 7th Street in Long Island City, a neighborhood in Queens just across the East River from Manhattan. That address no longer exists on any map. Today, the Hunters Point section of Long Island City is filled with apartment buildings made of glimmering glass and steel, with amenities such as a concierge and Peloton exercise bikes. The neighborhood is coveted by the young and upwardly mobile. However, the main selling point for these apartments is the view of the East Side of Manhattan. The iconic skyline is so close it seems you could swim there—that is, if the tidal current of the East River didn't suck you all the way to New York Harbor. When the Feehans moved there, Long Island City was a self-contained, working-class municipality with enough factories, warehouses, and rail termini to keep the local population employed. William Sr. found work as a janitor. Julia stayed home and took care of the children.

Though a good percentage of Irish immigrants took on menial jobs, they didn't face the same discrimination they had a generation earlier. The Irish who came in the 1840s and 1850s, the ones who encountered "Irish Need Not Apply" signs, were the first who not only assimilated but, thanks to Tammany Hall, the Democratic political machine, rose to positions of power in politics and civil service, especially in the police and fire departments. The first Irish Catholic mayor of New York City, William R. Grace, was elected three years before the Feehans arrived in Queens. Of course, Grace was of the "lace curtain" variety of Irish Catholic, a disparaging term for Irish of means, not one of the huddled hordes like the Feehans. There is no indication that William Sr. explored any avenue that would lead to a civil service career. Instead, he would be a janitor for the rest of his working life.

———

In the winter of 1891, eight years after they'd arrived in New York, Julia found herself pregnant again. By then some of the older children had moved on with their lives, which afforded the family more room in the apartment and perhaps a few more dollars. Julia was forty-three, and though it was not unusual then for women her age to give birth, the pregnancy came ten years after her last one. As mentioned, she lost some children in infancy, and records aren't clear, so maybe the gap was not as pronounced. Regardless, just when she must have thought she was through with teething and diapers, another bundle of joy was on the way. William Patrick arrived on July 29, 1891, the only one of the Feehan children who was American by birth.

Much like the street on which he grew up, William Jr.'s early years are lost to posterity. We do know that he was a tough kid from a roughneck, waterfront neighborhood. For a time in his youth, he wanted to be a boxer. He fought at the amateur level, probably for the local Knights of Columbus boxing club. Though his dream of a boxing career wouldn't come to fruition, long after he'd hung up the gloves he could still punch.

Much later, he would demonstrate his boxing technique to his two teenaged sons. "You give 'em a short chop," he'd say. The instruction would then be followed by a demonstration.

"He didn't realize how much it hurt," son Jim remembered. "He had the strongest hands."

———

At some point in his midtwenties, around 1915, Julia became sick with cancer and William's attentiveness toward her increased. The belief is he was exempted from the draft during World War I to take care of her. On June 5, 1917, he went to the local draft registration office and filled out a draft card. There is, however, no record of William serving in the military. Instead, he took a local job as a shipping clerk and then a mechanic for General Vehicle. What the Ford Motor Company was to Detroit, General, which made electric vehicles, was on a lesser scale to Long Island City. Electric cars made up nearly a quarter of the forty thousand vehicles that crowded the New York City streets at the time. The company employed around two thousand people, a number that would balloon to eight thousand in 1917 when the military fitted the plant to make airplane engines for the war effort.

Whether or not William had set his sights on a career with the car company we don't know. We do know, however, that his employment at General Vehicle would come to an abrupt and unceremonious end sometime after the First World War. Even though he was an auto mechanic for the company, he didn't own a driver's license and wouldn't have known the difference between a gearshift and a coat rack. One day a supervisor, obviously oblivious to his lack of driving credentials, asked him to move one of the company's trucks. William Patrick did what he was told and nearly put the vehicle into nearby Newtown Creek.

———

In his mother's last years, William was the man of the house. His brothers and sisters had all moved on with their lives and records indicate his father lived at a separate address in Woodside, Queens, some distance away. Though the reason for the estrangement of his parents is not completely clear, there are indications that the elder Feehan liked his drink, as the Irish might say. William lived with his mother until she succumbed to cancer in October 1921. When his father died of a stroke four years later, he was thirty-three and without a family or a career of his own. It is here in our story, however, that a higher power would intercede and change William's life forever.

———

Though William was nearly middle-aged when his life path turned toward a fire service career, the organization he was about to enter still held fast to its ribald and colorful adolescence.

Historians point to 1865 as the birth of the modern New York City Fire Department. It was then that reform politicians replaced a patchwork of volunteer departments with a paid force called the Metropolitan Fire Department. Before that, the volunteer fire brigades acted like rival street gangs. Intensely territorial, they would battle each other, sometimes while a building was burning, for access to the limited water sources like hydrants, and the glory that awaited the brigade that put out the fire. In 1850, government officials divided the city into eight districts, each with its own "fire tower" that would alert brigades to a fire by ringing a bell. Only two brigades were supposed to respond to the fire, but the ordinance did little to smother the smoldering animosity between the volunteer departments. One letter to the *New York Times* in 1865 about volunteer departments read in part, "And all classes of the community, except the 'roughs,' are shocked and disgusted by the horrible scenes of disorder attendant on every fire in New York—the shrieking, yelling, hallooing, confusion, absence of all discipline and subordination." However, it was a riot in July 1863 and not a published complaint that sounded the volunteers' death knell.

The Civil War was unpopular in many quarters of New York City, especially among the city's working class, who believed Black men, a portion of whom had escaped the slavery of the South, were trying to take their jobs—they called the war between the states "Lincoln's Nigger War." Many volunteer firefighters, some of whom worked on the docks and as skilled laborers, vehemently opposed the war. The genesis of what would become known as the Draft Riots occurred in March 1863, when the U.S. Congress passed the Conscription Act, the nation's first federal draft. Up until then, because of the service they provided to the community, volunteer firemen in New York City had been exempt from being drafted into military service. The Conscription Act did away with that exemption. The first round of the Civil War draft lottery included several members of the "Black Joke," a name taken from a bawdy Irish tavern song, and an all-white and particularly violent fire brigade. It was then that the simmering anger against the war and Blacks exploded into the bloodiest civil unrest in U.S. history.

According to some historians, the riots began when members of the Black Joke descended on the draft office and set it on fire. Over the next four days, the riots held lower Manhattan in a bloody grip. According to some estimates, over fifty thousand became involved in the fighting. President Lincoln had to send in federal troops to impose martial law. Though the estimates vary, when all was said and done, some estimates said over a thousand people lay dead, including hundreds of Black men, women, and children who were murdered because of their race.

The Draft Riots were the final straw for the Republican-controlled New York state legislature. In 1865, state lawmakers replaced the citizen fire brigade with the Metropolitan Fire Department. Though volunteers made up the bulk of the new department, one of the first orders the department gave them was to forcefully remove from the firehouses those volunteers who didn't become part of the paid force. As you might imagine, these evictions didn't go smoothly, and brawls were commonplace. Though the paid fire department would eventually win out and its arrival would mark the end of the volunteer brigades, a fire in July 1865 proved to be an appropriate epitaph to the most colorful era in New York City's fire service history.

P. T. Barnum's American Museum in lower Manhattan was one of the country's most popular attractions and is still known as perhaps the most bizarre in the history of New York City. Along with animals of every stripe, including two adult whales kept in water tanks, Barnum's museum was home to a host of circus performers, from tiny Tom Thumb to the Gigantress, a woman purported to be eight feet tall and weighing four hundred pounds.

The fire began in a basement office around noon, perhaps from a discarded cigarette, and spread quickly to the upper floors. Two competing fire brigades ran alongside horse-drawn apparatus. It's not too far of a stretch to believe, as they arrived on the scene, that they immediately knew the fire was going to be one of epic notoriety. So of course there was the obligatory brawl for first dibs to fight it. Meanwhile, flames shot from the museum's windows while scores of monkeys who'd escaped the conflagration ran past them and disappeared down the cobblestone streets of old Manhattan, some "never to be seen again," according to one report. The volunteer firefighters were right about the notoriety. Thousands of New Yorkers watched the fire and the antics of the volunteers from the street. According to historians and newspapers of the day, volunteer fire eaters carried wax figures out of the blaze, believing they were human. One of them threw a likeness of Jefferson Davis wearing a dress out of a window. Another firefighter supposedly carried the Gigantress to safety. Miraculously, no one was killed inside the museum. The two adult whales, however, were boiled alive in their tanks.

———

New York City's fire service would be known as the Metropolitan Fire Department for only three years. In 1868, New Yorkers elected John T. Hoffman as governor, the only former New York City mayor to accomplish that feat. Hoffman was a Democrat with ties to Tammany Hall, the crooked and powerful Democratic political machine that represented New York City's immigrants and working class. Perhaps the person most thrilled with the election of Governor Hoffman was the de facto leader of Tammany, William Magear Tweed, incorrectly called William "Marcy" Tweed, but known by all as "Boss Tweed." Colorful and corrupt, Tweed was an ex–volunteer fireman himself and had bristled when the Republican state government took control over a city agency, especially one so near to his heart. With an ally now in the governor's mansion, Tweed had the power to push through a state charter that gave the reins to the fire service back to the city and Tammany Hall. Maybe the most memorable language in the charter, however, was the change of the name of the agency. The Metropolitan Fire Department was supplanted by the appellation Fire Department of the City of New York, which gave birth to the universally known acronym FDNY.

———

Of course, Tammany was responsible for a lot more than the fire organization's famous initials. The very ethnicity and exclusionary nature of the FDNY have their roots in the Democratic machine. With the exception of the Catholic Church, there was perhaps no other institution in New York City that could trace its members' roots back to Ireland with more frequency than the New York City Fire Department. In the late 1880s, 44 percent of the city's population was Irish-born or first-generation Irish American. Some 75 percent of the city's fire department was Irish Catholic. Irish Catholics also dominated the fire and police departments' upper echelons. Thanks to Tammany, at least in civil service, the Irish had climbed the ladder.

Though some Eastern Europeans and other ethnicities managed to crack the ranks, the fire department remained mostly an Irish American entity for most of the twentieth century. It also remained nearly entirely white. A horse groomer named William H. Nicholson became the first African American in the fire department in 1898. Nicholson hadn't planned on being a horse groomer for the department—he thought he was going to put out fires and help save people. When he showed up at Engine Company 6, however, he was told to report to the veterinary unit, where he would remain shoveling out horse stalls for the rest of his career. Sixteen years later, in 1914, John H. Woodson became the second. Woodson's career was marked by many transfers and a spectacular rescue of a woman and her baby from a fiery apartment. Four years after Woodson came Wesley Williams, perhaps the most qualified recruit the department had at the time. He passed both the written and physical parts of the examination with a nearly perfect score. His father, James Williams, was the head Red Cap baggage handler at Grand Central Station. His job allowed him interactions with the rich and famous, including the Rockefellers and Vanderbilts. James Williams became especially friendly with Theodore Roosevelt. The former U.S. president wrote a letter of recommendation to the fire department for his son Wesley. Yet Tammany Hall had Williams on a waitlist for over a year while they hired less qualified white men in the meantime. Finally, on January 10, 1919, Wesley Williams received his appointment letter and was assigned to Engine 55 in the Little Italy section of Manhattan. He would be the first Black firefighter to achieve rank, but well into the 1930s there were still only four Black New York City firemen.

Aside from Wesley Williams's career, one of the most significant events for the fire department in the early part of the twentieth century was the advent of the firemen's union. In 1917, a Brooklyn fireman named Albert Guinness organized the Uniformed Firemen's Association. Under his leadership, the union brought its members' workloads down from an inhumane 151 hours a week to a two-shift system and an 84-hour workweek. Later the union won pay raises for firemen. Guinness and his union's rise in influence wasn't welcomed by everyone. John Hyland, the Tammany-backed mayor of New York City, for one, saw it as an impingement on his power. Out of spite, he had Guinness transferred from Brooklyn to City Island in the Bronx, an excruciating thirty-two-mile commute by bus and subway. To the union membership, however, Guinness remained a hero. When he retired in 1925, the union members presented their founder with a diamond-studded badge. Guinness died at fifty on March 11, 1927. Led by the department pipe band, two thousand firemen marched alongside his coffin driven by a hearse to its final resting place in Greenwood Cemetery in Brooklyn.

———

In Long Island City, the parish church William attended was St. Mary's, one of the oldest and largest Catholic churches in Queens. Mass on Sunday at St. Mary's was crowded with so many parishioners it looked like the casting call for the movie *The Ten Commandments*, only without the sandals. At its zenith, the congregation numbered eight thousand or more. William was devout in his faith, attending Mass every day of the week. Perhaps it was his devotion that caught the eye of a young parishioner with a sweet round face who worked in a local grocery store.

Catherine Cashman grew up not too far from the Feehans on Vernon Avenue in Long Island City. Her father, Maurice, pronounced the Irish way, like Morris, had arrived in New York from County Cork in the 1880s. Like many before him, he traveled to northeastern Pennsylvania looking for work in the coal mines. Very quickly, however, he realized that digging chunks of anthracite coal out of the middle of a mountain was a horrible way to make a living. If you survived the mine collapses, you'd die of black lung. One family story has it that Maurice's brother was injured in a mine and the event was the impetus for his early retirement from his coal mining career. Whatever the reason, Maurice soon found himself back in

New York in Long Island City. There he took a job as a night watchman in a lacquer manufacturer. Maurice might have been a better miner than watchman. One night, the factory he guarded burned to the ground. Though his work life had proved troublesome, he seemed to be lucky in love. Sometime just before the turn of the twentieth century, he met and married the former Nora Sullivan. Nora would give birth to five children, only three of whom, James, Nelly, and Catherine, would survive.

———

Though we don't know a whole lot about the romance between Catherine and William, given the time and place it undoubtedly burned no hotter than a votive candle. If one had more of an influence on the direction of the other's life, it was Catherine on William's. William was seven years older than his girlfriend and owned a much more serious outlook on life. Catherine was known for her sense of humor and a smile that gave the impression that she was keeping something funny to herself. She, through a member of her family, was also integrally instrumental in opening the door to William's lifelong career.

Traditionally, the Roman Catholic Archdiocese of New York has owned an outsized influence with the city's fire department. In William's time, only Tammany itself rivaled the church's sway with the FDNY. Sometimes the church had even more power than the political machine. In her book *Firefight: The Century-Long Battle to Integrate New York's Bravest*, Ginger Adams Otis tells the story of Wesley Williams's promotion to lieutenant, and the problem it posed for the department's bosses, especially Fire Commissioner John J. Dorman. The rank and file of the department had made it clear that they would refuse to be subordinate to a Black man. The brain trust at headquarters came up with what they thought was a perfect solution by creating a new "Black firehouse" in Harlem. It wasn't an original idea. In 1872, the Chicago Fire Department created Engine 21, a Black firehouse, though the Windy City's firehouse was led by a white captain. The FDNY's idea would have Williams in charge of a Harlem firehouse where the few Black firemen then on the job would be transferred. The department would then hire a few more Blacks to fill out the ranks. Problem solved, they thought. Except for one thing: Williams wasn't about to let it happen. "I have had to take orders from a white man, and the white men will have to learn to take orders from a Black man," he said when the department approached him with the idea. With those words, the situation ballooned from a department problem into a political kerfuffle. At the time, New York governor Al Smith, a Tammany man, was gearing up for a run for the presidency of the United States. Tammany bosses went to him to help block William's appointment. For Smith, it seemed like the prudent political move. There were plenty of racist voters to appease. Before he could act, however, William's father dashed off a note to his friend Cardinal Patrick Hayes, the archbishop of New York. As we said, being the head Red Cap at Grand Central Station was a position with proximity to enormous power and in just about every realm. Commissioner Dorman received a phone call from the archbishop soon thereafter, and Lieutenant Wesley Williams was assigned to Engine 55 in Little Italy. Al Smith might have been running for president, but as far as the hierarchy of sway in the FDNY was concerned, an archbishop beat a presidential candidate every time.

———

St. Mary's had its own specific connection to the fire department. One of the priests assigned there was a part-time chaplain for the

FDNY. His name was Father Jim Cashman, Catherine's older brother. Throughout its modern history, the FDNY chaplain's position has been held in the highest of esteem and influence. Maybe the most famous chaplain the New York City Fire Department has known was Father Mychal Judge. Father Judge was beloved in the FDNY. A mostly closeted gay man, he navigated a prevalent homophobia in the department by coming out to those to whom he thought his struggle with sexuality would help. His ministry to AIDS victims during the height of that plague was nothing short of saintly, and in fact there is now a movement under way for his canonization. He was one of the first members of the fire department killed in the 9/11 terrorist attack on the World Trade Center. Reverend James Cashman is not remembered with quite the same saintly glow as Father Judge. Not that Father Cashman was a bad man—he wasn't. Let's just say he was a bit more colorful than your average priest.

If Sunday Mass at St. Mary's rivaled a Cecil B. DeMille epic movie, Father Jim was one of the film's stars, Edward G. Robinson. Like the actor, the priest was both diminutive in stature—only five foot three—and larger than life. He certainly dressed like a movie star. Though priests then were rarely seen in civilian clothing, Father Jim managed to accessorize his priest getup with panache. He built a collection of no fewer than nineteen black overcoats from Rogers, Peet & Co., the tony Fifth Avenue haberdashery. He also owned an array of expensive watches from the swanky Black, Starr & Frost jewelers in Manhattan that would have made a Rockefeller jealous. Presumably the clothing and jewelry were gifts from parishioners, though labeling them as "gifts" might not capture the entire nature of the offering. Priests at the time dispensed favors like union bosses. Most had enough leverage with city agencies to arrange sought-after jobs and promotions. Though perhaps short of a kickback scheme, these quid pro quo transactions kept some priests, like Father Jim, in silk underwear and old scotch. Blood, however, is thicker than both silk and scotch. So when it came to doing a favor for his sister's boyfriend, no such compensation was necessary.

Although New York City is far from unique in this regard, the Big Apple has helped set the standard for the shadow system of arrangements and favors within civil service agencies. Usually these unofficial contracts are made by someone of rank or influence. In the NYPD, cops call such a person a "rabbi." Firefighters call them, somewhat appropriately, a "hook." The only hard-and-fast rule with these secret pacts is that you don't divulge the identity of, or as they say in the department, "give up," your hook. Of course, with retirement and the passage of time—or after a few beers—the grip on the conditions of the bargain begins to loosen. Some hooks, however, take the contracts to their graves. Whether or not the Reverend James Cashman was involved in William's appointment to the fire department is impossible to know for sure. But it is equally impossible to believe that he stood by and did nothing for the man who had asked his sister to marry him. What we do know is that in late February 1926, William reported to Engine 21, and less than a year after that, on February 21, 1927, he married Catherine at a nuptial Mass celebrated by Father Jim at St. Mary's. No doubt with his brother-in-law's help, William went from being an adult orphan to a married man with a career in under a year. It was a career, however, that would worry his wife sick for the next thirty.

———

By the time William joined it, the FDNY had established itself as the finest and best-equipped fire department ever assembled. In

April 1921, an article in the *Brooklyn Eagle* hailed New York City's fire department as being "the most efficient in the world." By then, the superannuated horse-drawn fire wagons had been replaced by seven hundred motorized apparatus (one model of fire engine was "capable of throwing three streams of water over the Woolworth Building," then the tallest skyscraper in the world). The department added ten fireboats, and a telegraph fire alarm system, the first of its kind. For all its innovations, however, the FDNY was also an organization that nurtured a culture of exclusion and narrow-mindedness born in the coarse-grained days of the volunteer fire departments of the 1800s.

––––––

Before he was assigned to Engine 21, probationary fireman Feehan had spent about a month and a half in "Fire college" and "Drill school," as the fire academy was then called. Located on East 67th Street in Manhattan, the academy occupied a space that had been a prison attached to the rear of the old 25th Precinct house. He was given probationary badge number 3995 to wear as a frontal piece on his helmet and instructions to buy a training uniform. The old prison had rows of cells that ringed an open common area. Instructors drilled the recruits indoors. There was enough height inside the structure to raise ladders and simulate ladder rescues, and ample space to practice stretching hose lines and using the nozzle. Along with drills, William studied tenements, frame dwellings, and loft fires. He learned about lighting oil and varnish fires, a central problem of the day. There were classes in marine and boat fires. Twenty years earlier, a paddleboat called the *General Slocum* had caught fire on the East River, killing over a thousand people from a German church group out on a pleasure cruise. Though the equipment was antiquated by today's standards, the basics of fighting city fires was mostly the same as it is now. Still, there was one element of fighting fire that no amount of training could teach a proby. As it happened, William came onto the job with plenty of it. He had the courage of a lion.

It was lucky he did, because the business he was about to enter was as dangerous as any. The first line-of-duty death in the paid New York City Fire Department came a little over a month after the P. T. Barnum Museum fire. On August 24, 1865, Robert Wintringham died of injuries he'd suffered ten days earlier. According to fire department data, he was thrown from his rig and run over by the fire wagon. Two hundred and seventy-five more firemen would die by the time William joined the department. Fourteen would perish during his first full year on the job. His was a dangerous profession.

Civilians often wonder what propels firefighters into burning buildings. What possesses someone to run up the stairs of a 110-story tower that a hijacked jet airliner has just crashed into while everyone else is running down for their lives. Although there is no definitive way of verifying this, there is something inherent in firefighters whose instinct for helping others comes with little regard for their own safety. The percentage of firefighters who possess this quality is also not quantifiable. Our guess is that more have it than don't. But there is a smaller segment of firefighters who always seem to find themselves in the most perilous situations. In department parlance, it's called "chasing fire." For these firefighters, the fight is personal. Very early in William's career, it became evident that he was one such fireman. In the coming years, he would go face-to-face with the red devil often. And on several occasions, it would be the devil who'd win the fight.

# THREE

# Taking Its Toll

Though it might have taken a while for him to find his true calling, once he did, William's job consumed him. For most of his early career, he insisted on taking the nozzle. At the point of attack, the nozzleman, along with positions above the fire, is the most dangerous of all firefighting roles. A large part of the area that Engine 21 covered was the slums of the East Side of Manhattan. Today the section is filled with high-rise buildings with apartments that cost millions. In William's time, though, it contained row after row of five- and six-story tenement buildings crowded with the city's poor. The old adage goes, where there's poverty there's fire. The saying was correct in William's time, and it's true today. On January 9, 2022, a malfunctioning space heater sparked a fire in a Bronx housing project that killed seventeen people. Though working-class, many of the residents in the building needed federal rental assistance to survive. Safety doors and sprinklers in the building failed, sealing the victims' fate.

When Fireman Feehan joined the East Side engine company almost all of the fire action in Manhattan occurred within the blocks covered by his firehouse. Tenement buildings, since they began lining the streets of the poorer sections of New York City in the nineteenth century, have produced some of the most challenging fires to fight. Narrow hallways, confined stairwells, lots of occupants, long and crooked distances to stretch hoses, and flimsy wooden construction all combine to make the multifamily dwellings potential death traps. In 1905, a tenement fire on the Lower East Side killed nineteen people and injured twenty more. The landlord had locked the door leading to the roof to keep tenants from going up there. Tenants blocked apartment windows leading to fire escapes to keep burglars out, or used the fire escape landings as storage spaces. The bodies of most killed in the blaze were found huddled in front of those useless exits. In tenement buildings, engine companies often have to navigate several rooms to get to the fire seat. In heavy smoke and intense heat, it can be a nightmare. Although the 1905 fire brought attention to fire safety in tenements, and regulations began to be implemented, by the time William joined the fire department the only real change in the buildings was that they were twenty years older.

In December 1928, the fire department promoted William to first grade fireman, a rank he would hold for the rest of his thirty-year career in the FDNY. This was not from a lack of ambition. William loved facing a raging fire with a nozzle in his hands and saw no reason to do anything else. His mindset was not all that unusual in the FDNY. There were and are many firefighters who wouldn't think of trading an active firefighting role for a promotion that would take them away from fighting fires.

For Catherine, however, her husband's dedication to his perilous job was a constant source of consternation. They'd moved into a small apartment at 146 11th Street in Long Island City, not too far from where both had grown up. Six days a week, William worked fourteen-hour shifts. He'd drag himself home reeking from the stench of smoke and with stories of narrow escapes and harrowing fires. When Catherine became pregnant in early 1929, her worries only increased.

More than once throughout his career, fireman Feehan's love of his job would directly conflict with his wife's wishes. By all accounts, the relationship he had with Catherine was much the same as he had with his mother: He was devoted to her. William was not a self-ish man. The last thing he wanted was for his wife to suffer. And yet when it came to a choice between his Catherine and the fire depart-ment, the fire department always seemed to win. There were times, however, when he was able to satisfy her demands while holding on to what he wanted. The first of these creative maneuvers came in April 1929.

At the time, the FDNY was in the process of opening sixteen new firehouses in Queens to accommodate a population spreading out from the city center. One of the new structures was in Asto-ria, a neighborhood growing with new apartment buildings and businesses that included a movie studio later called Paramount. Chances are, William's transfer to Astoria was an organizational decision—the firehouse needed the manpower. When her husband brought home the news that the department was sending him to a docile, suburban setting bordering Long Island City, Catherine was thrilled. Not only would William be safer, but he'd be closer to home. William, it seems, went along with the transfer without argument. After all, his wife was pregnant with their first child, and according to family stories, Catherine was not having an easy preg-nancy. William wanted to support her in any way he could. He had no intention, however, of staying in the Astoria firehouse for long.

On September 29, 1929, Catherine gave birth to a healthy baby named William Michael Feehan. Two weeks later, much to Cath-erine's consternation, her husband transferred back to twenty-one engine and the cauldron of the East Side. How he managed the quick turn of events is not clear. By then he had begun to form an impressive reputation as an active fire eater. Perhaps some sympathetic fire chief saw William's courage being wasted rescuing cats from trees in Queens and brought him back where his talent could be put to use. Though William was able to outmaneuver his wife's wishes to get back to the firehouse he loved, Catherine wouldn't give up in trying to steer her husband's career to safety. She had good reason to worry about him.

———

After the stock market crashed in 1929, sending the United States spiraling into the Great Depression, fires on the East Side of Manhattan increased dramatically. One cause of the fires was alcohol stills that people built in their apartments. As "bathtub gin" increased in popularity, so did the number of contraptions that implemented an open flame. The city put together a task force of tenement inspectors, at least 250 men responsible for Manhattan's apartment buildings. However, the force had a limited effect on illegal operations, as many offenders received suspended sentences or fines of just two dollars, about thirty dollars today. Fires in tenements had been prevalent enough without what was tantamount to a lit fuse burning in them. By one count, in 1927 there were twenty-five hundred stills operating in Brooklyn alone, and that was before the Depression. Most of the bootleg booze apparatus was for personal use, but moneymaking operations proliferated. Explosions in apartments became so commonplace that cops wouldn't even write them up in reports. For William, who never touched a drop of alcohol in his life, fighting fires caused by stills not only brought more danger to his job but was the height of irony.

It wasn't a still fire, or even one in a tenement, however, that would nearly take William's life for the first time. That would happen in a brownstone on a fashionable block off Fifth Avenue.

The morning of October 27, 1931, was quiet in William's firehouse. The guys drank coffee and talked about the stories in the newspapers. A few days before, a judge had sentenced Al Capone to eleven years for tax evasion. Sportswriters wrote about Babe Ruth asking Jacob Ruppert, the Yankees' owner, to renew his eighty grand per annum salary. One newspaperman reportedly asked Ruth to comment on his salary being more than President Herbert Hoover's. "I had a better year than him," Ruth quipped. The New York State governor, Franklin Roosevelt, attended the opening ceremony of the newly finished George Washington Bridge. By then, William was a battle-hardened fire eater. Four-plus years in a busy engine company will do that to you. The nozzleman position is usually one that rotated among members of the fire company. William, however, was so fearless at the job that it was hard to ask him to give it up. He'd be on the nozzle the first time a fire almost killed him.

Often compared with London's Bond Street, West 46th Street between Fifth and Sixth Avenues was lined with upscale clothing shops housed in old town houses and lofts. It was early morning when the alarm came in. Had the fire started even an hour later, the streets would have been a snarled mess of cars, trucks, and double-decker buses, but with little traffic at that hour, the engine truck reached the burning town house in a matter of minutes. The blaze, however, moved faster than they did. By the time Engine 21 turned onto West 46th, fire had consumed the top floors of the structure.

William jumped from the rig and helped run a hose line into the building and up the stairs. He wore a rubber trench coat, a wool coat underneath, heavy cloth pants, and cut-off rubber boots. Though the outfit might have been appropriate for a February sleetstorm, it did little to protect a fireman from a blaze. Nozzlemen often walk on their haunches to stay under the smoke, which leaves the upper thighs and groin area especially susceptible to burns. The outfit William wore also made a nearly unbearably hot job even hotter. Deep red fire burns at over a thousand degrees. White flames can reach temperatures of two thousand degrees or more. Underneath his rubber coat, William was soaked in sweat. His wool coat was as heavy as cement. As he moved, smoke as thick as tar hung just overhead. He didn't wear gloves. Few firemen then did. The retired fire chief and author Vince Dunn tells the story of being instructed to buy his own pair of gloves when he graduated from proby school in 1957. "Look at this guy with gloves!" Dunn remembers a fireman yelling, as if he'd shown up at the firehouse wearing a mink coat. He also remembers not getting to use the gloves very much, as they had a habit of ending up in other firemen's lockers.

If William used any type of breathing apparatus at all, it would have been rudimentary. It was only after World War II that the Scott Air-Pak, used by fighter pilots at high altitudes, became part of the firefighters' equipment in the FDNY. Even into the 1950s, however, many firefighters refused to use them because they thought they were cumbersome. The superheated atmosphere singed William's nasal passages. The fire devoured the oxygen in the room, leaving him little breathable air. Unconsciousness came without warning. The big firefighter's blood oxygen level dropped dangerously low. Respiratory failure and cardiac arrest are the most common causes of firefighters' demise. William was within a breath of becoming part of those statistics.

William's fellow firemen pulled the nozzle from his hands and dragged him out of the burning room. They summoned an FDNY physician named Harry M. Archer. Dr. Archer was either nearby or on his way to the fire, because he arrived quickly. Out on the sidewalk, he worked for over an hour to keep William alive, using two tanks of oxygen attached to an early resuscitator called a pulmotor. Still, the burly fireman barely clung to life. A regular resting heart rate is between 60 and 100 beats a minute. William's had fallen to 20. Firemen ran to the rectory attached to St. Patrick's Cathedral, just a few blocks away. They returned with a priest who gave William the sacrament of Last Rites. As the back doors of the ambulance closed and he was transported to the Polyclinic Hospital on West 50th Street, his company pals were sure it would be the last time they'd see him alive. A news article about the fire stated that "little hope is held for [William's] recovery."

But William would survive, perhaps miraculously. The family story goes that the nurse tried to take off his scapular medal, colloquially known as Catholic dog tags, and William nearly jumped out of the hospital bed to stop her. There's no way of telling whether or not his faith in God saved him from an early worldly exit. We do know that his near-death experience did little to dissuade him from running into burning buildings. In a five-alarm blaze a few months later, William inhaled sulfur fumes and found himself in the hospital again. Two years after that experience, he was buried in a building that collapsed during a fire and ended up in the hospital again. Each time he lay in a hospital bed, Catherine would come to see him and make him promise he would not put himself in danger again. Each time, William would nod to ease her worry, all the while knowing that the next time the opportunity came, he would grab the nozzle again.

Not every fire run he took was death-defying for William. In fact, the stories of his antics and hijinks could fill a binder and have been told so many times since in the Feehan family that they're rounded at the edges.

After a spate of deadly and spectacular theater fires across the country, mostly caused by the gas lamps of the day, New York City enacted regulations that required a uniformed fireman to be posted at all theater performances. Before the show, the fireman would check the fire alarm, the self-closing fire doors installed in all theaters, the proscenium arches, and the nonflammable curtains put in place due to earlier fires. During the performance, firemen made sure the aisles were clear and the fire exits accessible.

For a busy fireman, theater duty was a chance to take a breather and see a show. One night in the early 1930s, William volunteered to do fire duty at a theater featuring an up-and-coming singer named Ella Fitzgerald. Noting her name, he told his pals in the firehouse that he was in the mood to hear some good Irish music. On another evening, the detail put him in an uptown opera house. The performance that night was by an Italian composer and set during the days of the Roman Empire. Just before the performance, several of the extras on the show called in sick with the flu. The director found himself in a real bind. When William arrived for work, he saw his way out of it.

The local firehouse captain would do rounds each night to check on the firemen who were on theater duty. On this particular evening, the captain happened to be accompanied by his boss, a deputy chief. When they arrived at the opera house, William was nowhere to be found. They looked near the exits, in the lobby, even in the wings. As the search continued, the deputy chief became more and more aggravated.

"Where the hell is he?" the chief demanded of the captain.

"He must be here somewhere," the captain answered. "Feehan's a good man."

It was at that point that the captain's eyes fell on the performance. "There he is!" he exclaimed.

"Where?"

"The third Roman soldier from the left," he said, pointing at the back of the stage. "The one with the spear!"

The friendships William made in Engine 21 would last his entire life. There was Mike Imhoff. Five foot five on his tiptoes, Mike was built like a fireplug but was as nimble as a dancer. And then there was Eddie Keeley, a chauffeur on the rigs who would drive the engine in bare feet because he had a better feel for the clutch and brake pedal that way, he said. Rough and tough like William, Keeley worked the docks as his second job. One day, after he'd retired, William sent his son Bill to the waterfront to deliver Eddie a message. Bill was then a college student and dressed, as male students of that day often did, in a suit and tie. When he asked a dockworker if he could speak to Eddie, the man looked him over suspiciously. At the time, television networks were broadcasting the Kefauver Committee hearings on organized crime. The Senate investigation had partly to do with the Mafia's control of the docks in New York. Thinking young Bill might be a federal agent, the man gave him the runaround. Only when young Feehan said that his father knew Eddie from the fire department did the man relax his guard.

Catherine, too, had plenty of friends, all of them from the neighborhood in which she grew up. There were the Brady sisters, Lol and Nel, and a girl named Mamie O'Rourke, just like the one from the song "The Sidewalks of New York." Still, caring for the baby, she spent many hours alone at night while William was working. At least outwardly, Catherine wasn't emotionally frail—she was a city kid from a tough neighborhood. But she had to have had moments at night where frightening scenarios played in her thoughts—all firefighter spouses experience the feeling. And although she didn't have the close camaraderie of the firehouse that her husband enjoyed, she did have one person in her life on whom she could always rely, her sister. And much to William's dismay, that relationship was going to become a united front against him.

———

For many in New York City during the Great Depression life was miserable. Shantytowns called "Hoovervilles," named after the unpopular president, swelled in Riverside and Central Parks. Many of the homeless who lived in Hooverville had worked in the trades. Masons built sturdy homes of brick and cement in the parks, while the unskilled in labor lived in slapdash structures made of tin sheets and plywood. Unemployment in Harlem reached 50 percent. Food lines and violent demonstrations were commonplace. For the most part, however, William's civil service job, and his yearly salary of $3,000, kept the Feehans immune from the financial rapaciousness of the Depression. But the poverty of the time brought even more overcrowding, squalor, crime, and fire to the response area of Engine 21. In 1935, a Broadway play by Stanley Kingsley called *Dead End* drew the world's attention to the street urchins who roamed the blocks under the Queensboro Bridge. Mayor Fiorello H. La Guardia steered New Deal federal money into slum clearance efforts on the East Side. Families living in the tenements were relocated to housing projects on the Lower East Side, the Bronx, and elsewhere. The plan brought needed work to carpenters, electricians, and roofers. One of those projects would eventually become one of the most exclusive stretches of real estate in the world— Sutton Place. The neighborhood once ruled by the junior toughs portrayed by Huntz Hall and Leo Gorcey onstage would become home to the likes of the Pierpont Morgans and the Vanderbilts. It would also be the scene of one of the most spectacular blazes Engine 21 fought.

In the middle of the afternoon on April 4, 1935, a roofer kicked over a flaming tar kettle on the roof of 505 East 55th Street. The blaze caught quickly and began to consume the building and spread to adjoining structures, one of which sat on the East River's bank. Engine 8 from nearby 51st Street was the first fire company to arrive. By the time Engine 21 and William got there, the fire was winning the battle. Thick black smoke poured from the structure, and flames licked upward from the blown-out windows. As William entered the building, the structure's support walls began to give way and the wall facing the street buckled. Bricks rained down on him and his mates. The ensuing collapse partially buried Engine 8's rig and most of William's company.

There is no official departmental record of the event. For many years, the FDNY's record-keeping system was limited to journals kept by captains in individual firehouses. Even when a uniformed member of the department died in a blaze, the fire department did little post-fire analysis. Other than the captain's journals, firemen relied on oral accounts usually shared at mealtimes. As you might imagine, details would shift, be misconstrued or exaggerated. Only in 1998, when Congress funded a study to investigate firefighter deaths, did official written records supplant the oral history tradition. Newspaper reports, however, tell us that the collapse of the building on 55th Street was so catastrophic that it pushed most of the adjoining building into the East River below. The fire reduced the other structure to a hollowed-out shell. There aren't records of William being hospitalized, but it's hard to imagine he wasn't injured when the wall fell on him. The department would honor him for his actions later that year by placing him on the Roll of Merit, a list of firemen who had performed above the call of duty. On Valentine's Day 1936, William was injured again, this time in a fire at Hunter College on the East Side. An iron radiator fell through the ceiling and fractured his skull. For Catherine, it was the last straw.

William had remained a devout Catholic, and would light a candle in church on his way to every shift. But even with faith as deep as his, with the close calls in the fires of West 46th and East 55th Streets, it seems he had started to wonder if he was cheating death. In the kitchen of the apartment he set up a shrine with votive candles where he would pray for an hour after dinner. He had a three-foot tall wooden statue of Our Lady with a kneeler in the bedroom. He carried a missal the size of a thumb that his parents had brought from Ireland. In the late 1600s, English invaders banned the Catholic religion and hunted and brutally murdered priests. Worshippers printed the tiny missals so that they could be easily hidden. Much later, William would give his to his granddaughter Elizabeth. And he still received Communion most days.

Catherine, too, would rely on the church in the hope of keeping her husband safe. But she also took more temporal steps in pursuit of William's well-being. Without her husband's knowledge, she went to her brother the priest and asked if he would use his influence to get William transferred to a quieter firehouse, preferably nearby in Queens.

We don't know if William protested the machinations of his wife and priestly brother-in-law, but if he did, he didn't put up much of a fight. Son Jim can't remember one time when his father raised his voice to his mother. Though he wasn't demonstrative in his objection, that didn't mean he hadn't a say in the matter. He'd handle it his own way. He wasn't about to let them ship him to a camp.

At the time of the proposed transfer, William had accrued enough seniority that he could've worked his own connections to derail it. He knew, however, that to do so would cause an uproar on the home front. He needed to find a middle ground to appease both his wife and his need for fire action. Once again, he found a way to fulfill her wishes and do what he wanted. Catherine wanted William to work in Queens, and he promised her that he would. She didn't, however, specify where in Queens she wanted him to work. It was through this loophole that William stepped into the most active part of his firefighting career.

In 1936, the fire department had instituted a three-tour system. This change in the chart created openings in companies across the city, including ones in specialty units called rescue trucks. The FDNY initiated the units around 1912 when several fires presented obstacles for which regular companies were not prepared. One of those incidents occurred in the early morning hours of January 9, 1912. At a soaring nine stories, the Equitable Life Building, as it was known, on lower Broadway was considered the first skyscraper in New York City. The blaze had started in the Café Savarin on the bottom floor of the tower and spread up the elevator shaft to all parts of the building. From its onset, the fire had firemen at a distinct disadvantage. Icy, gale-force winds with gusts that measured 65 miles an hour injected oxygen into the fire as though from giant bellows. By eight o'clock that morning, the entire building was sheathed in flame. Black smoke filled the narrow downtown streets. Water from the hoses instantly froze on the building, and then melted from the flames. According to newspaper accounts, firemen performed heroically, entering the burning building several times to carry semiconscious victims to safety. By hacksawing through heavy steel bars, they also rescued a man who had locked himself in a bank vault in the basement, but others died in the vault. Several firemen, who had somehow made their way to the roof, rappelled down the side of the structure to attempt a rescue of three men clinging to an outside ledge as orange flames shot from the window behind them. The firemen would not reach them in time, however, as the ledge gave way and the three fell to their deaths. Firemen battled the conflagration for nearly four hours before they had it somewhat under control. In all, six people would perish in the fire, including an FDNY battalion chief.

The Equitable Building fire, and a series of subway and subway tunnel fires, added to the need of a unit that would specialize in difficult rescue situations, especially for the rescue of other firefighters. Robert Adamson, the fire commissioner at the time, called for firemen who were also top-notch electricians, mechanics, and welders who could use their skills in complicated rescue operations in factories, trains, and other mechanical settings. On March 8, 1915, Rescue 1 went into operation. Quartered on Great Jones Street in downtown Manhattan, they fitted a Cadillac touring car with a welder's torch and a line-throwing device called a Lyle gun. They had jacks and Z bars that could lift up to thirty-two tons for subway car rescues. They even carried Draeger masks, a self-contained breathing apparatus that looked like an early diving helmet. There's a photo of William wearing one that makes him look like a character out of a Jules Verne novel. They had first aid for burns and oxygen for smoke inhalation victims. For the casual onlooker at the time, the rescue vehicle must have been like something out of a Batman comic book. It was also an immediate success. Less than a year after the unit was instituted, Rescue 1 firemen sawed through steel bars with a German-made Blau-gas torch to save a trapped and unconscious fire captain. The unit worked out so well that the department formed a second rescue truck in Brooklyn on March 1, 1925. Rescue 3 in the Bronx and Rescue 4 in Queens followed on June 1, 1931. Staten Island would get its own rescue truck in 1948.

———

On October 2, 1938, the fire department transferred William to Queens Rescue 4, the busiest company in the entire borough. The men assigned to the unit were some of the best and bravest firemen the department had to offer. Instead of retrieving cats from the leafy trees in suburbia, as Catherine might have hoped, William was racing to the most daring, dangerous, and emotionally draining emergencies. One of the more brutal calls concerned a neighbor's daughter who had been fatally hit by a train after falling onto the subway tracks. On another run, a pump at a gas station exploded, practically incinerating an attendant. Rescue trucks at the time carried nasal catheters that administered oxygen to victims with badly burned faces. Jim remembered his father saying he'd wished someone had shot the poor man to put him out of his misery.

Though William was a brave man, putting his job and need of action ahead of his wife's emotional well-being was unquestionably self-serving. He wasn't unique; firefighters have been selfish in this way for about as long as there's been smoke. They'll tell you that someone has to put out the fires, a statement that is hard to argue with. A spouse or family member might counter with: Well, why does it have to be you? It is between those two mindsets that the friction in firefighters' families exists. In William's time, however, given the diminished power of women then, Catherine had no voice in the matter. Yes, she could try to maneuver behind his back. But in the end, William always did what he wanted when it came to his fire service. Though Catherine lost battle after battle to her husband's love of the fire department, a move out of Long Island City would soothe the sting.

———

Nelly, Catherine's older sister, was never married and lived with her parents. Sometime in the early 1930, she moved with them to a neighborhood called Jackson Heights in Queens. Then, in 1933, her mother, Nora, died, followed by Maurice six months later. Nelly found herself in a two-family home all by herself. Soon after Maurice died, Catherine became pregnant again. During her first pregnancy, Nelly had been just a short walk away and always willing to lend her sister a hand. And although Jackson Heights wasn't across the country, psychologically at least for Catherine, her sister now seemed more than just a subway ride away.

In the spring of 1935, Catherine gave birth to James, named after his priest uncle. The apartment in Long Island City wasn't big enough for the new addition to the family. When Nelly suggested to her sister that she and William move in with her, Catherine thought the idea was the answer to her prayers. William, however, wasn't quite as enthusiastic. He was wary of the close relationship his wife had with his sister-in-law. He began calling them "the Dolly Sisters," after an identical-twin vaudeville act. He began to envision them teaming up on him about his job, the risks he took, and the hours he worked. Nelly especially would needle William, but always behind his back. One time, much later on, Catherine's granddaughter was taking about a boy in school she was interested in but didn't think was very attractive. "Well, looks aren't everything," Nelly said. "Take your grandfather, for instance." But though William was at first reluctant to go, in time began to see that the upside of the move out of Long Island City.

As with other parts of the outer boroughs of New York City, the neighborhood of Jackson Heights experienced a housing boom in the Roaring Twenties. Just two decades earlier, the mayor of New York City, William J. Gaynor, had called the section "the cornfields of Queens." With the extension of the subway and the Queensboro Bridge opening, however, the area became prime property for investors. One of the first to see the real estate potential of the area was a man named Edward A. MacDougall. Today, Jackson Heights is the most culturally diverse community in the United States. Within its confines, some 170 languages are spoken. The community MacDougall imagined and went about developing, however, wasn't nearly as diverse. In fact, according to researchers, MacDougall built houses and apartments specifically for white, non-immigrant Protestants of a certain means. One of the apartment buildings he built, called "The Towers," featured seven-bedroom flats as expensive as any in Manhattan. MacDougall's project was an immediate success, and Jackson Heights as a whole became a bustling hub of middle- and upper-middle-class commuters.

———

On a fireman's salary of $3,000 a year, there was little chance William could afford to buy a house on his own in Jackson Heights. But Nelly, whom they now called Nennie because baby Jim couldn't pronounce "Nelly," could. In 1939, she put a thousand dollars down on a three-story brick and shingle home a few blocks from the two-family in which they'd lived. Though we don't know what sort of financial arrangement existed between William and his sister-in-law, what we do know is that when Nennie moved into her new house, he and Catherine moved along with her.

The house, part of MacDougall's vision, was massive and sat on a street as wide as a boulevard and lined with soaring maples and oaks. It was the perfect place to raise a family. It certainly was a step up for the Feehans.

Some of their neighbors included the Slatterys from Slattery Construction, who lived down the block. Slattery Construction built the tunnels under the East River, and later would help construct the United Nations headquarters, the Lincoln Center for the Performing Arts, and the World Trade Center. A doctor lived across the street who was also Father Jim's best friend. Jim Feehan remembers a dentist on the block giving him money to teach his son to play stickball. Jim took the cash and told the kid to sit on the curb and watch. Even the public school custodian who lived in the house next door seemed to have an endless supply of disposable cash. If you're wondering how a custodian could afford a big house in an upper-middle-class neighborhood, you must not have read the New York tabloids for most of the last half of the twentieth century. Stories about kickback schemes that proliferated due to lack of oversight of public school custodians ran about as frequently as advertisements of sales at Macy's. "He made more than the mayor," Jim Feehan said of the janitor.

Another family in the neighborhood was particularly standoffish, or at least the Feehans believed they were. It turned out they were more secretive than aloof. The man of the house's income was even more mysterious than the custodian's. Once, when he was gone for a considerable time, his wife explained her husband's absence as an extended business trip. The extended business trip, however, was actually a stretch in an upstate jail. Jim remembered that the couple later had a row in the street in front of their home, complete with flying pots and pans. They moved from the neighborhood soon after.

Catherine, William, and the children took the spacious and luxurious first two floors of the house. The first floor was cavernous. Jim Feehan remembers playing catch with his brother Bill in the living room. Though Nennie was the house's legal owner, the king of the castle was her roommate and brother.

Nennie and Father Jim shared the top floor of the house, which had been remodeled into a one-bedroom apartment that included a dining room, living room, kitchen, and bath. "Shared," however, is a generous description of Nennie's living arrangement. Father Jim was as demanding as he was pompous. When the church transferred him to a parish in the Hamptons on Long Island, he became a part-time lodger in the house in Jackson Heights. Yet the bedroom waited empty and tidy for his arrival. Nennie was relegated to a daybed in the living room. Father Jim had a buzzer system installed to summon Nennie when she was downstairs. Watching her run up and down the stairs so many times, William began to wonder what would wear out first, the buzzer or Nennie. And most of those trips were for things like making a cup of tea or ironing his trousers, simple tasks that he'd have no trouble doing himself.

The priest drove an old Plymouth that looked like it was once owned by Bonnie and Clyde. At five-three, he could barely see over the steering wheel and never learned how to parallel park, a necessity in New York City. He would drive in from the Hamptons in those days on two-lane highways and winding roads, a journey that would take him four or five hours. Before he left, he would call Nennie and give her his approximate time of arrival. As the prescribed time drew near, she would dutifully put on her coat and stand in the street in front of the house, keeping a parking space open on the corner for him so he could pull straight in.

For the most part, modern American women have obtained a

considerable amount of independence, so it might be difficult from a contemporary perspective to understand why Nennie would allow herself to be treated so poorly. But well into the twentieth century, the expectation for many Irish Catholic daughters was one of self-sacrifice and subservience to the men in their families. The Blessed Virgin Mary, and her devotion to her son, was the ultimate role model for them. Though we don't know for sure if there were specific pursuits Nennie abandoned to serve her brother the priest, it certainly seems he gave little or no consideration to her needs. Nennie was never able to break free from the bonds he placed on her.

———

Though not thrilled to have a sister-in-law and brother-in-law living with him, William had no problem with the accommodations. The house in Jackson Heights was a castle compared to the tiny apartments in which he had lived most of his life in Long Island City. In time, he even got used to living under the same roof with Nennie and Father Jim. But there was one thing he would never get used to, and that was the feathered housemate who lived on the top floor.

The mynah belonged to Father Jim, although he delegated the care of the bird to Nennie. It chattered and cawed incessantly. It was dirty and smelled. William despised the bird, especially the cageling's sarcastic streak. Every time he'd go to the top floor, the mynah would greet him with the same refrain:

"Who are you? Who are you?"

For a proud man who lived with his family in a house his sister-in-law owned, the words had a particular bite.

"I'll show you who I am," he would grumble. "When I throw you out the window."

For Catherine, living with Nennie almost made up for the worry she expended on William. Often the Dolly Sisters would go on sojourns into the city to shop at Macy's or Gimbels. They'd be gone for hours and then blame the Northern Boulevard bus for keeping them out so long. When William's sister Ellen, also a spinster, moved in, the Dolly Sisters became a trio. When you added the bird, two small children, and the demanding priest with his buzzer into the mix, the house could be like Grand Central Station on a Friday rush hour. It was no wonder William couldn't wait to leave for work.

––––––

On December 7, 1941, William was a fifteen-year veteran of the fire department, had three years in Rescue 4, and was fifty years old. He was also fiercely patriotic. Any notion that he didn't want to serve in the First World War is dispelled by his action during the second. After the Japanese attacked Pearl Harbor, he tried to enlist in the U.S. Army. Well over the maximum age, he lied about it on the form, listing his birthday as July 27, 1896, instead of the actual date, July 29, 1891. He wouldn't get the chance to fight, however. We don't know if the Army saw through his ruse or the fire department simply wouldn't let him go.

During World War II, younger members of the FDNY joined the armed services in droves, much to the consternation of Mayor La Guardia. A fire buff of the first order, La Guardia thought they would perform a better service by keeping his city safe from fire and air raids, which never materialized. Because of the shortages in manpower, however, the department needed as many men as they could hold on to and doubled the work chart for the firemen like William who stayed home. Fireman Feehan was back to working eighty-four-hour weeks as he did when he first came on the job, and he did so without a pay raise. The city also suspended civil service promotional exams during the war. To fill the vacancies in the upper ranks, FDNY brass appointed firemen on an interim basis. William was made an "acting lieutenant." The job came with all the additional responsibilities, but without an actual promotion or any additional compensation for the higher rank.

Though he wouldn't go to Europe or the South Pacific, William fought plenty of battles at home. Because of the hours, and the war-thinned department membership, his fire service during the war was incredibly grueling. And with each set of stairs he climbed, each blaze he faced, each inhalation of smoke, his body broke down a little more. There is perhaps no other profession more physically and emotionally demanding than a firefighter's in a busy specialty squad or firehouse. William was as tough as they come on the job, but even he wasn't immune to the physical decline that befalls every active fire eater. Meanwhile, the fires he fought remained dangerous and at times spectacular.

———

The SS *Normandie* was the pride of France. Christened in the spring of 1935, the ocean liner was the biggest, fastest, and most luxurious of its day. The ship's dining room was a hundred yards long and adorned with bronze and cut glass walls and lights made of Lalique crystal. The galley served food as good as any restaurant's on the Left Bank. Promenades that lined the ship's perimeter were wide as city streets. Movie stars and millionaires filled the first-class cabins, some containing four bedrooms. The *Normandie*, however, would sail for only four and a half years. In 1939, at the start of the war in Europe, the ship was docked at the West Side piers in New York, a berth in which the great liner would stay for the rest of its short, tragic life.

After the Vichy government took control of France, President Franklin Roosevelt ordered the French liner seized and converted into a troopship. On February 9, 1942, work on the vessel was nearly completed when a fire began. Stacks of lacquered wood being removed during the conversion provided more than adequate fuel, and the fire spread with astonishing speed through the opulently appointed staterooms and dining area. The sprinkler system was not functioning, and in a futile attempt to stop the spread of the blaze, workers formed a bucket line and used wet blankets. By 3 p.m., much of the ship was engulfed in flames.

Word of the fire spread almost as quickly as the blaze. Across town, the bells atop Bellevue Hospital sounded their city-wide catastrophe alarm. Mayor La Guardia left in the middle of a radio speech and sped to the fire. Hundreds of onlookers lined the docks watching as flames licked at the grey sky above.

The fire department responded with alacrity. By 3:01 p.m., a second alarm had already been sounded. The first of what would grow to a small regatta of fireboats arrived soon after. The fire commissioner, Patrick Walsh, ordered a "surround and drown" effort by the fireboats and the battalion of firemen on the dock. Engine companies shot arcs of water at the hull from dry land. Fireboats did the same on the ship's port side. Still, rapacious flames, driven by a cold wind off the Hudson River, consumed the *Normandie* throughout the afternoon.

William's company arrived at the third or fourth alarm. By then the ship's quarters and common areas were an inferno. The French-made fittings on standpipes had stymied the first engine companies to arrive. Helpless to fight the fire, firemen instead focused on saving those aboard. The conversion of the liner to a troopship had taken months longer than planned, and, as the war continued to escalate in Europe, an army of workers had been assigned to the task. The rescue effort performed by the firemen and other volunteers was herculean.

The blaze spread so quickly that some people had to escape by lifeboats or by jumping into the freezing water, to be rescued by scores of tugboats and other vessels that had arrived to help. Still others climbed down seventy-five-foot extension ladders placed on the bow. The temperature had dipped well below freezing. One unimaginable news report told of firemen having to chop off a man's frozen hands from an iron ladder to save him from being burned alive. A temporary hospital was set up nearby on the dock in front of the *Queen Mary* and *Queen Elizabeth*. Miraculously, only one person would die in the flames and smoke that would injure two hundred.

The fifth alarm included fire companies from Greenwich Village and Harlem. Firemen would gain control over the inferno only after the fire had consumed practically everything that could burn.

William and his company worked the fire throughout the night. Early the next morning, he stood on the dock and watched as the ship began to roll. Inadvertently, the fireboats had pumped much more water into the hull's port side than the engine companies did into its starboard. At 2:45 a.m., the great ship, port side down, would sink into the mud at the bottom of the Hudson River.

In the wake of the fire, rumors of sabotage gripped the nation, and for good reason. Just a few months before, a Brooklyn court had sentenced thirty-three German spies to a total of three hundred years in prison. German U-boats had already sunk ships off the coast of Long Island. One U-boat had sailed right into the mouth of New York Harbor. It took months for FBI investigators to determine that it was a spark from a welder's torch that set fire to a stack of highly flammable life preservers and not a spy's fuse that started the blaze. In the meantime, paranoia held the city in its grip. Ironically, Alfred Hitchcock's film *Saboteur* was in post-production at the time. The great director took advantage of both the city's unease and the tragedy. In her book *Over Here!: New York City During World War II*, Lorraine B. Diehl writes, "Seizing an opportunity to sharpen the plot, Hitchcock obtained a newsreel of the burning *Normandie* and had Norman Lloyd, who played the German agent, ride in a taxi down the West Side Highway. As he passes the stricken ship, Lloyd looks out the window and smiles smugly, indicating to the audience that yet another act of sabotage has succeeded."

———

Over the course of the war, more than eighteen hundred New York City firefighters enlisted into the armed services. Forty-one would die in action. As the soldiers returned home, they again filled the positions they left behind, and William was "demoted" back to his rank of fireman first class. After the war, Fireman Feehan's work-week shrank to an almost manageable sixty hours. He cherished the time off and spent much of it with his sons. He would take Bill and Jim to the Sunnyside Gardens Arena in Queens to watch the prize-fights, where he'd root for anyone with an Irish name or a shamrock on his shorts. They'd go to baseball games at Yankee Stadium or the Polo Grounds to watch Joe DiMaggio, Yogi Berra, or Bobby Thomson play. One day at the Polo Grounds, Jim remembers a pitcher walking a batter to face a lesser hitter who was up next. William was incensed. "He's being cheap!" he shouted at the top of his lungs. When the next batter came up and hit a home run, the big fireman nearly jumped out of his seat with joy. He had a place in his heart for the underdog.

Sometimes they'd go to Dexter Park, a baseball stadium in

Woodhaven, Queens, to watch the Brooklyn Bushwicks of the Negro League. There they'd see Josh Gibson or Cool Papa Bell play exhibitions against Lou Gehrig and Hank Greenberg. Jim remembers going with his father to Dexter Park to watch the famous Israelite House of David team play. Members of a strict religious cult, they wore their hair down to the waist and full beards. Though when they first started out on the barnstorming circuit the players were all from the religious community, by the 1930s, and with growing popularity, the team began signing notable baseballers such as Satchel Paige and Grover Cleveland Alexander. When the Feehans went to see them, they were sort of an all-star team filled with professional and professional-caliber ballplayers.

William was protective and gentle toward his sons. One day Jim came home from school with a report card that wasn't up to Father Jim's standards. When the priest began to criticize Jim, William interceded. "Leave the boy alone," he said. "He'll be just fine." If Bill's or Jim's hair had grown too long or was unkempt, he wouldn't chastise them or demand they get a haircut. Instead, he would say something like, "You look like you're coming down with something. Are you feeling okay?" Jim remembers one day when an argument he had with his brother escalated into a wrestling match. His father pulled them apart.

"You know why your cousin Lenny is lame?" William asked. "He got into a fight with his brother."

———

Although by all indications William treated his sons equally and loved them both, very early on a special bond began to form with his oldest boy. According to family lore, young Bill's interest in the fire department began when the Feehans still lived in Long Island

City. It's said that as young as four, he would run after fire trucks that went by, perhaps because he thought his father might be on one. As he grew older, the childhood fascination became more of an obsession. Much of his budding passion for the profession came from the way he viewed his dad. Because of the long hours his father worked, Bill wouldn't see William for days at a time. When his dad did come home, Bill would sit transfixed listening to his fire stories. He couldn't wait to experience the feelings his dad described. When there was a massive fire in a coalyard near the house in Jackson Heights, William took his boys and Father Jim to see it. The coalsmoke smell and burning eyes were too much for Jim and the priest to endure, and they couldn't wait to leave. But Bill and his father were mesmerized by the scene. In his early teens, Bill would listen to FDNY's radio alarm broadcast. When his father came home from work, he'd pepper him with questions: "What's the box's location that was pulled?" "What companies responded?" "Who covered the second alarm?" He read his father's *WNYF* (*With New York Firemen*) magazines incessantly. The fire story that fascinated the young Feehan most, however, was the one that occurred on the morning in July 28, 1945, an event that would foreshadow the FDNY's darkest day.

The shroud of fog had descended so low over Manhattan that it obscured many of the taller buildings. In his B-25 Mitchell bomber, Lieutenant Colonel William Smith had taken off from an Army airfield in Massachusetts to pick up his commanding officer at Newark Airport. At some point Smith became disoriented in the fog and unwittingly altered his flight path. He then made the disastrous decision to try to drop the plane below the low-hanging clouds to gain visibility. At an altitude of one thousand feet, he realized his mistake just moments before his plane slammed into the seventy-ninth floor of the Empire State Building.

Though assigned to Rescue 4 at the time, William was covering for a fireman in his old company, Engine 21, that day. Less than ten blocks from the skyscraper, he was one of the first firemen on the scene. At the time, his son Bill was sixteen. Bill's eyes lit up as William told him about the torrents of high-test gasoline that flooded the seventy-eighth and seventy-ninth floors and poured down one of the elevator shafts. They widened further when he was told of the plane's landing gear penetrating an elevator shaft and plummeting seventy-eight stories "like a bomb." As would happen in the attack on the World Trade Center fifty-six years later, the plane tore a hole right through the famous skyscraper, with engine parts landing on the roof of an adjacent twelve-story building. There were other similarities. An article published in *Fire Engineering* magazine in October 1945 had this to say: "Among other things, the tragedy demonstrated the need of effective liaison and communications between fire-fighting and other emergency units at the scene of the catastrophe, and between these units and their respective headquarters." New York City, however, did not heed the warning. Difficulties with communications between agencies at the World Trade Center would prove catastrophic. There were also big differences between the two events. Because it occurred on a Saturday, fourteen people died in the Empire State Building crash, compared to the nearly three thousand in the twin towers. And of course, the Empire State Building withstood the impact. Both, however, exposed the vulnerability of New York City's skyline.

A dramatist, perhaps, would punctuate Bill's fascination with the B-25 crash as a forewarning of things to come. But he did recount the story often throughout his long career, and the most intricate details of it never seemed to fade from his memory. The last time he told the tale about the plane hitting the Empire State Building was during an interview just a few months before the World Trade Center attack.

———

On June 1, 1946, the department transferred William to the Special Service Squad, the combustibles division, sort of an offshoot of the rescue companies. During both world wars, the department organized these specialty squads to increase the response to major fires and disasters, and, during World War II and after, to handle combustible materials. William's squad would escort explosives being transported over the bridges of New York City. He would stay in the squad for a decade. His last stop in the FDNY came on July 1, 1956, when the department transferred him to the record maintenance Bureau of Fire Prevention. By then, William was nearly sixty-five, had been a fireman for over thirty years, and was part of the walking wounded. He couldn't straighten his back, and suffered constant pain in his both of his legs from the burns and grueling positions he had put his body in to fight fire. It wouldn't be until the 1990s that New York City firefighters were finally given protection for their thighs and groin area. William would get severe headaches from the fractured skull he'd suffered. He wore a grimace most of the time. Ultimately, a firefighter always loses the battle against the red devil. Sometimes the fight is lost in a moment. Fire, smoke, and heart attack can kill instantly. But the fire devil can also be a patient foe, taking down the fireman in increments. Sooner or later, every firefighter realizes this. William took his last transfer without protest.

———

Though out of the action, William was still in the job that he loved. The fire department instituted the fire prevention division in the wake of the 1911 Triangle Shirtwaist fire, which also gave rise to the FDNY's elite rescue units. But regulations to prevent building fires predated the city itself. In 1625, the Dutch West India Company had a set of rules that dictated how and where in New Amsterdam you were allowed to build. To monitor fire hazards in existing buildings, the fire department created the post of "superintendent of buildings" in the late 1700s. In 1938 the city established the Department of Buildings. From its inception, however, the fire prevention division was unpopular with New York City landlords and building owners. With authority vested by the city, the fire bureau demanded expensive improvements to buildings, such as fire escapes, sprinkler systems, internal alarms, and standpipes. Powerful real estate lobbyists wrested some of the authority away from the bureau during its early years. In 1932, fire prevention was wholly removed from the FDNY and placed under the auspices of the Department of Buildings and Tammany Hall. Reformist mayor Fiorello La Guardia returned the authority to the fire department in 1938.

In short order, William began to enjoy working in fire prevention. He liked being out in the field inspecting buildings and businesses. With thirty years of firefighting experience, he knew better than most how fires started and spread. Much to his friends Keeley and Imhoff's delight, who would enjoy the spoils during visits to William's home, he was also inundated with bottles of scotch. Business owners would give him the booze in the hopes of currying his favor, a miscalculation on two fronts. Fireman Feehan still didn't drink, and he had seen too much pain and suffering from fires to intentionally overlook something that might cause one. William liked the regular hours, and by all indications he would have stayed in fire prevention until they carried him out on a stretcher. A new fire commissioner, however, would institute regulations that would put an end to William's career.

New York City mayor Robert F. Wagner appointed Edward Francis Cavanaugh as fire commissioner on January 1, 1954. The son of privilege, Cavanaugh had played polo at Georgetown and studied law at Harvard. He was known for showing up at a fire scene in a baseball cap, à la the colorful Navy vice admiral William F. "Bull" Halsey.

Though the rank and file was cool at best to Commissioner Cavanaugh, under his watch the fire department made great strides in modernization. He oversaw the department's first digitized fire statistics and false alarms. At headquarters, an IBM machine would collect fire data such as type and occupancy of buildings involved. The department would then rely on the data to determine the manpower and equipment needed for affected areas. Cavanaugh was the driving force behind the Super Pumper, a combination of fire truck and trailer that could pump up to ten thousand gallons of water. Though his extensive contributions to the fire department are undeniable, he took an aloof posture when it came to his relationship with the rank and file. Some of them resented him for his outsized ego. In Brooklyn back in the day there was an expression that perfectly captured the firemen's sentiment toward Cavanaugh: "He thinks who he is."

What bothered William about the commissioner was not his emotional detachment, however, but his strict adherence to the rules, especially the mandatory retirement age of sixty-five. Simply put, William didn't want to retire. One reason was, with both his sons grown and out of the house, he didn't want to be trapped at home alone with Nennie and Catherine. He also didn't want to let go of the camaraderie and friendships the fire department had given him. But more even than those reasons, he didn't want to leave because the fire department defined him. He didn't know what he would be without it.

––––––

Inexorably, William's time to leave came. On June 8, 1958, William Patrick Feehan was granted terminal leave prior to retirement, and he officially retired from the New York City Fire Department on September 14, 1958. He carried only a few things when he left the job: the frontal piece of his helmet, a photo or two, and a grudge against the commissioner that he would nurse for the rest of his life. Ultimately, however, William would enjoy the last laugh. Long after the commissioner was dust in the ground, there would be a Feehan wearing the shoulder patch of the FDNY.

––––––

By all indications, William's relationship with his wife, always loving, became especially tender in retirement. At some point after he retired, Catherine had a minor heart attack. Where she'd be the one waiting on her husband hand and foot, after the medical episode it was William who assumed the nurturing role. Though she wouldn't let him near the kitchen to cook, he would run the errands for her and make sure she didn't overexert herself. "He wouldn't let her do anything," his granddaughter Liz remembers. Still, spending so much time with his wife took some getting used to. One day, Catherine talked him into going to the city to see the film *The Barkleys of Broadway* with Fred Astaire and Ginger Rogers, not exactly William's fare. But he decided to go for Catherine's sake. At one point in the story, as the fate of Ginger Rogers's character hung in the balance, Catherine nearly ripped the lining out of William's fedora, which she was holding. When she swooned at Ginger's travails on the big screen, William had had enough.

"That's it," he said, sounding like Ralph Kramden from the *Honeymooners* TV show, "from now on, you go to the movies with your sister."

————

When Nennie and Catherine headed to the city on one of their sojourns, leaving him alone, William would protect and cherish his solitude. He'd wear his old fireman's turnout pants with the suspenders and a moth-eaten sweater that had a hole in one elbow. If the doorbell rang, he'd grab a wrench he kept nearby. Be it a Jehovah's Witness or a Girl Scout selling cookies, his delivery was the same.

"I'm only here working on the boiler," he'd say. "The lady of the house isn't in."

Every now and then he'd invite his old pals Eddie Keeley and Mike Imhoff, also retired, over for a visit. Imhoff would have to take a bus all the way from the Bronx to Jackson Heights. Partly, one might surmise, he made the trip because of the adult beverages his host served. Because William never touched a drop of alcohol, he had no idea of the correct ratio of a mixed alcoholic drink. He'd serve water glasses filled to the brim with scotch. But the men would also spend hours reliving their years together in the firehouse. The large living room in Jackson Heights would fill with laughter, nostalgia, and a kind of love those outside the fire department can't really understand. And, at least for a few hours, they would recapture the firehouse connection they once shared. When it was time for his friends to leave, William and Catherine would watch from the doorway as Imhoff walked haltingly down the driveway toward the subway. He would always stop when he reached the sidewalk and turn back to doff his cap.

As time went by, William saw his firefighter friends less and less often. There was something wistful about him in his later years, more than the usual feelings of lost youth and aging many go through. Firemen have such a clear mission. Their contribution to society is immediate and can literally make the difference between life and death. The void that is left when a job of such importance disappears can never really be filled. Certainly, there are firefighters who are content in retirement, and it isn't as if William was unhappy in his later years. But he had lost something that gave as much meaning to his life as anything else. Still, he had it better than some of his superannuated brethren. For the rest of his days, a Feehan would carry his mantle.

# FOUR

# Kids from Queens

It's impossible to tell Chief Bill Feehan's story without telling his wife, Betty's. They were always a team, called Betty and Bill, or Bill and Betty, never one name without the other. Their romance is sealed in the amber glow of the 1950s—quintessentially New York City outer borough and Irish Catholic, but a universal love story nonetheless. Though, as with his father, the fire department defined Chief Bill Feehan's life, Betty was his reason for living.

Elizabeth Keegan came from a town called Maspeth in Queens. Newspaper columnist Jimmy Breslin once remarked that four times as many people were dead and buried in Queens than there were alive walking around on its streets. Maspeth's little corner of the borough does little to dispel the newspaper legend's assessment. A two-and-a-half-square-mile section in the western part of Queens, the town is bordered on three sides by cemeteries, and on the fourth by Newtown Creek, which was once so polluted that there was nothing alive in it either. The house she lived in was just down the block from a crematorium. This is not to say that Betty's childhood existed under a shroud. Quite the opposite. Cemeteries and crematorium aside, the town in which she grew up was nearly ideal.

The story goes that when Betty's father and mother, Bernie and

Elizabeth Keegan, went looking for houses to buy, Bernie's rich aunt lent them her car and driver. Being chauffeured around Queens to hunt for houses is sort of like wearing a tuxedo in a laundromat. Still, they might not have found the house on the tree-lined street without it. Maspeth is what is known in New York as a "two-fare zone." To get to anywhere important, say, Manhattan or downtown Brooklyn, you had to take a bus (a trolley in Betty's day) to a subway stop in Woodside, Queens. Though not ideal for commuters, or house hunters, the lack of a subway gave Maspeth an isolated, small-town feel. Many of the residences in Maspeth are one- and two-family houses made of wood and brick. Rosemary Feeney, Betty's best friend from childhood, said the Keegans lived in an "Archie Bunker house."

Though there were plenty of homes in Maspeth that resembled the one from the 1960s sitcom set in Queens, the description isn't entirely fair, especially the inside of the house. Elizabeth had a gift for interior decorating, a talent she'd pass down to Betty. Neatly and colorfully, she blended couches, chairs, and rugs perfectly. She also had an inventive way of adding finishing touches. Each summer, Bernie would rent a bungalow in Rockaway. One time, the tiny cottage he leased sat inside the grounds of an amusement park called Playland. Bernie was a steamfitter and worked nights. Alone in the evening, Elizabeth would carry Betty, still in diapers, around Playland until she'd fall asleep. While making the rounds, she got in the habit of stopping at a carny booth where you pitched pennies for prizes. She became so proficient at the game that she won a complete dinner service for eight. The dishes never failed to draw compliments from her guests.

———

Betty's independent streak began to appear very early in her life. A supermarket called Bohack's sat at the bottom of the block the

Keegans lived on. When Elizabeth went food shopping, she would bring Betty in a baby carriage. By the time she was three or four, Betty was done with being pushed around in the buggy. If her mother wouldn't let her walk into the store under her own steam, she'd throw a tantrum.

She inherited some of this self-reliance from her father. In the years before he was married, Bernie was a sport. Handsome and jaunty, he was a familiar face in the clubs and saloons on the Lower East Side. Though he was in "the trades," as they call the skilled construction industry, he also booked a little action on the side. The story goes that Bernie first took Elizabeth out when she was only fifteen. He was twenty-four. Though they might have drawn judgmental looks from those who saw them together, time would prove those who questioned his motives wrong. On Elizabeth's sixteenth birthday, Bernie took her to a restaurant and ordered a bottle of champagne. He then gave her sixteen gold coins as a present. Elizabeth, it's said, went home sick to her stomach from the bubbly but certain that Bernie was the man with whom she'd spend the rest of her life.

It was early in grammar school when Betty began emulating her dad. During World War II, Bernie took a job in Ohio at a factory that made power trains for military vehicles. Once he realized that the job, and the war, would last longer than he thought, he sent for the family. They enrolled Betty into second grade at a local Catholic grammar school. One day the nun teaching her class went around the room asking the students what they wanted to be when they grew up. Betty told her she wanted to be a Rockette. The nun, who presumably wouldn't know a Rockette from a rutabaga, smiled sweetly and said, "That's nice, Elizabeth." During class talent shows, Betty was known to sing the bawdy saloon songs her father had taught her.

After the war, the Keegans moved back to Maspeth, and, as her sister Vera and brother had before her, Betty attended St. Stanislaus grammar school. The late 1940s and the 1950s were the golden era, at least in attendance, for parochial schools. Nationwide, Catholic schools enrolled over five million students. Today that number is less than two million. In 1957, one out of every four children in New York City attended Catholic school. Back in the mid-twentieth century, the church, flush with cash, didn't need to accept funds from state governments like the Catholic school "academies" of today. They operated autonomously and with impunity from the social movement away from corporal punishment in schools. Catholic schools then were notoriously strict. Girls with rebellious streaks like Betty's would often find themselves staring up at a red-faced nun. But the sisters of St. Stanislaus couldn't break Betty's spirit.

The group of friends Betty made in grammar school would remain close the rest of her life. Back in the day, Stokes ice-cream parlor on Grand Avenue was their headquarters. After school, they would sit sipping fifteen-cent cherry colas while they gossiped and giggled about boys. But from a very early age, Betty sought to break the provincial bonds of her neighborhood. A part of Maspeth sits on a plateau, and on clear days the famous New York City skyline is painted on the horizon. At night it twinkled like a magic kingdom. For Betty, Manhattan beckoned like Oz.

———

As young as nine or ten, Betty and her friend Rosemary would take the trolley and then a subway into the city. Rosemary says she was actually the ringleader and something of a bad influence on her friend. One time, she was caught skipping school and forged her mother's name on a note excusing her. Still, when it came to going to Manhattan, Betty was a willing accomplice. They'd stroll the theater district or head to the movies on 42nd Street. Rosemary remembers seeing double features, even a live show and a movie for the same quarter. For a nickel they could buy a hot dogs at Nedick's and marvel at the ten-story-high Mr. Peanut advertisement, or the one for Camel cigarettes, just as big, with the fellow who blew giant puffs of smoke.

———

By high school, the discussions at Stokes ice-cream parlor became strategy sessions about meeting boys. Rosemary tells stories about how the girls would dash around the corner after school to roll up the waists of their plaid skirts. That way, they could show off more of their youthful legs. Though Betty was something of a late bloomer when it came to dating, once she started, she made up for the lost time. Witty and unpredictable, she had an engaging and magnetic personality. She and Rosemary went to St. Joseph Commercial High School in Brooklyn, an all-girls Catholic school. The "commercial" part of the school's curriculum prepared students for careers as secretaries and stenographers. She'd begun dating a Polish boy in secret, as such a mixed coupling was strictly forbidden by her father. Though the crush on the Polish boy would fade, Betty's propensity for going against accepted social norms only became stronger.

It was while at St. Joseph's that she began to think seriously about becoming a journalist, specifically writing for magazines. For a young Queens girl from that era, hers was an ambitious goal to say the least. Still, if you asked anyone who received a letter from Betty, they would tell you she certainly had the talent to be a professional writer. And in high school, where she wrote for the school paper, Betty showed a good reporter's indomitable spirit. No story, it seemed, was too big for her.

Her time at St. Joseph's coincided with McCarthyism and the House Un-American Activities Committee. For Betty, the "Red Scare" was page one material. One day, she and Rosemary cut school and headed to the *Daily Worker*, the Communist Party newspaper with headquarters near Union Square. The plan was to get an interview with a real live commie. At some point, the intrepid reporters realized they might not be wearing the most appropriate outfits for the mission. The green jumper and tan cap of St. Joseph's seemed more suited for marching in the St. Patrick's Day Parade. Like most good journalists, however, Betty was resourceful. At her behest, they stopped in a fabric store and bought ribbons of red material, which they pinned to their uniforms in the hope that the color would make them seem sympathetic to the Communist cause. They did manage to talk their way into the building. Once inside, however, the plan began to wobble. Though cordial to them, the Communists showed no interest in giving interviews to a high school reporter.

––––

Bill's and Betty's paths would converge in Rockaway, which is no surprise. For a particular generation of native New Yorkers, at least those of Irish and Jewish extraction in the outer boroughs, romance in the beachside community in Queens was a rite of passage.

In one way, the moment was preordained. Father Jim had arranged a summer job for Bill working for the New York City Parks Department. The fire department wasn't the only agency in which the good father had influence, which is a nice way of describing the pressure he could exert. Jim Feehan remembered one instance when

Father Jim had sent him to nearby Calvary Cemetery in Maspeth for a summer job. At first the foreman seemed uninterested in hiring the young man. But when Jim mentioned his uncle's name, a helpless expression fell over the man's face.

"When can you start?" he said with a shrug.

Though Bill was happy for the work, the job wasn't exactly convenient. A trip from Jackson Heights to Rockaway took well over an hour and spanned the entire width of Queens. In those days, you had to take the Long Island Railroad, a local train that made dozens of stops. Bill took the trip so often that he memorized the order of the stops the conductor announced and would recite them for years afterward to entertain his children.

Still, with the sunshine, ocean spray, and pretty girls, he couldn't have asked for a better place to work.

As luck would have it, Betty, too, had taken a job with the parks department in Rockaway. Bernie had done well enough in the trades to send his family to Rockaway for the entire summer. In those days, it wasn't that large of an outlay of cash. Now known as the Irish Riviera, the Rockaways was not exactly the Hamptons. Still, the Queens beach was a whole lot better than Maspeth in July and August. One night, right after Betty graduated from high school, Bernie held a party at the bungalow he'd rented. The revelry stretched deep into the night. Betty was starting her new job early the next morning. At daybreak, with little sleep, she dragged herself up to the boardwalk. She thought she'd caught a break when she ran into a coworker who told her the supervisor didn't make his rounds until later in the morning and that he was never on time. With the sun rising over the glistening Atlantic, Betty curled up in a ball for a little catnap on a bench. As fate would have it, Bill was filling in for Betty's supervisor, and Bill was always on time.

*Look at the shape of this one*, he thought to himself as he passed Betty on the bench.

———

At the time, Bill was enrolled at Cathedral Preparatory High School and taking classes at Cathedral College in Brooklyn. He had set his sights on becoming a Catholic priest, or, rather, Father Jim had set his sights for him. "He didn't have much of a choice," Bill's brother, Jim, remembered. "Our uncle was grooming him to be the next cardinal. The school adhered to a strict regimen of academic and religious study. A portion of the students were enrolled in a minor seminary for the Archdiocese of New York. The school sequestered the wannabe priests, like Bill, from the rest of the study body. It was only on Wednesdays that the seminary students were allowed to mingle with the other students. It was also on Wednesdays that the cloth of Bill's calling began to fray. Jim remembers seeing his brother escorting several young ladies around Jackson Heights at the time. Bill himself would later admit that the idea of becoming a priest evaporated when he realized the girls in nearby Bishop McDonnell High School were more interesting than Gregorian chants.

Though family stories here get somewhat convoluted, one narrative has it that Bill continued seminarian studies when he enrolled in St. John's University in Queens. By sophomore year, however, the path to the priesthood was behind him. In college, he majored in American history, a subject of which he would remain a devotee for the rest of his life.

The next time Bill ran into Betty was at St. John's. She had enrolled there, ostensibly, to follow her dream of writing and journalism. According to one family story, she'd received a scholarship to attend Columbia University, but the principal at St. Joseph's told her she'd lose her faith if she went there. How much time Betty actually spent at St. John's, however, is now debated in the Feehan family. Some say she completed two years of study, while others insist she left before her second semester. What we know for sure is, she was at the school long enough to experience her second encounter with her future husband.

At the time, Bill was a senior and the manager of St. John's basketball team. Though he was a pretty good athlete—he played baseball in high school—he wasn't good enough to compete at the level played at St. John's. In the late 1940s and early 1950s, the university's basketball team was as popular as the New York Knicks. Hardwood legends such as Al and Dick McGuire starred on those teams. Even practices were well attended, including by a segment of the coed fans.

It was at one of these practices where Bill noticed a girl who seemed vaguely familiar. When it dawned on him where he'd seen her, he found himself thinking that she looked a whole lot better than the morning he had found her asleep on the bench. He also realized then that he knew her older brother, and that was information enough to start a conversation.

"I know you," he said to Betty. "You're Bernie Keegan's kid sister."

As opening lines go, Bill's wasn't exactly movie dialogue material. In fact, it didn't impress Betty at all. She was a college freshman, for goodness' sake. She was going to be a journalist. She didn't want to be known as anyone's "kid sister."

"Thanks a lot," she said, and left in a huff.

———

Given her independent streak, Betty's initial reaction to Bill wasn't surprising. Still, one has to believe she was at least a little interested in the team manager. Photos of him then show a handsome, athletic young man with eyes that seem to gleam. He was popular, an important part of the basketball team, and a senior! So when Bill asked, chances are she quickly agreed to go out with him. One date, as these things go, led to another, and soon they were a steady item. By then, Betty's friend Rosemary had married a soldier and moved to Texas. Betty introduced Bill to her via a letter and enclosed a photograph of him wearing a bathing suit and T-shirt, sitting on the railing on the Rockaway boardwalk.

"She was effusive," Rosemary remembered of Betty's description of Bill. Her view of her new boyfriend had progressed a long way from that first, awkward encounter.

The budding romance, however, would have its challenges. The biggest of these was an event seven thousand miles from Queens. The Korean War and Uncle Sam had left Bill with only two choices: Enlist or get drafted out of college. Almost immediately after he graduated from St. John's in 1952, he found himself in a U.S. Army uniform shipping off to the Korean Peninsula.

Once again, stories as to how the romance withstood the separation diverge. Some friends say that Betty—beautiful, independent, and social—wasn't one to sit at home and wait for her soldier boyfriend to return and remember her dating other guys while Bill was away. Others, however, insist that Betty changed when Bill went into the Army. This camp points to the letters she wrote to him every week. Betty would make notes all week long of things to include. When she sat down to write, she would spread the notes onto the table and weave them into a story.

Purely from a practical standpoint, it makes sense that Betty would wait for Bill. After all, he was hardworking, wasn't a big drinker, and was a guy you could count on. Besides, how realistic was it for Betty to stay footloose and fancy free? Catholic girls who came from Queens then didn't finish college. A popular saying of the day was that girls went to college to get an M.R.S. degree. It wasn't only Queens that felt this way. The marriage rate in the 1950s in the United States was at an all-time high and many young women married right after they graduated from high school. Still, nowhere was the societal pressure of the day more prevalent than in the blue-collar borough across the East River from Manhattan. In Queens, if you were a young woman like Betty and single at twenty-three, friends and family were already applying pressure on you to get married. By the time you were twenty-five, they might even start to whisper about you becoming a spinster—a fate worse than death.

Still, saying that the culture was the only reason for Betty wanting to marry Bill discounts a considerable body of evidence to the contrary. The stories of Bill's wit, charm, and storytelling prowess abound. He had a self-deprecating sense of humor that put people around him at ease. There was also his reflexive desire to help others that nearly propelled him to become a priest, and was the main reason he became a fireman.

In Korea, Bill fought with the 7th Regiment, a unit that saw more action than any other. In his division alone, over two thousand soldiers were killed, with nearly nine thousand more injured. He saw heavy combat and was awarded several commendations. If he talked about his time in Korea, however, it wasn't to his family. Even career-long fire department friends would later say that he never discussed his time on the battlefield. Years later, after he'd climbed the fire department ranks, a poster hung on his office wall in headquarters. It featured a photo of an Army grunt patrolling a lonely road in Korea. "The war took Bill's boyishness away," Betty's older sister, Vera, remembered.

The fighting in Korea came to an end in July 1953, but Bill wouldn't return home until April of the following year. In the Army's convoluted way of showing appreciation for bravery on the battlefield, they sent him to Fort Dix near Trenton, New Jersey, to train recruits. But at least it was close enough for him to come home on the weekends.

It was on one of those weekends that he proposed to Betty. At the time, she was working as an executive secretary for Little, Brown and Company, an old, staid publishing house in Manhattan known for such classics as *Little Women*, the poems of Emily Dickinson, and a slim novel by J. D. Salinger called *The Catcher in the Rye*. Betty loved the job. She was an avid book reader and at Little, Brown she would meet Salinger, Gore Vidal, and the founder of Random House, Bennett Cerf, among other literary lights. Her dream of being a journalist was running out of steam, but a job in the book business was a pretty good second choice. Though she was able to break into publishing, the glass ceiling she encountered wouldn't crack. A manual at the time, *Lady Editor: Careers for Women in Publishing*, suggested that women trying to enter the field should pursue a position such as secretary, assistant, or stenographer. For the more ambitious gals, it advised, perhaps something in the children's book department. The manual also warned that publishers only hired females "who are pleasing, who possess tact, sincerity, enthusiasm, courtesy, and loyalty." It said successful applicants had to look like a million dollars on the smallest kind of salary and must learn to work with men. "She must learn not to be over-sensitive, not to brood outside of her job. And she must not be too emotional," the manual cautioned. However, even if you did check all the manual's boxes, there were few editorial opportunities for young women. Vassar and Radcliffe grads filled the ones that did exist.

Only ten years later, writers Helen Gurley Brown and Betty Friedan would help start the women's lib movement in America. It was then when the idea of women "having it all" became part of the national discussion. Betty's prospects might have been much different had she come along a decade later. Although the mores of the day were stacked against her, it wasn't as though she hadn't any support. The friends that Betty made in school, the ones who pined after boys in Stokes, all thought she had the talent to write or work in the book business. Rosemary, who would go on to have a career as a librarian, was an especially encouraging voice. The support from the Queens girls, however, was little help in the publishing towers of Manhattan. Though she never talked about it to her family, it's easy to imagine that Betty secretly lamented the missed opportunity. Instead, she neatly folded her dreams, locked them away, and followed the well-worn path taken by nearly all the other young women of her ilk.

Not that marriage was a consolation prize. By then her love for Bill was unquestionable, and on some level she knew she would find no better life partner. Still, somewhere in the deep recesses of her soul, there was always a quiet voice that wondered, what if?

———

Meanwhile, Bill began to chart a path to the FDNY. When he came home on the weekends, his father would have the latest fire department magazine and flyers given out by the department. Those periodicals listed civil service exam dates and other pertinent information. Together the two would pore over the material. Still, Bill becoming a fireman was far from a sure thing. Troops were home from Korea, including many returning members of the FDNY. Opportunities for appointment were tight and competition keen. The entrance exam would draw many applicants. As a just-about-to-be-married man, Bill knew he needed to make contingency plans. In the months before the fire department test was given, he took the New York City Police Department test, followed by an exam for a position as an investigator for the Department of Welfare, now known as the Human Resources Administration. When the FDNY test finally came around, he did extremely well on the written portion, scoring in the mid-90s. He also received five points for being a veteran. The Army had kept him in great shape, so the exam's physical portion did not pose a problem. All he needed was to pass the eye examination, and he'd be on his way to fulfill his dream. There was only one little problem. Bill's eyesight was poor at best. He'd already failed the eye test for the police department after he'd passed the cops' entrance exam. He needed a miracle, and when he walked into the examination room, he thought God had answered his prayers.

Part-time examiners from the city's Department of Personnel administered the eye exam. The fellow who was about to give Bill his was the track coach from St. John's University. For a few minutes, it was like old home week. The coach greeted him warmly, and they reminisced about their time together at the college.

Then Bill pressed his face against the eye test machine and began reading the Snellen chart. The last line of letters on the chart looked to him like blurry blobs. *Big deal*, he thought. With his pal the track coach, the exam was in the bag. Bill took a guess and leaned away from the machine, confident he was about to receive good news.

"Sorry, Bill," the track coach said in the same friendly tone he had greeted him with. "You fail."

So much for the alma mater.

# FIVE

# The Holy Ghost

The date is July 7, 1956. The wedding is captured in fading black-and-white photos with scalloped edges kept in plastic-bound folders and a grainy 8-millimeter film. In one photo, we see Betty and Bill standing on the steps of St. Stanislaus Roman Catholic Church. The bride wears a white gown that billows at the bottom, the fashion of the day. A delicate veil falls over one shoulder. Her hair is dark and cut short, a style that flatters her smiling round face. Though not classically beautiful, she's striking in the way that Judy Garland was, her daughter Liz would later remark. She's just twenty-two and holds the bouquet with both hands, seemingly for dear life. Friends say she had cold feet the night before, undoubtedly because of the independent streak Betty always had.

The groom is dressed in a morning coat with tails. Bill's shirt has a wingtip collar and is adorned by a striped ascot tie. Just back from the Korean War, he has dark hair worn Army short. His mischievous smile shows a set of slightly crooked teeth. His dark, handsome eyes hold a piercing gaze.

It's impossible, of course, to see in the faces of the just-married couple what was to come. In Betty's, we see none of the health issues, both physical and emotional, that would eventually consume her.

There is no indication of the loneliness and worry she would endure. Her smile shows no hint of the tragedy that would befall her, the worst a parent can imagine.

Bill's smile, too, belies what was ahead for him. There is no sign in his expression of the hundreds and hundreds of fires he would fight. We see none of the overwhelming sadness that accompanied the sight of young widows and children at the scores of firefighter funerals he attended. The handsome face shows no indication of his meteoric rise to the uppermost echelon of the FDNY, nor of his heroism and ultimate sacrifice on the FDNY's darkest day.

No, in the moment captured by the photo, there is none of that darkness, only the light of a future filled with possibility.

Bernie, always the sport, spared no expense on the reception. He hired out the Victoria House, a nearby upscale restaurant, to cater the event. By all accounts, it was a lively affair. Betty's mom ended up on the floor when she missed her partner's hand doing the Lindy. Betty, too, had a dancing mishap. The hoop skirt of the wedding gown came loose during a polka. The bride just stepped out of it, kicked it to the side, and continued to dance in her petticoat.

The next day, the newlyweds flew to New Orleans for the honeymoon. It was a rather extravagant trip considering their financial situation. How they paid for it is anyone's guess, but one can image that Bernie kicked in. In New Orleans, Betty wanted to tour the French Quarter and Bourbon Street, while Bill was most interested in looking at the local firehouses.

When they returned from the honeymoon, they moved into a tiny apartment in Rego Park, a predominantly Jewish section of Queens. Vera remembers Betty making the apartment into a "doll's house." She had the trait all good interior decorators possess, spontaneity. For their first apartment, they shopped for furniture at Macy's, where they purchased a contemporary set. However, a colonial set in the store's window caught Betty's eye on the way out. They went back in and changed the order.

"She was twenty years ahead of her time," Vera said.

She was all that, in a lot of ways.

———

Bill was crestfallen about failing the eye exam of the fire department test. The department's entrance exams are given about once every four years. But as a newly married man, he didn't have the luxury of feeling sorry for himself. He was offered and took the job at the welfare department, working in Harlem investigating fraud and abuse of the system. He enjoyed the sleuthing aspect of the job, but he didn't want to make a career out of it. Luckily, he didn't have to.

On one of the weekends he'd been home from Fort Dix, he'd read a story in a fire department magazine about the New York Fire Patrol. Privately employed by insurance underwriters, the patrol was charged with minimizing water damage from fire hoses during fires by spreading rubber tarps called "covers" on insured equipment and stock. They also removed valuables when possible. The story had piqued Bill's interest.

"Gee, I wonder how you get that job?" he asked his dad.

"We'll find out," his father said.

He took and passed the Fire Patrol entrance exam as a fallback. When the patrol offered him a position, he left the welfare department and took the job. It wasn't the FDNY, but it was the next best thing.

———

From its formation in 1867 to when it was disbanded in 2006, the Fire Patrol was intimately linked with the FDNY. Many of the patrol's members either once worked as New York City firemen or, like Bill, were hoping to someday get appointed to the city job. At one point, the patrol was, administratively at least, part of the FDNY. During World War II, the New York City fire commissioner was given control of the private agency, ostensibly to bolster the depletion of department manpower due to the draft or enlistment. When Bill joined the Fire Patrol, the chief of the agency was Joseph J. Scanlon, a former deputy chief in the FDNY. Fire patrolmen dressed like firemen—in Bill's day, with rubber coats, boots, and leather helmets with the extended rear brim—worked the same chart as firemen (9 a.m.–6 p.m., 6 p.m.–9 a.m.). But there were differences too. Fire patrolmen wore red helmets, and firemen wore black. And the patrol's equipment wasn't nearly as elaborate, nor did it pay as well or have the same benefits as the department. In a way, the Fire Patrol was like Triple-A baseball compared to the Major Leagues of the FDNY. Still, fire patrolmen took much of the same risks firemen took, including working above the blaze. Bill would find out just how risky his new job was on Valentine's Day, 1958.

———

Today, with its fancy shops and restaurants, cobblestone streets, and celebrities living in expansive lofts, the real estate south of Houston Street is some of the most expensive in the world. In the 1950s, however, the area was known to the fire department as "hell's hundred acres," a moniker hung on the neighborhood by William Feehan's nemesis, Commissioner Cavanaugh. The hundred-year-old loft buildings that lined the streets, the ones artists would soon inhabit, lay empty, as did makeshift factories housed in wooden firetraps. The Elkins Paper and Twine building, a six-story wood and brick structure at 135 Wooster, was one such edifice.

When Bill arrived for his night shift, he was fighting a bad chest cold, and the weather wasn't cooperating at all. The forecast had the night turning bitter, with a likelihood of heavy snow. Fire Patrol 2, his unit, was housed in a redbrick building with a single bay door on 3rd Street between Thompson and Sullivan, just north of SoHo. He climbed the stairs to the second-floor bunks. Undoubtedly, he was hoping for a quiet night.

The alarm rang twenty minutes after he arrived. Someone pulled the box on the corner of Wooster and Prince Streets. Simultaneously, workers on the first floor of the Elkins building saw reflections of the flames above them in the windows across the street and called the fire department. Bill slid down the pole to the bay and climbed onto the apparatus with the rest of his unit. The truck looked like a large pickup truck with an open cargo bed. They arrived on the scene minutes later. The fire was only four blocks from his firehouse.

———

Later, investigators determined that the blaze had started on the first floor, most likely by a discarded cigarette butt. The flame found its way into the air shaft, which blew like a fiery geyser up to the fifth and sixth floors. Bill remembered that fire was blowing hard out the windows of the top stories. His unit arrived just moments before Engine Company 13 and Hook and Ladder Company 20 from nearby Mercer Street. The firemen placed an aerial ladder against the building, and several of them climbed to the roof. Others ran hose lines into the building. Captain John J. Mullin, the commander of Fire Patrol 2, ordered his men to carry covering tarps to the third floor. He looked again up at the fire. He knew they were going to need help. In those years, the Fire Patrol didn't have two-way radios. He used a phone in a nearby building to call for more units.

Inside the building, the heat felt to Bill like it was melting his skin. Fire patrolmen didn't have self-contained breathing apparatus. The odor surrounding him was a toxic blend of burning rope, wood, tar, and chemicals. The room he entered contained heavy machinery, large bales of paper, and eight-hundred-pound rolls of twine. The air seemed alive with waves of heat. Fire Patrolman Feehan took his covers and climbed the massive roll of twine. At the top, he was only a foot or so from the ceiling. He could see the smoke seeping through from the room above.

After he finished covering the bale, he went down for more covers. By then, the street was filled with rigs and firemen. Hoses snaked into the building while water cannons fired at the top floors. On the roof, firemen used axes to hack holes for ventilation. Thick black smoke poured out of the openings they made. In less than half an hour, the blaze had progressed from one alarm to four. Ten minutes later, it would go to five. Meanwhile, the temperature outside began to plummet. Snow blew in icy gusts.

At Captain Mullin's beckoning, Fire Patrol 1 arrived and was sent into the building. Bill went up and down the stairs two more times. He felt a searing pain in his chest from the smoke. As the young fire patrolman started down again, a fireman was standing on the third-floor landing, putting on a mask and blocking the stairwell. When he saw Bill, he stepped out of the doorframe.

"You guys go ahead of me," he said.

The next thing Bill heard was a cacophony of wood snapping, bulbs popping, walls falling, and things crashing to the floor. Then came a deafening thunderclap. The last thing he remembered was the floor beneath him falling away. The rush of air caused by the collapse lifted him and blew him down the stairwell. Screams from inside the building were so loud people on the street heard them.

———

A forty-five-minute subway ride away, Betty, pregnant, lay in the Murphy bed under doctor's orders. Betty's first pregnancy had ended in a miscarriage. When she miscarried the second pregnancy, she began to believe a surgeon's prediction who had operated on her in high school for a gynecological issue. He had said her chances of getting pregnant were slim. Her family physician, Dr. Kelly, however, told her to keep trying, that there was no reason she couldn't have a child. He had known Betty for her entire life, and had treated her numerous times. When she got pregnant again, she took every precaution. Dr. Kelly ordered bed rest, and that's where she stayed.

Most of the time, she wasn't alone. Her mother and Vera came over to the apartment often to take care of her. Friends would stop by to cheer her up. Always the hostess, Betty would entertain them the best she could. The apartment was so small, she could stir soup on the stove without leaving the bed. However, at night, when Bill was working, worry and loneliness would creep into her thoughts.

Bill's stories brought her even more anxiety. Though he wouldn't make a big deal out of the close calls he had or dangers he faced, he couldn't keep them completely hidden from his wife. He'd come home with scrapes, cuts, and reeking from the pungent smell of smoke. She wouldn't allow herself to consider the possibility, however, that he could be seriously hurt, or worse. But when Valentine's Day night turned to the next day, she couldn't help worrying. He hadn't called, and that wasn't like her husband. Though he wasn't a teetotaler like his dad, Bill wasn't one of the guys who wrapped himself around a bar rail. He always came right home after work. Then, sometime the next morning, Vera called. She'd seen a report the night before on Channel 11 about a fire on Wooster Street.

"That's near Bill, isn't it?" she asked.

For Betty, the feeling first came as a knot in her stomach, as though she'd forgotten about an important date. The anxiety built with each hour that passed. Over the years of her husband's career, those emotions would become familiar. But she'd never get used to it. She would see a fire on the nightly news when Bill was working, or the phone would ring late at night, and a deep foreboding would grip her like a cold hand. Sometimes the worry would come without prompting. Betty wouldn't know if her husband was in the firehouse yukking it up with the guys or hanging from the ledge of a burning building.

"You don't know whether they'll come home at all," Betty said to Vera on the phone.

After her sister's call, Betty was nearly a wreck. Maybe they'd kept him at work because of the snow? His relief might have gotten stuck in the storm, she told herself. But, call it intuition, she knew deep in her soul that something was wrong.

———

Bill, still dazed, stood on the street and looked at the pile that had once been the Elkins Paper and Twine building. Flames shot from the back of the building, while the rubble toward the street smoldered. Icy snow swirled around him. Two other members of his unit, Ted Fosberg and Joseph Devine, had somehow also survived the collapse and had crawled from the pile. Devine's face was cut and covered with plaster. Captain Mullin ran up to them.

"Have any of you seen Patrol 1?" he asked breathlessly.

Bill didn't even know how he had gotten to the street. He vaguely remembered face-planting on the second-floor landing, but the rest was a blur. Then the fireman who stepped out of his way came to his mind. He wondered if he had gotten out alive. The four patrolmen of Fire Patrol 1, and two New York City firemen were unaccounted for.

They found the missing firemen first. William Schmidt and Bernard Blumenthal had been ventilating the roof when the building collapsed. They were sucked into the floor below and found buried up to their waists. Schmidt was killed instantly. Blumenthal, who had been on his honeymoon two weeks earlier, died on the way to the hospital. Meanwhile, with snow piling high on the streets, the search for the missing fire patrolmen continued.

It was Monday afternoon when Bill finally walked into the apartment. He'd called Betty at some point on Saturday the fifteenth to let her know he was all right. He told her about the collapse but not about his near-death experience. Once he was home, Betty looked at her husband's eyes and saw the fear and trauma. Dead tired, frozen, and caked with ash, the young fire patrolman dragged himself into the bathroom and took a long hot shower. When he was dressed, he kissed his wife and told her he had to go back.

"You can't," Betty protested.

"I have to," Bill said.

Fire Commissioner Cavanaugh had announced over the department radio a recall, an all-hands-on-deck order. Firemen and the Fire Patrol came from all corners of the city to help in the search. News reports said as many as five hundred or more would show up at the Wooster Street site. Bill worked shoulder-to-shoulder with them, digging through the pile into Monday night and Tuesday morning.

By then, the snow was piled nine inches high, and the temperature had dropped to near zero. What was left of the building and all the apparatus was coated thick with ice. Donald Blaskovich, who at this writing was the only still living fireman from the Wooster Street fire, remembers that the hoses all froze and that they had to bring them back to the firehouse on pallets. Meanwhile, the search for the others moved at a glacial pace.

It would be early Tuesday morning when they finally found Fire Patrolmen Michael R. Tracy's and James F. Devine's bodies. The others of Fire Patrol 1, Sergeant Michael G. McGee and Patrolman Louis J. Brusati, were found the following day. The collapse had swallowed them whole and sent them to the very bottom of the pile.

Eventually, as firefighters do, Bill would look back at the Wooster Street fire with a kind of gallows humor. He would joke that the Holy Ghost had blown him out of the building. But the near-death experience was like an invisible scar that he would always carry. He was a pragmatist. He knew the fatal element of the work he'd undertaken. But knowing it and experiencing it were two different things. Though throughout his career he would never shy away from any fire situation no matter the danger, after Wooster Street a haunting fear lodged somewhere deep in his subconscious. Not too long after the fire, his unit answered a call in a building near the Fulton Fish Market on the Lower East Side of Manhattan. The top floors of a coffee roasting house had caught fire. The building had a sheet metal hopper on the roof. Bill was covering stock with tarps on a level below the blaze when the hopper fell over with a thundering crash. He thought the building was coming down and ran as fast as his legs could take him. The firefighters on the scene looked at him like he was crazy. Many years later, he would downplay the fear that many firefighters silently carry.

"It's something that comes up," he would say, "[and] over time comes up again."

———

On August 20, 1958, a little more than two months after the Wooster Street fire, Betty awakened in the early morning hours with severe contractions. Bill grabbed the bag they had packed for the hospital stay and rushed to the street. "Misericordia Hospital, in Manhattan," he told the cabbie, "and step on it." When they arrived, the hospital lobby was empty, save a Catholic nun at a telephone switchboard. Betty was in severe pain. The nun rushed to them.

"I've got her," she told Bill. "You take over the switchboard."

"You want me to do what?" he asked.

"There's no one else here!" she said. "Someone has to answer the phone."

The nun took Betty by the arm and rushed down the hallway.

For a moment, Bill stood there, wondering what had just happened. Then the phone started to ring.

"Misericordia," he said, his voice a bit unsteady. "How can I help you?"

Betty gave birth that morning to a healthy baby girl named Elizabeth Ann, the third generation of Elizabeths in the Keegan line.

Though she wanted to believe Dr. Kelly's comforting words, it wasn't until she held her daughter in her arms that Betty's uncertainty completely disappeared. She wasn't as devout in her faith as Bill's parents, or Bill for that matter, but one wonders if she hadn't entered into a kind of spiritual bargain with her higher power. Later, she and Bill would volunteer at an orphanage in Brooklyn called the Angel Guardian Home. One of the duties they performed was transporting infants to doctors' offices and hospitals. They would continue volunteering at the home for years afterward. Maybe the charity work was Betty's end of the divine deal.

---

After a few years on the Fire Patrol, Bill retook the fire department entrance examination. Once again, he aced the written and physical parts of the test. When he arrived for the eye examination, he was relieved that the St. John's coach was nowhere in sight. This time there was no chitchat with the examiner. The older gentleman administering the test seemed to Bill to be all business. He'd gone to a family doctor who gave him an injection that would temporarily help his eyesight, but when he pressed his face to the machine he again had trouble making out the last lines in the chart. He squinted as hard as he could to bring the final letter into view.

"It's either a C or an O," he said nervously.

"It has to be one of them, kid," the man said softly. Bill knew his future as a New York City firefighter hung in the balance. He'd just turned thirty, and the next time the test came around, he might be too old to take it.

Throughout his career in the FDNY, he would tell the story of that eye test often. He could never remember, however, which letter he picked. Nor could he be sure that the letter he chose was actually the correct one.

————

Bill was just getting off his shift at the Fire Patrol when a New York City Fire Department investigator doing a background check called him. Firefighters are officially notified of their appointment to the department by letter, but a call from an investigator is the final step in the hiring process and an unofficial notification. When he hung up the phone, he had one thought in his mind—he had to tell Betty. He hurried out the door of the firehouse and took the subway home. The last leg of his commute was a bus down Woodhaven Boulevard to Rego Park. By then, he was so eager to see his wife he didn't want to wait for the bus and instead began to run the three miles to the apartment. Betty happened to be coming home from an appointment on the Woodhaven Boulevard bus, the one that Bill didn't take. From her window seat, she saw her husband running full stride on the sidewalk and thought he'd lost his mind. She made the driver stop the bus.

When Bill saw his wife coming toward him, he ran to her, picked her up, and twirled her around like in a scene from a movie.

"I'm in," he said, trying to catch his breath. "I'm in."

The date was October 10, 1959.

# SIX

# Family Man

O n his graduation from the fire academy, the department assigned Probationary Fireman Bill Feehan to Ladder 3 on East 13th Street near Union Square. Bill's firehouse was only a short walk from the *Daily Worker* where Betty had hoped for a news scoop, and Orbach's where she had burnished her fashion sense for her job in publishing. The fire station's first due response territory was eclectic and included the exclusive grandeur of Gramercy Park, the Flatiron District with its artists' lofts and photography studios, and the Bowery where the twenty or so flophouses packed down-and-outers into pens separated by chicken wire. The fire company also covered New York University's Washington Square campus, which had been the site of the Triangle Shirtwaist factory fire. In 1911, the sensational and catastrophic blaze in the clothing manufacturer took the lives of 147 mostly young immigrant seamstresses. Caught above the fire in a locked work area on the ninth floor, many of the young women died when they jumped from the windows. One of those who perished in the fire was a relative of the future fire commissioner Howard Safir. Most of the fires to which Ladder 3 responded, however, were located in the East Village, the northern reaches of the Lower East Side. There the building stock was an assortment of factories, commercial loft buildings, older tenements, and apartment buildings in various stages of blight.

Because of the architectural diversity of the neighborhood, Ladder 3 afforded Bill the opportunity of gaining experience in a variety of complex buildings and occupancies early in his career. But perhaps the most advantageous thing for Bill about Ladder 3 was that his best friend was already part of the crew.

Bill met James J. Marron when they worked together on the Fire Patrol. Both young, married Irish Catholic guys from Queens, Jim and Bill had much in common, especially their desire to fight fire. Marron had come onto the FDNY a few months before Bill and wasted little time making a name for himself. The department had already awarded him the Bella Stiefel Medal* for bravery. With just weeks on the job, he ran into a raging fire in a hotel lobby. There, at the end of a smoke-filled hallway, he found a semiconscious man and carried him to the street. The fire had burned the man so badly, witnesses reported, that his skin seemed to be melting off his body. The man would later die from his wounds.

Without some help, the odds of Bill getting sent to the same firehouse as his best friend would have been long, to say the least— the New York City Fire Department covers 302 square miles. His own father's influence in the department was limited by the firemen's rank at which he retired. Marron, however, had a "big hook." His wife was from a heroic FDNY heritage. Her grandfather, Edwin Quinn, won the James Gordon Bennett Medal. Now named after Chief Peter J. Ganci Jr., the Gordon/Ganci medal is

---

* A wealthy Manhattanite and fire department admirer, Bella Stiefel bequeathed $25,000 to the New York City fire commissioner to hold in trust for the purpose of awarding the eponymous medal. The first Bella Stiefel bravery medal was awarded in 1947.

the department's highest bravery award. Edwin's son, Andrew Xavier Quinn, was a legendary battalion chief, who happened to have spent many years stationed in the same firehouse that quartered Ladder 3. It's not a stretch to think that Chief Quinn had the connections to get Bill assigned to his son-in-law's firehouse.

Though he might have had help getting the assignment, from the moment he pulled on his turnout gear, Bill made sure to do everything he could to prove his worth. He knew both from his father and working alongside the FDNY when he was on the Fire Patrol what was expected of a proby firefighter. In a way, he'd been training his whole life for this moment. Both Marron and Feehan were so enthusiastic about being firefighters that they would practice rescues in between runs. One night, the captain on duty looked out his office window to see them rappelling from the roof of the firehouse on a rope.

There was plenty of opportunity for real fire experience too. In 1959, the FDNY responded to one hundred thousand calls, an increase of eight thousand from the year before. Some of those fires were spectacular. Just during his probationary period, Bill's company responded to two of the most famous fires of the last half of the twentieth century. On the foggy, sleety morning of December 16, 1960, a United Airlines DC-8 slammed into a TWA turboprop in midair over Brooklyn. The United jet fell from the sky, crashing in Park Slope, then a poor section of the borough. Fiery parts from the jet set a whole block on fire, including a funeral home, a church, and a number of brownstones. The TWA plane, which was nearly cut in half by the jet, came down in flames on Staten Island. The city mobilized twenty-five hundred first responders, including cops, doctors, civil defense volunteers, and firefighters. Bill, with Ladder 3, helped in a rescue effort that would prove futile. The crash killed all

134 passengers and crew on both airliners. Six more on the ground in Brooklyn died.

Three days later, Ladder 3 responded to a fire that tore through the aircraft carrier *Constellation*, then being built in the Brooklyn Navy Yard. Like on the SS *Normandie*, it was a welder's torch that sparked the conflagration. But this time it was fuel leaking from a damaged tank that caught fire. Workers were trapped in airtight compartments below deck. Firefighters had to use acetylene torches and rotary saws fitted with heavy blades to cut holes through two-and-a-half inch plates that made up the carrier's interior walls. The fire burned so hot that the water that gushed from hoses immediately turned to steam when it hit the hot metal. Fifty workers suffocated in the fire's poisonous fumes, many of whom were found stiff from death and still clutching their necks. A fire department chaplain told a reporter that he saw a small room filled with bodies "huddled like puppies." Like Bill, many of the same firefighters who fought the flames in Park Slope again responded to this disaster. The fire swept the ship from stem to stern, the equivalent of five city blocks. Wooden scaffolding formed a conduit for the flames. Eleven hours after firefighters arrived, the blaze still burned out of control in large sections of the carrier. Fire companies fought the flames for seventeen hours. As bad as it was, the disaster could have been much worse. The government had employed forty-two hundred people to work on the sixty-thousand-ton carrier to complete the job quickly because of the Cold War with Russia. The Navy had not conducted fire drills of any kind, and no "abandon ship" signal came from the carrier's horn. News of the fire traveled only by word of mouth. The fire disabled the electricity, plunging the labyrinth of twelve hundred rooms below deck into total darkness. Fire department aerial ladders saved 250 workers, and operators of the soaring cranes on the dock swept many from the deck to safety. The U.S. Coast Guard pulled men who had dived from the ship out of the East River. Fire officers led firemen, some without masks, into the belly of the carrier and carried unconscious workers out of rooms filled with noxious smoke. The ship had begun to list to the point that it would be unsafe for firefighters on deck. Unlike with the *Normandie*, however, river-water-filled ballasts were able to right the vessel. In all, thirty-five engine companies, five ladder companies, four fireboats, and ten specialty squad companies comprising over 450 firefighters responded to the fire. Bill was still there when firefighters carried the bodies of the victims out of the carrier and lined them on the dock. Not even what he'd witnessed in Korea could compare. "It was the largest amount of body bags I've ever seen," he told a reporter.

In the weeks after the fire, the U.S. Navy and the New York City Fire Department argued over the reason why the fire had been so extensive. The Navy blamed electronic equipment, gas from melted plastic cables, and workers' varnish for the fire's spread. Commissioner Cavanaugh said it was "sloppy housekeeping," and the scaffolding that fueled the rapacious flames should have been fireproof. By housekeeping he meant the reams of paper documents scattered about the ship. During an inquiry hearing the Navy held three weeks after the fire, an admiral dismissed Cavanaugh's opinion, stating that the fire commissioner was not what he considered an expert in fireproofing. Following the devastating fire, the Navy drastically cut back operations at the Brooklyn Navy Yard. In 1966, after 165 years as the Navy's foremost shipbuilding facility, a period that spans nearly the entire history of the branch, the Navy Yard closed for good.

———

Throughout his time in Ladder 3, Bill witnessed many more fire fatalities, including ones from his own ranks. Later in Bill's time there, a fire in a textile loft building on lower Broadway claimed the lives of three firemen and severely injured six more. The conflagration was so massive, it went to nine alarms—five in Manhattan and four in Brooklyn. To give an idea of how big the response was, a two-alarm fire summons 25 vehicles, including engines, ladder trucks, specialty units, and more, and over a hundred firemen. In all, some 350 ladder trucks and other apparatus, and three hundred firemen, including fifty called from the fire college, fought the raging flames in the loft.

Even with a lifelong fascination with the fire department, a father on the job, and four years on the Fire Patrol, there was still plenty for Bill to learn. The biggest upgrade from the Fire Patrol was the equipment and roles of the crew. Four firemen and a lieutenant or captain manned the rig. A chauffeur drove the ladder truck. It was his job to position the rig close enough to the fire so that the ladders could be utilized. A tillerman worked the steering wheel at the rear of the apparatus. A can man, usually the youngest and least experienced, carried a three-and-a-half-gallon tank fire extinguisher. A forcible entry team used the Halligan tool, or "the irons," to pry open doors. Named after Hugh Halligan, the chief who invented it, the tool is a combination ax and crowbar. An outside vent, or "OV," man would climb fire escapes in the building's rear and punch holes in the roof to draw out the fire and lessen the heat. To the untrained eye, the team's initial response to fire might appear as a bunch of guys running around in circles not knowing what to do. Nothing could be further from the truth. Every firefighter is trained until they know their role by rote. They work as a team and are keenly aware of their responsibility to the other fire-fighters. Each depend on the others, often for their lives.

As is the case with most fire companies, most of Bill's waking downtime was spent in the kitchen, the beating heart of any fire-house. Most probys spend a lot more time washing pots there than fighting fires. In this family setting, generational gaps are closed, new members are invited into the fold, and the oral history of the FDNY is handed down. Though some of those stories need to be taken with a grain of salt, or, depending on who's telling the tale, the whole salt-shaker, the fire department's very culture is preserved at mealtime. It is where the seeds of the unit's cohesion take root and the depth of the company's camaraderie grows. Now, it wasn't as if every-body always gets along. When you have a couple of dozen grown men sharing tight living quarters, hard feelings and rivalries are not uncommon. Most of these are ironed out by the firehouse hierarchy, with the older, most respected firefighters or fire officers laying down the law. Sometimes these old-timers do so in an inventive way. A fire chief who used the pen name Ben Franklin—the Founding Father is credited with starting the first volunteer fire department in the United States in 1736—tells a story in his book on firehouse manage-ment about a firefighter's grudge. In charge of cooking the meal that night, he slipped a poker chip into a hamburger meant for his nem-esis. Instead, the captain of the house grabbed the hamburger, took a huge bite, and cried out in pain. He opened his mouth to show four of his teeth broken in half. The cook was horrified and began apolo-gizing profusely to his superior. It was about then that the captain brought his dental bridge out of his pocket, to roars of laughter from his men. He'd watched the firefighter put the chip into the chopped meat and saw a unique opportunity to teach him a valuable lesson.

Culinary exploits in the firehouse, of course, have gained national attention through cookbooks, cable cooking shows, and even brand names and fast-food chains. Seasoned firehouse cooks are exalted and treasured. Such was not the case in Bill's first fire company, however, mostly because they didn't need one. The firehouse's bay door was directly opposite the rear of a famous German restaurant on 14th Street named Lüchow's. Each night tour at dinnertime, a couple of firefighters would carry four empty stainless steel pots across the street and knock on the restaurant's back door. The chef would fill the pots with soup, vegetables, potatoes, and whatever meat was the special of the day. One of the daily specials was meatballs, which the guys took to calling "Cropsey balls," apparently for their scary size. There's an old line, mostly delivered by New York cops, that goes: The only thing cheaper than a fireman is two firemen. The men in Bill's first company did nothing to dispel that belief. At Christmastime, they would chip in all of twenty-five cents apiece and present the magnanimous sum to the kitchen staff for the food they had received all year.

Lüchow's wasn't the only establishment willing to feed Ladder 3. There was also the Automat on 14th Street. If you're not familiar with the now-defunct fast-food chain, Horn and Hardart's Automat sold food from vending machines. You'd put a quarter in a slot and then open the door to a little windowed cubbyhole behind which sat a ham sandwich or a piece of lemon meringue pie. The Automat near Ladder 3 would close each evening at eleven. Firefighters from Bill's company would show up a couple of minutes after closing time and leave with a box of surplus sandwiches and pies for late-night snacks. They might have been a little dry after sitting there all day, but the price was right.

———

Firehouse humor is not for the sensitive or faint of heart. It is usually not as cerebral as, say, a *New Yorker* cartoon. One retired firefighter interviewed for this book likened firehouse humor to "being in grammar school." Traditionally, new recruits bear the brunt of the jokes. Today some call it "pranking the proby," a kind of initiation ritual that works to remind the rookie of his place in the pecking order. Some of the more enduring stunts include sending the newbie in search of a left-handed Halligan tool, or a hose stretcher, or some siren fluid, none of which of course actually exist. Every proby who goes through the baptism of fire, in turn, gets to inflict the same routine on the next incoming class, and on and on it goes. There also seems to be a correlation between the wit of a firefighter and the danger they face—the busier the firehouse, the bigger the laughs. Proby Feehan's turn in the barrel, so to speak, came early in his time in Ladder 3, and the joke had nothing to do with firefighters' tools.

Betty had asked him to find a new place for a night out with their friends, and Bill went to one of the old-timers in his crew for a suggestion. As his firehouse was surrounded by such culinary delights as those served by Lüchow's, Bill was confident that the old-timer would certainly steer him to a good restaurant. A rookie mistake.

Excitement ran high on the evening of the dinner. Four couples, including Betty and Bill, all dressed up for a night on the town, headed to an eatery in Manhattan. As they arrived at the suggested destination, Bill didn't give much thought to the dining room's unusual layout, with aisles that ran down each side ending in stairs that the led to a stage. Nor did he think it strange when the lights dimmed and a jazzy tune with trombone slides began to play. Only when the stripper draped him with a rather intimate unmentionable did the true nature of the place come into focus. "Bill turned as red as a fire engine," Rosemary, who was at the table, remembers. For years to come, Betty's friends would needle Bill about their night together in the strip joint.

———

On June 30, 1961, Betty gave birth to William, whom they called Billy. With Liz still in diapers and now infant Billy, the apartment in Rego Park—with the bed that folded into the wall—had begun to become an untenable situation. Finding a place on Bill's salary with enough room, however, was going to be a challenge. When Betty gave birth, Fireman Feehan was making $4,800 a year, with a $125 uniform allowance. Luckily, he had already begun to partake in an old firefighter custom—moonlighting.

For many New York City firefighters, one of the most appealing aspects of the job is the work chart. The basic workweek consists of two nine-hour day tours followed by two fifteen-hour night tours. The department, however, allows its uniformed members to engage in what is called "mutuals." The idea behind mutuals is simple: You're allowed to swap tours with someone else in the same company so you can work one day tour and one night tour back-to-back. In other words, you're on twenty-four hours straight, and then have seventy-two hours off. This type of scheduling, obviously, can only happen when your job comes with a cot. Mutuals allow firefighters to work all sorts of side jobs, from tending bar to landscaping to studying acting, as Steve Buscemi did when he worked in Engine 55 in the early 1980s. Today, many male firefighters with families work mutuals to take care of the kids while Mom is out making the big money.

When Bill worked for the Fire Patrol, he moonlighted for a messenger service that delivered packages to brokerage firms in the Wall Street area. He got to know every back alley and freight elevator from the Bowery up to City Hall. He continued at the delivery service after he went onto the fire department, despite the fact that moonlighting was then against department regulations. The restriction against a second job was ludicrous. Like Bill, most young firemen then were married and starting a family, or about to. The yearly salary was barely enough to pay the rent, put food on the table, and keep a baby in diapers, never mind put some money away. As was the case for many men of his generation and socioeconomic station, buying a house was the ultimate goal. Without a second job, home ownership for a fireman was a fantasy. Luckily for him and other eager firemen, a few years after Bill started at Ladder 3, the department, still headed by Commissioner Cavanaugh, bowed to pressure from the fire unions and relaxed the moonlighting regulation. Not only could he moonlight without worrying he'd get caught, but now he might even be able to find a side gig that engaged his intellect a little more than delivering packages did. As fate would have it, that's exactly what happened.

Bill graduated the probationary academy with a firefighter named Bill Barry, who was also assigned to Ladder 3. One day, Barry approached him in the firehouse.

"I'm taking the test for a teaching license," Barry said. "You got a college degree. Why don't you take it with me?"

A teaching job sounded a whole lot better than running up stairways and freight elevators.

Six months after he'd taken the test given by New York City's Department of Education, he received his license teaching common branches, the subjects taught in grammar school. For the next fifteen years, Bill would substitute teach in the New York City school system. He would work all over the city, but more often than not in poorer neighborhoods in the Bronx and Brooklyn. He even for a short stint taught at Spofford, a juvenile detention center in the Bronx. By all accounts, he was a natural in front of a classroom. An engaging story-teller, with a quick wit and a substantial intellect, he had all the tools. He certainly was in demand. His son Billy remembers the phone ringing off the hook just about every weekday morning with anxious principals asking if he could work for them that day. What inner-city principal wouldn't want a young, handsome fireman teaching class?

———

Though, for Bill and Betty, the idea of owning a home was more than appealing, there were still a couple of issues that needed to be addressed. First off, Betty didn't want to leave the city. She couldn't understand how her friends, one by one, could move with their fami-lies to towns such as Bethpage, Islip, and Levittown on Long Island, no matter how good the bargains were. For Betty, they might as well have been leaving for the North Pole. There were also some hurdles, including the not-too-small challenge of coming up with a down payment. Even with a second income, Bill couldn't seem to get the money together for the deposit. When Betty became pregnant again, the financial challenge became even greater. And that wasn't the only problem that arose. After her earlier pregnancies, Betty developed a form of postpartum psychiatric disease. After Tara was born in the summer in 1963, the darkness that descended on her was the worst she'd experienced. Her condition became so severe, she needed to be hospitalized. Along with her clinical depression, Betty was chronically anemic, with an immune system so weak she frequently developed infections, including pneumonia. Bill nursed her when he wasn't working. Her mother and sister would help out. But because of her depression, Betty's will to get better was as diminished as her natural defenses against the diseases.

And with each descent in the cycle of depression she suffered, she would recede further from the life she'd known. At first her life-long friends, the women such as Rosemary whom she knew since St. Stanislaus, thought it was just Betty being Betty when she wouldn't meet them for lunch or dinner. She'd always marched to the beat of her own drum. But then she stopped talking with her friends almost entirely. Bill would answer the phone when they'd call, and use the same excuses time and again: She was in the shower, or she was taking a nap. "She just wasn't herself anymore," her friends remembered. Betty's condition would become a secret held closely by the whole family. The children wouldn't talk about their mother's condition to their friends, other than to say she was sick again. Though civil servant families don't have the market cornered, they can keep secrets with the best of them. But, without question, Betty's depression weighed on the Feehan kids. They were always on guard, afraid to drop their defenses and let the skeletons out of the closet.

---

With Betty debilitated much of the time, Bill had to handle a household that consisted of a four-year-old, a two-year-old, and now, with Tara's arrival, an infant. When he was working, the care of his children became a team sport, with grandparents chipping in. Liz lived with Catherine and William for a while, and Aunt Nennie would ride two buses to bring her to grammar school at St. Mel's in Flushing in the morning, and the same two buses in the afternoon to pick her up and bring her back. Liz describes those days as a "very hard time" for everyone in the family, but especially her father.

And yet in the midst of all of the responsibility at home and at work, somehow Bill managed to find a house of both his and Betty's dreams.

————

As you might imagine, the neighborhood of Flushing has endured its share of jokes over the years. The odor that can emanate from nearby Flushing Bay at low tide only adds to the comic material. Historians believe, however, that the name is actually a corruption of Vlissingen, the original Dutch settlement on the land back in the days of Peter Minuit's $24 purchase of Manhattan. More recently, Flushing has become home to waves of Asian immigrants. The neighborhood is now mostly inhabited by first- and second-generation Chinese, Korean, and Indian newcomers.

Despite the jokes and low tide, there are parts of Flushing that are as lovely as any neighborhood in the entire city. Towering trees line blocks filled with brick Tudor-style homes fronted with flowerbeds and green shrubs. It was on one of these charming Tudors that Bill set his sights. Still, the problem of the money for a down payment persisted. Until he had that cash on hand, the idea of buying the home was little more than a pipe dream. Enter spinster Aunt Ellen. We don't know whether Bill went to his aunt or if she offered to lend him the money. Either way, she had the cash to give to him—by then, she'd worked for the telephone company for years and had socked away a tidy sum. Bill had his down payment.

————

Though the houses seemed more suited for the upper-middle-class enclaves of Bronxville, Forest Hills, or Rockville Center on Long Island, Flushing was decidedly blue-collar. A police officer owned the house next to the one Bill bought. The cop's wife worked as a nurse. A sales representative for Domino sugar lived on the other side. A police sergeant lived down the block, as did a city transit worker. Even the parish had a working-class name—St. Mel's. Many of their neighbors were of either Irish or Italian extraction, with names like Brady, Cannon, and Antonucci. They were the sons and daughters of lower-middle-class apartment dwellers, New York City's version of the generation who sought and found the American dream. It was an accomplishment they would protect at any cost. But neighborhoods such as Flushing became fortresses against what firefighters, cops, and other city workers believed was a takeover of the city by minorities and the liberal politics that supported them.

In 1969, John V. Lindsay, New York City's dashing and controversial mayor, came to Flushing to dedicate a playground that had just been renovated. Lindsay was then a Republican (he became a Democrat in 1971 to run for president), but a RINO well before the term was in vogue. Though a World War II hero, with five battle stars, he supported the anti–Vietnam War movement, and was friendly with Tom Hayden, the cofounder of Students for a Democratic Society (SDS) and a member of the Chicago Seven. The night after the Reverend Martin Luther King Jr. was assassinated, as Robert F. Kennedy had in Indianapolis, Lindsay helped soothe the simmering anger in his city. In his obituary (Lindsay died on December 19, 2000), the *New York Times* described his actions that night: "And when riots tore at Detroit, Newark, Los Angeles and other cities, he walked the steamy night streets of Harlem and other black areas, tie askew, jacket flung over the shoulder, taller than anyone else, talking to people with only a detective at his side: a calm figure of civic dignity. And while other cities burned, New York had only minimal looting and violence."

Lindsay was a product of New York City's privileged class; his father was an investment banker and chairman of a subsidiary of Credit Suisse Bank, and his mother was a Wellesley graduate with a lineage that traced back to the Revolutionary War. He rode crew at Yale, and as a congressman represented the city's silk-stocking district on the Upper East Side. But his station in life did not particularly endear him to hardscrabble city workers. One of the more contentious relationships Lindsay had was with the Transit Workers Union president, Mike Quill. On New Year's Day 1966, the new mayor's first day in office, Quill shut down the city's buses and subways over a contract dispute. In press conferences, the union chief would mispronounce the mayor's name as "Mr. Lindslay," the corrupted moniker delivered with a hint of an Irish brogue. Lindsay had Quill thrown in jail, a situation the union boss didn't seem to mind. Quill told reporters that he came from a family that was "a bunch of jailbirds." While he was incarcerated, Quill suffered a heart attack, and was dying as he negotiated terms for the new contract in an oxygen tent.

But Quill was only the start of the problems for Lindsay. Violent crime in New York City increased by nearly 25 percent and continued to spiral upward in Lindsay's third year as mayor. A blackout and then a blizzard crippled the five boroughs, especially Queens. Still, the mayor tried to downplay the trouble. In an interview the day after the MTA went on strike, Lindsay remarked to writer Dick Schaap that he still believed New York was a "fun city." His words were an affront to firefighters and cops who day in and out put their lives on the line in a city that grew ever more dangerous. In 1966 and into 1967, the firemen's union had battled the Lindsay administration for better wages and equipment. The rank and file of the fire department worked without a contract for nearly nine months.

During that time, a fire in the Madison Square section of Manhattan killed twelve firemen, after which public opinion lined up on the fire union's side. The dispute would ultimately be settled, but the tensions simmered on.

When the mayor came to Flushing that day, a parody of the bubblegum hit "Windy" serenaded him through a loudspeaker. Instead of the lyric "Everyone knows it's Windy," the loudspeaker blared, "Everyone knows it's Lindsay." Apparently the parody was an attempt to mock the mayor as effeminate, a category into which many in the city's blue-collar community placed hippies and the politicians who supported their causes.

Later that same year, in a televised speech, President Richard M. Nixon coined the term "silent majority" to describe the sleeping tiger of white conservatism in the United States. In New York City at least, Nixon was behind the curve. That majority had not only found its voice, but had begun to flex its muscles. In his meticulously researched book *The Hardhat Riot: Nixon, New York City, and the Dawn of the White Working-Class Revolution*, author David Paul Kuhn describes the day in May 1970 when construction workers left the half-built towers of the World Trade Center and descended upon a hippie antigovernment protest near Wall Street. While New York City cops folded their arms and watched from the sidelines, the hardhats beat the living daylights out of the mostly long-haired collegiate crowd. Some forty of the protestors suffered head wounds, including several who were knocked unconscious.

Since the days of Tammany Hall, the FDNY had been a bloc vote for the Democratic Party. Though it took fire union leadership some time to catch up, by the 1970s much of the department's white rank and file had become conservative Republicans. On November 3, 1969, in response to widespread antiwar protests, President

Richard M. Nixon said these words: "And so tonight—to you, the great silent majority of my fellow Americans—I ask for your support." In the sections like Flushing where firefighters and cops lived, he had it.

The beginning of the end of Lindsay's political career, however, would come not at the hands of hardhats or even Republicans. In early February 1969, a blizzard that dropped fifteen inches of snow crippled New York City and killed forty-eight people, most of them in Queens. The city was totally unprepared, primarily because the forecast had the snow turning to rain, which didn't happen. Still, Mayor Lindsay took the brunt of the blame. In 1971, he would enter the primary race for the Democratic nominee for president, but for all intents and purposes his political career ended in the piles of snow that blocked the streets in Queens. Though history has not looked fondly on Lindsay's years in City Hall, his mayoralty marked a sea change in New York City politics. His predecessor, Robert Wagner, was the last New York City mayor with ties to Tammany Hall. After Lindsay came a succession of progressive mayors, until 1994, when Rudolph W. Giuliani took the city's top office. And it wasn't until Giuliani that the fire department would have a friend in the mayor's office. The years prior to Rudy marked the most politically contentious period in the department since the days of Boss Tweed. And for much of that time, the city burned like never before.

Bill was certainly conservative in his life and political views. Years later, he wouldn't let Billy join the Boy Scouts because he didn't think the organization was manly enough for his son. Mario Cuomo was a classmate of his at St. John's, and Bill liked him as a person, but the future New York State governor's politics were far too liberal for his taste. But Bill remained a quiet conservative. As politics swirled out of control around him, he kept his focus on his job and family.

———

As a neighborhood to grow up in, Flushing was nearly ideal. With the working class comes children, and plenty of them. The street in front of the Feehan house was wide enough for football and roller hockey games, and there were enough kids to easily field the teams. Just a couple of blocks away was Browne Park, a twelve-acre village green that would turn into a wonderland with a frozen pond for skating and hills for sleigh rides in the winter. St. Mel's parochial grammar school was only a three-block walk from the house—so close that the Feehan children would come home for lunch on school days. Betty was a stickler about the family sitting together for dinner. Often, one or both of the sets of grandparents would join them. Bill would pick them up in the car and bring them home.

During this time, Bill found time to prepare for the lieutenant's exam. He studied mostly at home. Many firefighters use the downtime in the firehouse to study. But Bill didn't find it conducive, perhaps because, with two jobs and a house filled with kids, he needed the time to rest. On the days Betty was feeling better, she'd take the children out for a ride, or go over to visit her parents to give him time to study. Becoming a lieutenant in the New York City Fire Department is perhaps the most challenging civil service rank to achieve in the country. This is primarily because of the large number of people taking the exam and the small number of positions available. As with the entrance exam, the test is given once every four or five years. But Bill took the study habits he'd honed in Cathedral High School and St. John's University and applied them to the civil service test manuals. He aced the test, and would soon take the leap from firefighter to fire officer.

# SEVEN

# Lieutenant Feehan

By the mid-1960s, Betty would make one of her comebacks from her health issues. As she did, her relationship with Bill would regain some of the spontaneity, humor, and romance it contained early on. They loved Broadway and would dress up and head into the city to catch a show or play. Bill, thanks to his uncle Jim, developed a keen fashion sense early in life. Father Cashman would take him to Rogers Peet to buy suits. He brought his nascent eye for threads into his adulthood. He wore suits with wide lapels and coordinated ties, and topped the ensemble off with a fedora. Vince Dunn once said he dressed like Humphrey Bogart. Betty was even more stylish.

The few years Betty worked for the publisher, she would shop at Orbach's or S. Klein on Union Square to build her wardrobe. Though known for its bargains, Orbach's boasted a clientele that included celebrities and British royals. When they felt in a more avant-garde mood, Betty and Bill would attend shows Off-Broadway. One of their favorites was the musical *Jacques Brel Is Alive and Well and Living in Paris*, which ran at a small theater in Greenwich Village called the Village Gate. Though a carbon copy of his father as a firefighter, Bill was the opposite when it came to sharing the theater with his wife. They played the cast album at home for years afterward.

Sometimes on Bill's days off they would scour the bookstores in Greenwich Village, then have coffee and pastry at the famous Sutter's bakery. They would get into an argument, at times, usually about finances or Bill forgetting to pay the phone bill or Con Ed (though a stickler for detail in his job, Bill, for some reason, could be absentminded about running the household), and Betty would get so angry that sometimes she would throw dishes at her husband. More often than not the fights would end with both of them laughing. Still, there were times when Bill found it hard to see the humor in the situation. When Betty was behind the wheel was one of them.

When Betty finally passed the driver's exam, no one was more surprised than her. She immediately called her sister.

"I passed!" Betty exclaimed.

*After the ninety-ninth time*, Vera thought.

One day, when Bill was trying to give her a driving lesson, they were on the busy Van Wyck Expressway and he criticized something that Betty had done behind the wheel.

"You can't talk to me that way," she said, slamming on the brakes and getting out of the car. Bill watched his wife storm off the highway, leaving him sitting in the passenger seat as cars whizzed by.

Things didn't get any better after she passed her driving exam. When she was out on the road by herself, the calamities piled up like a multicar crash. She couldn't seem to line up the car correctly to go through a tollbooth. The shortcoming wouldn't be so bad if she didn't have any tollbooths to contend with. But if you lived in Flushing and you wanted to drive to a destination even a medium distance away, there was usually a tollbooth involved. It would take her multiple times to get the car lined up correctly, and with each failed attempt the drivers behind her would become more agitated. She also didn't pay much attention to extraneous features of the car, such as the gas gauge. For Betty, running out of gas was an act of God. One day the car sputtered to a stop on a highway. She left it and walked to a nearby side street. There she saw a fire alarm box. That night Bill was livid.

"Why would you pull a fire alarm?" Bill asked in a pained voice. "How could you embarrass me like that?"

Betty couldn't understand why he was making such a big fuss. Pulling the alarm seemed perfectly logical to her.

Some of her driving problems weren't of her making. The family car was an old Nash Rambler that had a bum starter for most of her early driving career. When Betty would visit her parents in Maspeth, she'd have to leave the car running.

Still, she loved taking the kids on road trips. She would scour the newspapers for destination ideas. One day, she drove with her children and Vera's daughters, Kathy and Mary, to a state police barracks in New Jersey. She'd read an article about an exhibition of police dogs they were giving. The plan, though, might have been a bit ambitious. Traveling from Queens to New Jersey isn't the easiest trip for even an experienced driver. It involves two bridges (and tollbooths), tricky mergers, and high-volume highways such as the Grand Central Parkway and the East Side Drive. Yet, miraculously, Betty made it all the way over the George Washington Bridge into New Jersey without incident. It was exiting the bridge where the problem started. Somehow she got turned around on the exit ramp and ended up going through the same tollbooth three times. On the last attempt, the toll-taker didn't have the heart to charge her.

When Bill wasn't working or studying for the next civil service exam, he would take the wheel for the day trips. Bill was a history buff, especially of the Civil War era, so Gettysburg in Pennsylvania was a favorite destination. They also went to Martin Van Buren's house in upstate New York, and the Kutztown Fair, also in Pennsylvania. In those happy times, Betty's personality would sparkle like lights on a Christmas wreath. From the Rambler's front bench seat, Bill and Betty would lead the kids in a singalong to the Bob Hope and Bing Crosby song "On the Way to Apalachicola Bay."

Still, for Bill, and to some extent the Feehan children too, lying just underneath the merriment was a foreboding feeling that the good times wouldn't last. When Betty gave birth again, they nearly disappeared for good.

———

As a newly minted lieutenant, Bill engaged in a system called "covering." Often when you're promoted to lieutenant, captain, or battalion chief, a permanent assignment isn't available right away. Instead, you're placed in fill-in positions to cover for other lieutenants, captains, or battalion chiefs who are out for an extended period because of sickness, vacation, or other reasons. You might be placed in the Bronx and a month later you're commuting to Staten Island. You're working in midtown Manhattan and the next thing you know you're in Corona, Queens. Although not the most ideal situation for the covering fire officer, "carrying the bag," as the practice is called, offers a rare opportunity. From the high-rise office buildings in midtown to the two-family homes in Queens, from the apartment houses with courtyards in the Bronx to tenements and taxpayers, buildings with businesses, in Harlem, a covering fire officer can accumulate an impressive array of fire service knowledge. Bill soaked up all he could in a couple of different ladder companies in downtown Manhattan, but still yearned for a house to call home. In August 1964, he would find one in Ladder 6 in Chinatown.

New York City's Chinatown in the mid-1960s posed a unique set of problems for firefighters. The Lower East Side has been home to many generations of a struggling immigrant populations. Since the turn of the century, multiple tragic fires in this densely populated area resulted in the reform of residential building codes to include fires escapes, air shafts, and building materials standards. However, the prevalent stock of aging four-story tenements with their notorious "railroad flats," several connected rooms without a hallway, has remained a most significant hazard to residents and a lifesaving challenge for firefighters to this day. Moreover, access to the narrow, irregular streets below Houston Street handicapped the responding fire companies in the area. Because of the relaxation of immigration laws in the mid-1960s, waves of Chinese people from Hong Kong, who were escaping civil unrest at home, packed these tiny apartments over the neighborhood's stores and restaurants, making the possibility of deadly fires all the more probable.

Still, it would be two fires just outside Ladder 6's first due response territory that would be the most memorable in Bill's time as a lieutenant. The first of those was a five-alarm blaze that would go down in the annals of FDNY history as the department's most tragic event until 9/11.

The blaze had started around 9 p.m. in an art store's basement on 22nd Street, in the Madison Square section of Manhattan. Firefighters didn't know that the previous owner of the building had recently reconfigured the basement to accommodate the art store by removing a load-bearing wall and erecting a four-inch cinderblock partition. The modified basement was filled with lacquer, paint, and other highly flammable supplies. The blaze in the cellar devoured what support was left under the floor in the drugstore that abutted the art dealer and faced 23rd Street. Engine 18 arrived at the second alarm. They began to run hose lines through the drugstore. As they did, the concrete floor beneath them gave way. Ten firemen dropped into the fiery pit. In a later report, an investigator wrote that the collapse occurred with a "suddenness that precluded even an attempt to escape." Two other firemen were incinerated by the flashover that blew up from the exposed basement.

Only two members of Engine 18 survived the fire. According to eyewitnesses, one was the chauffeur who had been assigned to the rig but was late changing into his gear when the call came in. The other was a fireman named John Donovan who'd been detailed earlier that evening to ticket cars blocking fire hydrants in his firehouse's district. When he heard that his company had responded to the fire on 23rd Street, he joined up with nearby Engine 5 and took the nozzle on a line they'd run into the building. In the thick smoke, he didn't see that the floor had given way and fell into the abyss that had swallowed ten members of his company. Miraculously, Donovan managed to hang on to the hose. Firemen saved him from falling into the flames below by pulling him out by his Scott Air-Pak's straps.

Ladder 6 arrived on the second or third alarm. Bill worked all night and into the next morning in what had first been a rescue operation, then, as the hours went by, one of recovery. As they would after the attack on 9/11, firemen formed bucket brigades to remove the rubble. With the others on the line, Bill stood silently as firemen carried out each of the charred bodies of their twelve dead brethren. The fire left twelve women without husbands and thirty-two children without fathers. In a little over eight years of fire service, including his time on the Fire Patrol, Bill had personally seen sixteen firefighters die in the line of duty. By the time he was an FDNY lieutenant, he knew the odor of burning flesh. He'd seen the frozen expressions of horror on the faces of dead firefighters.

He'd seen grizzled old-timers weep uncontrollably at firefighter funerals, and watched helplessly as widows and fatherless children tried to comprehend the incomprehensible. All active firefighters develop a fireproof skin that covers the difficult feelings and hurt. They wouldn't be able to continue to perform if they didn't have this protection. But the skin doesn't remove the scars and heartbreak. It merely hides the wounds from others. During the early days of the New York City Fire Department, before radios or transmitters were in use, the department signaled a fireman's death in the line of duty by sounding from headquarters five bell strikes repeated four times. The "striking of the four fives" is still in use today over department radio when a firefighter has fallen. When firefighter hear those solemn sounds, their hearts clench and tears fall. But those emotions are most often shown only to other firefighters.

———

The second of these memorable fires for Bill burned not in a basement, but thirty-three floors above him. For most of the 1960s, Wall Street boomed. Yet despite the strength of the stock market, downtown Manhattan was in severe decline. Corporations fled to the suburbs. Nearly 30 percent of the Fortune 500 companies headquartered in the city fled for safer and newer environments. As early as 1960, the physical stability of the financial center was in jeopardy. From the dust left behind by the stampede, David Rockefeller decided to build a sixty-story tower just two blocks north of Wall Street as the headquarters for his Chase Manhattan Bank. A strong case can be made that without One Chase Manhattan Plaza, the revival of the financial district in the 1960s might not have happened, nor, perhaps, the construction of the first World Trade

Center in 1968. The revitalization of downtown Manhattan, however, came at a steep price for some.

In order to build the towers, the Port Authority of New York and New Jersey would have to remove what was known as "Radio Row," a thirteen-square-block ecosystem of mom-and-pop stores, many Jewish-owned, that sold everything from fuses to vacuum tubes to transistors and every other imaginable surplus electronic gadget. At the height of its popularity in the fifties, the center would draw tens of thousands of customers a day. Some thirty thousand people worked there. Despite community protests, which included a widely publicized mock funeral replete with a coffin containing a dead "Mr. Small Businessman," the city went about a cold, systematic campaign to remove the stores. In a cruel twist of fate, one of Bill's first assignments as lieutenant was to ticket the electronic shops for fire code violations to add pressure on them to leave so the towers could be built. Bill was not happy with the task. He'd rather have been fighting fire and he identified much more with the working stiffs than with those erecting the soaring towers of finance.

Just as the finishing touches were applied to the twin towers, another newly constructed building at the very southern tip of Manhattan, 1 New York Plaza, opened its doors to its first tenants. The fifty-story tower would expose the flaws in high-rise fire safety construction at the time, including in the twin towers.

It was August 5, 1970, when the fire started in a locker that housed telephone equipment on the thirty-third floor. An elevator that contained three building workers stopped unexpectedly on the fire floor. The pocket of air in the stalled car sucked in smoke like dust into a vacuum. Two of the three men in the car would die of smoke inhalation.

A second alarm brought Ladder 6 to the fire scene. As Bill rode in the cab, the rig raced from Chinatown down East Broadway to lower Manhattan. Halfway there, steam started blowing out of the truck's engine. An air hose line had split, causing the rig to lose power. For Bill, the idea of missing the fire was not an option. He sent a firefighter to a hardware store to buy duct tape to patch the hose. The jury-rigging worked, and they were back on their way. Meanwhile, the radio crackled to life with the dispatcher asking the company's location. Lieutenant Feehan said they were three blocks away, a lie. They arrived at the fire ten minutes later.

Directing the operation was the chief of the department, John O'Hagan—perhaps the most controversial, legendary, and innovative fire chief the FDNY has ever known. He's credited with bringing to the department such innovations as lightweight air masks, infrared sensors to detect fires in walls, the "jaws of life" for victims in car crashes, and bucket "cherry-picker" ladders for high-rise rescue. Later, when Mayor John Lindsay appointed him as fire commissioner, he kept his chief-of-department rank and became the only person to hold both positions simultaneously. The rank-and-file firefighters disliked him for budget cuts and the closing of firehouses, but respected him for his firefighting knowledge and experience. Later, he would, literally, write the book* about fighting high-rise fires.

Buildings taller than the reach of aerial ladders posed a unique set of problems for firefighters. Search-and-rescue units have to climb stairways in the towering structure; engine companies must rely on standpipes installed in the building for water sources. They also have to depend on internal communication systems, which can

---

* John T. O'Hagan, *High Rise Fire Safety* (Tulsa: Pennwell Corporation, 1977).

fail. Building codes then demanded that construction in high-rise buildings prevent fires from spreading from one floor to another. However, the flames in 1 New York Plaza found their way to the ventilation shafts and shot to the floors above. O'Hagan sent engine companies to the floor below the fire to stage a base of operation. It took nearly twenty-five minutes for the engine company to reach the thirty-third floor and hook up a hose line to the standpipe. Meanwhile, the fire intensified and spread. The heat blew out the windows on the south and east sides of the thirty-third floor and vast plumes of flames billowed from them.

O'Hagan sent Bill's company into the building twice that night. When they first arrived, he ordered them to the floor above the fire to see if there were open access stairways through which the fire could travel. Entry was impossible, however.

"Lou, it's just too hot," one of the grizzled firemen told him. "We got to get out of here."

When they returned to the command area, Bill delivered the bad news to O'Hagan.

"If you can't get in, you can't get in," the chief said as he ordered another company to try.

Bill felt like he had failed in his duty. As a young lieutenant, he was always trying to measure up with more experienced guys he worked alongside. He wanted to be respected by them, and also didn't want to let them down. A short time later, he would get another chance.

This time, O'Hagan sent Ladder 6 to the top of the building. There were reports that civilians and construction workers were trapped on the roof. Bill's company took an elevator to the thirty-second floor, under the fire. Using an elevator during a tower fire can be a precarious proposition. One elevator in the building would stall that night, trapping an entire fire company inside. Thankfully, no one was hurt. The elevator Ladder 6 took, however, made it without incident. The crew then climbed the stairs the rest of the way—twenty-eight floors. By the time they got to the top of the building, a police helicopter had already rescued the few civilians and construction workers from the roof. O'Hagan then gave Bill the order to search and vent the floors on the way down. It was an exhausting process. Each window in the new building had five locks, which needed a special wrench to open. The firefighters had to use screwdrivers, which took time. Each floor contained offices and partitions that slowed the task down even more. It took them hours to make their way back down. At one point they stopped between two floors. Sweating profusely, one of the old-timers sat in the stairwell and looked up at Bill.

"You and your damn duct tape," he said.

Lieutenant Feehan remembered being so dehydrated it was like having sandpaper in his throat. Deep into their descent, they came across an executive dining area. The sight before them, brand-new stainless steel appliances and huge refrigerators, was like an oasis in the desert. They couldn't believe their eyes. The refrigerators had locks that posed little problem to pop. Once they were open, however, the company's collective enthusiasm deflated. The refrigerator contained only ten small cans of fruit salad. The men inhaled the contents of the cans and drank the little juice they contained. It was better than nothing, but just barely.

————

Meanwhile, below them, the fire had spread to the thirty-fourth and thirty-fifth floors. Dozens of firefighters were now in the building fighting the blaze in the thick black smoke. The fire burned so hot it melted the metal bases of the office furniture. Far more ominously, the super-intense heat began to warp the structural steel supports of the building. Two years before, New York City's fire code had begun allowing a type of spray-on fireproofing that hadn't been fully tested under extreme circumstance. The same fireproofing was also used in the construction of the upper floors of the World Trade Center towers. In both cases, the fireproofing failed to protect the building's structural support. The only difference was the extent of the failure.

It was eleven o'clock at night before Bill's company made it safely back down to the staging area. An assistant chief of the department, a man who had a reputation as a tyrant, immediately called Bill over. The first thought that entered the young lieutenant's mind was that there must have been surveillance cameras in the dining room that had captured the unit pilfering the fruit cups. That thought was followed by one that told him his career was over. The chief, however, just wanted Bill to apprise him of the conditions inside the tower.

Lieutenant Feehan sat on the sidewalk, soaked in sweat, his helmet on the ground next to him. He had no way of knowing how close he and the other firefighters in 1 New York Plaza had come to unimaginable disaster. When the heat-warped support beams separated from their connections, the building had begun to collapse. Unlike the World Trade Center, however, concrete slabs that made up the floors buckled but refused to give way. Had they failed, scores of firefighters and office workers would have died. The fire in 1 New York Plaza killed two and injured twenty-six firefighters and a dozen civilians. In his book *Command and Control of Fires and Emergencies*, published in 1999, Vince Dunn wrote about the dangers that high-rise fires pose. He had fought high-rise fires in midtown Manhattan for fifteen years. He'd witnessed firsthand the deficiencies of high-rise buildings, and was amazed that a calamity of more significant proportions had not yet occurred.

"It is my opinion," he wrote, "that the fire service has been lucky."

Two years after his book was published, that luck would run out.

———

While developers were breaking ground in downtown Manhattan for towers that would change the skyline, other neighborhoods of New York City were descending into a cauldron of racial tension. Just before the department promoted Bill to lieutenant and assigned him to Chinatown, a white off-duty New York City police lieutenant shot and killed a fifteen-year-old Black high school student. The killing triggered a race riot first in Harlem and then in the Bedford-Stuyvesant neighborhood in Brooklyn. The New York riots would be the kindling to deadly racial unrest that would blaze across the country throughout the 1960s and after. Though most of the ire of the Black community was directed at the cops, firefighters weren't immune. As with inner-city neighborhoods in Los Angeles, Newark, and Detroit, firefighters in Harlem were targets. Residents in poor communities would start fires in buildings, then block the firemen from fighting them. On its face, it seems ludicrous that residents would do this, but most of these structures weren't owned by people who lived locally but by absentee landlords who cared little about the communities in which their buildings sat. They let them fall into disrepair, and they gouged people with rent. And as soon as they squeezed the last dollar out of the property, they left it empty. On one hand, then, you couldn't blame the residents for their action. On the other, however, forcibly keeping firefighters from fighting fire was the height of societal dysfunction. When he was chief of the department, O'Hagan testified about the issue before a state panel. There he described what he called "guerrilla tactics" by inner-city youths. They would lure firefighters by false alarms and other methods into confined areas, then pelt them with bricks, cans, and "even kitchen refrigerators," he said.

In his book *Black Firefighters and the FDNY: The Struggle for Jobs, Justice, and Equity in New York City*, David Goldberg cites nine separate incidences of bullets fired at firefighters in 1967 alone. Just in July of that year, there were 160 reported attacks against them. According to several stories published in New York City newspapers, firefighters began to arm themselves with blackjacks (short, easily hidden leather clubs) and other weapons.

Back in Chinatown, however, Bill and Ladder 6 didn't have to worry about riots or being attacked. Business organizations (a generous way of categorizing the group) called tongs ran the neighborhood with an iron fist. The Chinese secret societies employed young toughs just off the boat from Hong Kong and proficient in martial arts as enforcers. Nothing happened in Chinatown unless the tongs allowed it to happen. Separated from the rest of the city by organized crime, language, and custom, New York's Chinatown in the 1960s might as well have been a neighborhood in Hong Kong. Though the local residents treated the firefighters with respect, outside of fighting a fire there was little interaction between the firehouse and the community. There was one relationship Ladder 6 forged with a local resident, however, that Bill would talk about for the rest of his career.

Most firehouses have buffs, civilians who are obsessed with the milieu of fire service, from a historical perspective to the latest in gear and apparatus. Buffs hang around the firehouse, run errands and help out when they can, and, at least back in the day, get to ride on the rig every once in a while. In New York City, the practice stopped after a rig was involved in an accident and a buff was severely hurt. Ladder 6 had a buff whom they named Charlie, an older Chinese gentleman. Charlie, whom the firemen referred to as "Charlie the Chinaman," spoke very little English but somehow had struck up a friendship with several of the firefighters who worked with Bill, and began visiting the firehouse daily. Unlike the average buff, Charlie had no interest in the fire service at all and was not impressed by any of the equipment or the firemen for that matter. Still, he was very protective of them and the firehouse of Ladder 6. When the company would go out on a run, Charlie would close the bay doors after them and sit at the watch desk until they returned. During major fires, when companies from several firehouses in the area had to respond, a "located company" from a distance away would fill in in the firehouses out on the call so the area wasn't stripped of fire service. Though Charlie would let them into the firehouse, he wouldn't allow any of the firefighters to sit at the watch desk or touch the journal. It's standard procedure for a located company to sign in to the firehouse, but Charlie would chase them away with his cane. He'd answer the phone at the watch desk by saying, "Nobody home," and hang up. When Bill first arrived at the firehouse, the men in Ladder 6 told Charlie that their new lieutenant was married to a Chinese woman. Though not the worst of racist humor, it was indicative of the narrow-mindedness of the day. Still, from that moment on, Charlie brought Bill almond and fortune cookies so many times, Bill's kids still can't eat them.

———

At one point, Charlie stopped coming around. The firefighters close to him became so concerned that they checked the local hospital.

Sure enough, they found out that he was in Bellevue Hospital after being injured in a hit-and-run car accident. The guys from Ladder 6 went to the hospital regularly to visit him. When he was released, he went back to his apartment in a tenement on Allen Street in Chinatown. But Charlie wasn't very mobile after the accident and couldn't visit his friends like he used to. On the Thanksgiving after he left the hospital, the guys in the company got the idea that they would go pick him up and bring him to the firehouse for Turkey dinner. They put Charlie in a Stokes basket, one of those aluminum-tube stretchers that you see in helicopter rescues, and carried him down the stairs to the rig.

At dinner that day, it was decided, instead of sending Charlie back to his apartment, they would let him live in the firehouse. There was a small room in the basement that the firefighters used to watch TV. They moved Charlie in that night. Though Charlie was thrilled, the captain had gone along with the plan reluctantly. "He dies down there you're putting him back in the Stokes basket and getting him the hell out of here."

Though Bill's work life was interesting and rewarding, the atmosphere at home turned grim. Betty gave birth once again. Baby Michael was born healthy, but developed a medical issue when he was about four months old. We know that Michael's condition was serious enough that it required surgery, but was also not life-threatening. Though the procedure was somewhat routine, a mistake with general anesthesia occurred. The infant never gained consciousness and died on the operating table.

Betty's world collapsed after Michael's death. She'd draw the shades in her bedroom and stay there for days at a time. Nothing seemed to be able to shake her from her despondence. One day, Bill walked into the bedroom with Billy, hoping to cheer her up. Earlier,

Billy had played a soccer game and scored two goals. But when he told his mother the good news, Betty turned her head away.

"I want Michael," she said.

Bill put an arm around his son's shoulder and walked him out of the room. When Betty acted like that, Bill would tell the kids that their mother had a biological condition and didn't know what she was saying to them. But Betty's problems were far more than just biological, and her emotional fragility snapped with her child's death. In a way, Betty lost all hope for the future when Michael died. Tara was too young to understand, but Liz and Billy bore the brunt of that emptiness. They would lean on their father for emotional support. And Bill would always be there for them. Whether it was cooking dinner, driving Tara to twirling, or attending Billy's soccer or Liz's step dancing, he did what he could to fill the void. And so did the children, especially Liz, who guarded her dad's feelings. In some ways, she felt responsible for him. Even today, long after their dad is gone, the Feehan women protect their father's legacy.

# EIGHT

# The War Years

In Bill's time, and to some extent today, the New York City Fire Department was divided in two. You're either a truckie or an engine guy. Some ranks reside above those designations, of course, and specialty squads such as Rescue and Hazmat exist outside of them, but nearly all firefighters in specialty squads or of rank once worked on trucks or in engine companies, and many still identify themselves as such.

To use a football analogy, firefighters on ladder trucks are like the flashy position players, the wideouts, running backs, and quarterbacks. They get the applause, the dramatic photos in the newspaper, and, at the risk of political correctness, all the pretty girls. Okay, maybe they didn't have an exclusive on cute girls, but they certainly received more attention from the outside world. This is not to say the job on a ladder truck is easy. Along with making dramatic rescues, truckies, as they're known, are called upon for several essential tasks. They're charged with forcible entry into buildings and ventilation of the fire scene. They also perform what's called "overhaul," making sure fire hasn't seeded in the walls and ceilings of the structure.

Engine companies, on the other hand, are like the linemen. They're at the point of attack, nose-to-nose with the red demon. The nozzleman is the center. The backup and guys on the line are the tackles and tight ends. They're burly and dirty and do most of the heavy lifting, which includes running hose lines from a water source directly to the seat of the fire, no matter how arduous or dangerous the journey. After a severe fire, the saying goes, truck guys go to Medal Day, while engine guys go to the burn center. It might come as little surprise, then, that a subtle rivalry exists between a truck and engine companies. Actually, it's not so subtle.

In February 1972, the fire department promoted Bill to captain and assigned him to Engine 59 in Harlem. At evening mealtime his first day in his new company, a freshly minted Captain Feehan walked into the kitchen in the firehouse to see the members of his company, burly veteran firefighters, sitting around the table naked. Completely. No boots, no pants, no shirts, no underwear. Birthday suits. The first thing that came to Bill's mind was that it wasn't a pretty sight he was looking at. He then realized that this was an inflection point. How he reacted would set the tone of how they perceived him as their superior. He decided the best action was inaction. Without so much as a second glance, he filled his plate, sat, and began eating his dinner. When he finished, he left the table and went up to his office, without ever saying a word.

Bill might have passed the engine company's initiation, but as far as the men in Engine 59 were concerned, the new captain was a ladder guy until proven otherwise. As it happened, there would be plenty of opportunities for him to do so.

It's commonly held that during game two of the 1977 World Series, while a helicopter-mounted television camera captured a huge blaze in a public school a few blocks from Yankee Stadium, Howard Cosell announced to his TV audience, "Ladies and gentlemen, the Bronx is burning." As the writer Joe Flood once pointed out, it would have been a great quote if he actually said it. As is often the case with pithy phrases, ones such as "Houston, we have a problem," or "Play it again, Sam," Cosell never actually said those words. He did wonder aloud how many alarms the fire was (five). He told the viewers that the "fire department has its work cut out for it." But the words "the Bronx is burning" never tumbled from the bombastic sportscaster's lips. They gained infamy, however, because they aptly captured the reality of the moment. Throughout the 1970s, in large sections of the Bronx, fire and abandonment consumed over 95 percent of the building stock.

In his book *Strong at Heart,* Tom Von Essen describes his time working in Ladder 42 in the South Bronx. His firehouse was so busy, the future fire commissioner writes, that dispatchers would remind chauffeurs on the rigs not to stop at other fires on the way to the ones to which they were responding. By the 1970s, his firehouse received twenty to thirty calls a night, an unbelievable and exhausting number. Still, the phrase doesn't tell the full story. The Bronx wasn't the only section of New York City that was burning. City-wide, the fire statistics during the 1970s, an era known in the FDNY as the "war years," were staggering. In the 1950s, the yearly average of fire alarms was about sixty thousand. By 1975, that number had exploded to four hundred thousand. Flames engulfed the South Bronx, Brownsville and Bedford-Stuyvesant in Brooklyn, the Lower East Side and Harlem in Manhattan. Arson was the talked-about culprit. And though it was true that fire insurance policies were sometimes worth more than properties, and that some slumlords ripped anything of value, such as appliances, telephones, and copper wiring, out of the buildings before punching holes in the roofs so the fire would travel and then setting them ablaze themselves, arson was not the main reason for the devastation. In fact, it made up only a very small percentage of the fires. In his wonderful book *The Fires: How a Computer Formula Burned Down New York City—and Determined the Future of American Cities,* author Joe Flood details the closing of firehouses in lower-income areas in New York and the city's reliance on a misguided computer-generated strategy—devised by the military think tank the RAND Corporation—to predict fire and assign manpower. Following RAND's computer models, Commissioner O'Hagan closed nearly fifty firehouses in all. When you added the fact that the city's infrastructure was falling apart because of neglect and a lack of funds to fix it—some estimate that over a quarter of the fire hydrants didn't work—it was no wonder the fires had the upper hand.

The reasons the city was on fire, however, mattered little to the firefighters in the trenches. In Engine 59's first response area, lightning-quick tenement blazes would devour the structures from the inside out. Yet time after time, fire after fire, the engine company would run hose lines into the burning buildings and climb the stairs. The fires came so frighteningly fast, the joke went, that all you needed was sneakers and a raincoat to be a Harlem firefighter then. For Engine 59, the fight was personal. They fought so many tough five-story tenement fires, blazes that always seemed to start in the same, hard-to-access location in the building, that the company came up with a motto: "Five floors up, and five rooms deep." They'd go to wherever the fire took them. After the first few fires Bill fought with Engine 59 he was convinced he would never get out of the place alive.

The seventies also marked perhaps the broadest division between firefighters and the people they were charged to protect, primarily those in the poorer sections of the city.

The conditions in the poorer neighborhoods of New York City

were brutal during the seventies. City sanitation practically stopped picking up garbage in those neighborhoods because they were so dangerous. Illegal drugs were pervasive, and cops refused to patrol areas. Vince Dunn was the captain in a firehouse just south of Bill's. He remembers a cop being shot and killed on the street and, to the best of his recollection, no one ever being arrested for the crime. In 1975, police distributed a pamphlet at the airports and train stations entitled "Fear City," which warned tourists of the dangers of visiting New York City. One of the pamphlet's bullet points stated that there weren't enough firefighters to fight all the fires.

Older neighborhood residents lived in a constant state of fear of both drug addicts and the police. One day, Dunn's company responded to a call in a tenement walk-up. The occupant, an elderly woman, had called the fire department because, she said, she'd smelled smoke. When the firefighters arrived, she asked them to check the fire escape because she thought there was someone out there.

Still, unlike the police, who had to interact with the community daily, firefighters were like jet pilots on sorties. They would fly as fast as they could to the fire and then head back to the firehouse nearly as quickly. Where cops of the era had an "us against them" relationship with the inner city residents, firefighters' connections to the poorer neighborhoods were more of a "there's us and there's them" dynamic. The neighborhood and FDNY inhabited two different worlds, and firefighters would only venture into the other when it was burning.

Adding to this divisions was that, by the 1970s, much of the department was living outside the city limits. They were also nearly all white. Helped across the finish line by the Uniformed Firefighters Association, a repeal of residency restrictions cleared the way for a commuting class of firefighter. They moved in droves to Long Island or Rockland County or Orange County north of the city, and drove in to work. They were young fathers with growing families. They saw how bad the city was getting and wanted no part of it for their own children.

Many of the firemen who worked during the war years had been in the department during the social unrest of the 1960s. For Harlem firefighters, the scars from the fires of the sixties had barely healed when the fires that torched the seventies descended upon them. Many white firefighters held a simmering resentment toward the people in Harlem. By the seventies, the spate of physical attacks had lessened, but sick voyeurism, which was no less dangerous, took its place. Vince Dunn remembers drunks and addicts setting fire to buildings to watch the flashing lights and streams of water. And not all of the arson was just a light show. In July 1977, a twenty-five-year-old fireman named Martin Celtic was fighting an arsonist's blaze on the fifth floor of an abandoned tenement on the Lower East Side. As Celtic made his way up to the fire, the same arsonist who set the original fire returned and set another one below him. Celtic tried to escape the inferno the apartment had become by jumping into the bucket on a ladder. He fell seventy feet to his death.

———

Of course, the resentment on both sides mostly had to do with race and the extreme underrepresentation of the Black community in the FDNY. Because of this, it was easy for everyone to become entrenched in their own point of view, further cultivating the us-against-them dynamic. In 1966, the department numbered 13,500 uniformed and civilian employees and only 600 were Black. Those stark numbers made Mayor Lindsay's choice for his first fire commissioner all the more unexpected. In fact, the appointment sent shock waves through the fire department and the city at large. On January 1, 1966, Robert O. Lowery became the first African American to head a fire department in any major American city. He had been the president of the Vulcan Society, a line organization or brotherhood that led efforts toward reversing discrimination by the department's overwhelmingly white membership and in its unfair hiring practices.

The Vulcan Society was formed in the wake of Tammany Hall by a small group of Black New York City firefighters. During the Depression, a reform administration led by Mayor Fiorello LaGuardia displaced the Tammany Tiger, as the political machine was called. With LaGuardia, and Franklin Delano Roosevelt on the national stage, a movement toward equal employment opportunities took hold. Still, systemic and inherent racism ran strong throughout New York City civil service. In William Patrick Feehan's time, it was not unusual for a firehouse to have a "Black bed," where Black firefighters would be relegated to sleep. More often than not, the Black bed would be placed next to the bathroom. But as Tammany faded from view, progressives scored minor victories toward racial equality in the FDNY. In 1937, the FDNY appointed fifteen Black firefighters, a number that had been unimaginable just a few years before. Those pioneers rode the liberal wave in New York City politics by forming the Vulcan Society, which in turn set the stage for Lowery's appointment.

In August 1963, Lowery led a contingent of the Vulcan Society in joining Dr. Martin Luther King's March on Washington, where they acted as marshals along the parade route. During his tenure as commissioner, he piloted programs that helped train high school students and high school dropouts for a career in the FDNY. He also pushed for community outreach by Black firefighters so that young men could see that people who looked like them could work for and succeed in the FDNY.

In a speech to a conference of Black firefighters, he said that minorities made up a third of New York's population and that half of the department's responses were in minority sections of the city. Yet Blacks and Hispanics made up only 8 percent of the fire department's workforce.

Lowery increased the promotion of Black men within the department, and transferred them to work in Black neighborhoods, a practice that would bring an intense backlash from white firemen and the fire unions.

————

Lowery's time as fire commissioner proved more polarizing than anything else. His attempts to tear down the racial divides in the department mostly failed because of the entrenched white culture of the FDNY. In 1970, the *New York Times* interviewed him about the bitter and heated response to his efforts at a more integrated department. He seemed despondent in the news story. "I think maybe we should go back to the old ways," he said, talking about the days when the races in the department were fully segregated. He knew intimately about that time. When he joined the fire department in 1941, Black firefighters still weren't allowed to sleep in the same room in the firehouse with whites, or even to use the same utensils.

Though Lowery was once an ally of the Uniformed Firefighters Association, his relationship with the union soured in the years afterward. Attacks by the union became relentless when he tried to take firefighters on night shifts out of slow firehouses in lower Manhattan to work in busy Brownsville ones.

Despite the bitter divide, the first Black fire commissioner remained a firefighter at heart. Three of the twelve firefighters who died in the 23rd Street fire were members of the Vulcan Society. The loss devastated Lowery, who was seen crying while he toured the ruins of the building. He had responded to the fire early and took unwarranted blame for the chaos that had occurred in fighting the deadly blaze.

Ultimately, racism defeated Lowery. What started as a single union member spreading rumors of the commissioner dealing drugs and selling answers to promotional exams grew to a scandal that was reported in the press. Though none of the stories were remotely accurate, they helped to accomplish their intended purpose. Lowery resigned on September 29, 1973, after an apparent internal power struggle, and John O'Hagan took the top job. In a speech to the Vulcan Society, Lowery had this to say: "Always remember that America—including many white firefighters—will never let you forget that your recognizable ancestors were brought to this country in chains and that they believe you are inferior."

———

Lowery wasn't the only member of the FDNY defeated by the times. By the early 1970s, morale within the department had hit perhaps its lowest point in history. Day in and out, firefighters literally put their lives on the line to fight an unceasing inferno. In return, they received little thanks from the communities they served and layoffs and pay freezes from the city. The anger was palpable. Laid-off firemen picketed Fire Commissioner O'Hagan's home. O'Hagan's wife, Kaye, took to serving coffee to the protesting firefighters. The gesture did little to soothe the tensions. In October 1973, the union sent ballots to its members, asking them if they wanted to strike.

Not only once unthinkable, a firefighters' strike would also be illegal under a state statute called the Taylor Law, which would impose heavy fines on the union. It would also be contrary to the core instinct that calls people to become firefighters in the first place. And yet when the ballots were counted, the union members voted overwhelmingly to strike, at least according to Richard J. Vizzini, the Uniformed Firefighters Association president.

A stocky, balding man, Vizzini looked more like an accountant than a union boss, or a firefighter, for that matter. Though outwardly unimposing, the union chief had paid his dues in the fire fields. He spent the first twenty-two years of his career as a chauffeur and firefighter in the South Bronx. He brought the same tenacity and love for his fellow firefighter to his role as union president. In 1973, the base pay for firefighters was a little over $14,000 a year. It was a livable wage, but a stretch for firefighters with growing families. From his first moment in office in the spring of 1973, he fought for a $2,000 raise for firefighters. Demanding a raise from the city then was like asking a subway panhandler to loan you a hundred bucks. The city was shutting firehouses down, not giving out raises.

The strike took place on November 6, 1973, and lasted only five hours. Battalion chiefs, captains, and lieutenants took to the trucks and engines to fill in for the striking firefighters. The department took probys out of the academy to help out. This makeshift firefighting force answered some 330 calls during the five hours of the strike. The *New York Times* told of striking firefighters showing up at one fire to taunt the probys who had responded to the call.

From any vantage point, the walkout was an ugly episode. It would cause a fissure between the men who struck and those who wouldn't leave the firehouses unattended. It damaged the fire department's reputation for years to come. And it would expose audacious deception on the part of union leadership.

An investigation found that UFA members had not voted overwhelmingly to strike. In fact, as revealed under a court-ordered recount, they had voted against the strike. Vizzini and his top lieutenants in union leadership had unilaterally made the decision.

Vizzini later would plead guilty to a charge of reckless endangerment, and the state court sentenced him to three years' probation. Yet he remained union president, would be elected to a second term, and would ultimately win a raise of $950 a year for his members.

As a captain, Bill was a member of the Uniformed Fire Officers Association and did not go out on strike. Still, the walkout put him in a difficult position. He was a firefighter first and foremost. He certainly knew from personal experience how little the city paid firefighters for putting their lives at risk. But the strike wounded him because it had damaged the department he loved.

Still, it was hard for Bill to be mad at the guys with whom he had worked with for so long. He had come a long way with them since the naked meal he shared on his first day as captain. One of his favorites in the firehouse was a tough firefighter named Paddy who wore his hair and mustache long, the style of the day. The coif might have been stylish, but it was the bane of a battalion chief stationed at the firehouse who would constantly tell Paddy to trim his locks. In response, the firefighter would shrug and say he'd love to but that he moonlighted as a musician in a rock band. Though a stickler on appearances, the chief knew that Paddy had a family, and he wasn't going to take the bread off the man's table. Then one day Paddy hosted a barbecue for the truck company and invited the battalion chief. When the chief struck up a conversation with Paddy's wife, he asked about the band.

"What band?" she asked.

It was Paddy who sealed Bill's initiation as an engine guy. One time, a chief had dressed down Bill for some action he'd taken at a fire. Chief Feehan took it hard, but afterward, Paddy threw an arm around his captain. "Don't worry, Skipper," he said. "He's just another clipboard-carrying, noncombatant clown."

————

Out of all his assignments, Bill perhaps liked his time in Harlem the most. Later, in interviews, he would speak of the men he worked with there with deep respect. He'd compare his engine company with the Arnold Schwarzenegger–type body builders he saw proliferate in the ladder companies during the seventies. Bill would say that many of the ladder guys spent their downtime lifting weights and drinking protein shakes, while the short, dumpy engine guys would sit in the firehouse smoking a Lucky Strike. And yet when the bell rang, Bill would rather be alongside the short, dumpy engine guy every time. Because it wasn't brawn, or even brains, that was the main ingredient of a good firefighter. It was heart. And for his money, engine companies had more heart than anyone else in the department, and he knew that long before he'd even joined the fire department. He knew it because he saw that heart in his father.

————

Often the Feehans would pile into the family car and drive to Jackson Heights to have dinner at Bill's parents' house. William would make chocolate milk in plastic cowboy boot cups for his grandchildren. He'd pile ham on rye bread to have himself a sandwich. "I like 'em high and dry," he would tell the kids. One day at home, he'd had an appendicitis attack. The doctor had told him they either had to remove the appendix or he'd have to be on a bland diet. William understood the directions to mean for him to stay away from mustard. By then, William was completely bald, and with deep, dark circles under his eyes, and large, leathery hands, some of the grandchildren were frightened by his appearance. But he would disarm them with funny stories about the fire department. "I lost my hair in a fire" was one of his favorite lines.

At some point during the evening, Bill and William Sr. would begin to "talk fire," as they called it. Those conversations would be held at the dinner table, or afterward in the living room. The family, seated all around them, might be chattering on about something else, but one ear was always tuned in to William and Bill's conversation. As he did when he was a kid listening to his dad's tales of the firehouse and the calls he went on, Bill cherished these moments. But now he was the one telling the stories, while William listened intently. Certainly, advice was still offered by the elder Feehan, but most of the time William was fine with letting his son hold court. In one way, they were very different firemen. William was content with the nozzle in his hand, facing down the seed of the fire. His son, on the other hand, couldn't wait for the adventure the next rank would bring. Still, undeniably, they shared one trait, and that was the love of what they did for a living.

William Patrick Feehan died on February 2, 1975. Emphysema was listed as the cause on his death certificate. He never smoked a cigarette or cigar in his life. Bill had always seen his father as indestructible, and the loss struck him deeply. He had wanted to be a fireman like his dad from almost before he could walk. A photo exists of Bill, about one or two standing in front of his father who was wearing his dress uniform. In a way, his love for his dad and his love for the fire department were one and the same.

The funeral Mass was held at St. Joan of Arc's Catholic Church in Jackson Heights, and was filled with two generations of firefighters— the few old-timers still alive from William's time, and the engine men from Harlem. As he was lowered into the ground at Calvary Cemetery in Queens, Bill saluted him. It was a humble service, just the way William would have wanted it.

———

In most firehouses, the captain of the engine company is called "the captain of the house." He's responsible for all repairs and maintenance to the firehouse. In that role, Bill would experience one of the more interesting interactions he would have with the neighborhood. One time in the Harlem firehouse, Bill had the floors in the bay replaced. While the work was taking place, the chauffeurs parked the rigs in the fire zone across from the firehouse. Harlem streets then were notorious for lack of places to park. Car owners disregarded alternate-side parking rules. Abandoned cars, and ones that sat on rims, lined the streets. For the kids in the neighborhood, fire zones were a perfect basketball court. They could fix a hoop to a streetlamp and play all day and night without worrying about some junkheap being parked in the way. But when Captain Feehan ordered the apparatus parked there, the kids ran out of luck. At least when it came to having basketball games. City kids, however, adapt quickly. Instead of playing hoops, they began to use the trucks as jungle gyms. One activity was to climb up onto the cab and then jump to the street below. Aside from them scuffing up his trucks, Bill became increasingly concerned that one of the youngsters would jump in front of the cars that were always racing down the block. He walked over to the nearby police precinct and presented his dilemma. The cops cordoned off the fire trucks and posted an officer to watch over them. Problem solved. At least for Bill. For one prominent resident, however, Bill's solution was economically untenable.

Soon after the cop was posted, Sonny, a high-profile community member, walked into the firehouse and asked for the captain. "You're killing my business!" he said to Bill. Along with being a neighborhood stalwart, Sonny was also one of the biggest illegal numbers runners in Harlem. Having cops posted in one of his more popular spots hit him right in the rubber band that held his wad of cash.

"I'm worried about the kids," Bill answered.

"You won't have to worry about that," Sonny assured him. "Just get rid of the cop."

The saying goes, captains run the fire service. Vince Dunn says that a captain makes more decisions in a day than a chief will make in a month. Some of those decisions are made in the heat of the action, while others can be pondered and weighed. In this instance, it didn't take long for Bill to make up his mind.

"I'll see what I can do," he promised Sonny.

Captain Feehan asked for the cops to be removed from the post. The next day, surrounding the rigs were four of the most enormous human beings he'd ever seen in his life.

From that day forward, Sonny sent fresh turkeys on Thanksgiving and Christmas to every firefighter in Bill's firehouse.

———

Bill spent less than five years as captain of Engine 59, but he would carry for the rest of his career his experiences in the Harlem of the seventies. He wasn't a bleeding heart. Far from it. He'd called the bad actors who populated the streets around Engine 59 "mutts" or "skels." There were plenty of skels then in Harlem. A heroin epidemic had a stranglehold on the community. But he also knew that Harlem was filled with loving, hardworking people who struggled day in and out in a society stacked against them. At the time, Harlem folks raised families with little money and in horrible living conditions. He'd see mothers carrying babies and fathers coming home from work after overnight shifts. He saw families dressed in their Sunday best walking to church. It's easy to stereotype people, especially from behind the firehouse walls, and Bill would later admit he could be as narrow-minded as any firefighter. Harlem, however, would open his eyes. Often, when he'd have a weekend day off, he'd load the family, which now included John, born two days before Lindsay's snowstorm in 1969, into the Rambler and drive into the city. He'd point out to his kids the real Harlem, not the one they saw each night on the evening news, the one bathed in the light from cop cars and fire trucks. He would show them the brownstones and churches, the businesses, and tell them about the people who lived and worked within them. He was not an equality crusader—not at all. He just wanted them to see it for themselves.

―――――

In May 1976, the department transferred Bill to Engine 28 on the Lower East Side, then one of the city's busiest fire companies. His tenure in twenty-eight engine, however, would last only a year. He had studied for, taken, and passed the promotional exam for the rank of battalion chief. On May 28, 1977, he was promoted to the position and would begin a meteoric rise through the upper ranks of the FDNY.

# NINE

# Moonlight Bill

B ill called the battalion chief "the workhorse of the department," and being in charge of five or six fire companies can
undoubtedly keep a chief busy. But if you asked him what was the
biggest change the promotion brought to his career, he would have
told you it was his driver.

The primary reason the New York City Fire Department assigns
a driver to ranks of battalion chiefs and higher is to allow the chief
the freedom to coordinate resources on the way to a fire or incident.
Though an aide's first duty is to drive the chief, the position com-
prises several administrative and communication functions. The
best of aides act as an extension of the chief they serve. They should
anticipate his every move and be professional in appearance and
attitude, as their actions reflect upon their immediate boss. Most
important, they should provide strong, silent support on which the
chief can rely under the most pressure-filled situations.

Then there was John "Yappo" Grant.

For the first couple of weeks that they were together, Bill thought
his new aide was nearly obsequious, perhaps because he was feeling
his new boss out.

*I don't understand why they call this guy Yappo*, he wondered to himself.

A few weeks after they'd been together, however, the reason for the nickname started to become abundantly clear. Once he started talking, Grant didn't stop. Behind the wheel, he would regale Chief Feehan with story after story. One of his favorites was about the time he took the lieutenant's exam. Back then, a local radio station would broadcast the answers to the test a few hours after it was given so those who took the exam could assess their performance. Yappo hurried home to listen. As the announcer gave the last answer, he began jumping up and down. "I passed! I passed!" he yelled so his family would hear. It was only later that he realized he'd been listening to the answers for the transit patrolman test. Yappo had an inventive vocabulary. On a television interview at a fire scene one night, he told a reporter that the blaze was a "highanus conflageration."

He loved playing practical jokes on his boss. One day early in his time with Bill, they went to a fire in progress. A ladder truck and engine company had already responded to the call and had the fire under control. The lieutenant of the ladder company told Bill that they would open up a wall in the apartment. One of the duties of ladder companies is to make sure there is no fire or potential for fire hidden behind walls or ceilings. Out of an abundance of caution, Bill decided to order another hose line stretched into the building. He got Yappo, who was still in the car, on the radio.

"Start a second line," Bill instructed.

"Ten-four, Chief," Yappo responded, "transmitting a second alarm." A second alarm would bring eight more fire companies to the scene of a fire almost under control.

"Negative, negative," Bill said. "Second line!"

"Transmitting second alarm now."

Bill nearly fell down the stairs trying to rush out of the building to stop him from sending out the second alarm. When he got to his car, Yappo was inside reading the *New York Post*. He looked up at Bill with a smile on his face.

"Thought I was gonna do it?" he asked. "Didn't ya?"

From that moment on, life for Bill in the fire department was never the same.

Yappo was born and raised in Red Hook, Brooklyn, back when it was a tough waterfront neighborhood made famous by Marlon Brando and the movie *On the Waterfront*. He came from a long line of firefighters. His grandfather originally worked for the Brooklyn Fire Department before the consolidation and joined the FDNY when the city was incorporated in 1898. His father was also a Brooklyn firefighter. John spent ten years in the U.S. Navy, four of them during World War II. He joined the department in 1955 and worked in busy firehouses after that, including a specialty squad in Brooklyn. Yappo had been an active, heroic fireman. In 1970, on his day off, he rescued two of his neighbors trapped in a blaze in their home. His son, William, a captain in the department, duplicated the feat forty years later when he saved his neighbor from a raging fire in her home in Staten Island. When Yappo left the Brooklyn squad, the men in the company awarded him a plaque for 10,500 fire runs he'd made over his career, an astronomical number. By the time he'd begun working for Bill, however, his active career was all but burnt out. Not that he wanted to retire. He was having too much fun to do that.

One of Chief Feehan's favorite stories about his aide was when they went to a fire scene in Red Hook, the neighborhood where Yappo had grown up. While the chief was inside coordinating a second sweep of the premises, Yappo was catching up with some of his old friends. One of them was the owner of the building where the fire occurred, a woman named Mrs. Sullivan. When Chief Feehan started to inform her about the status of her building, she shushed him.

"Just a second, sonny," Mrs. Sullivan said to him. "I'm talking to the chief."

"Dummy up," Yappo whispered to Bill. "They all think I got your job."

From then on, when they went to Red Hook, Bill would drive and Yappo the aide would ride in the back of the chief's car.

Though Yappo always seemed to always have the upper hand on his boss, every now and then Bill would land a jab. The chief's office at the 31st Battalion office was attached to a police precinct building. One night, Yappo looked out the window to see two men trying to pop a lock in a car with a slimjim. He jumped from behind the desk, put on a threadbare coat, an old Navy watch hat that he wore all the time, and rushed out the door. "He looked like a homeless person," Bill remembered.

"Police!" Yappo yelled at the men. "What do you think you're doing?"

The two men, it turned out, were detectives who'd locked their keys in the car. When Bill came down to the parking lot, the cops were about to arrest him for impersonating a police officer.

"Tell them who I am," Yappo pleaded.

"Never saw him before in my life," Bill said.

———

By the time Bill was promoted to battalion chief, daughter Liz was attending Marymount Manhattan College, where she studied sociology. Billy had enrolled in Catholic University in Washington, D.C., where he played soccer. He grew up playing the game in Flushing. Because a significant part of the neighborhood's population was

In William's day, the breathing apparatus for firefighters looked like something out of a Jules Verne novel. Here he is wearing one sometime in the late 1930s. *(Courtesy Catherine Cole)*

The crew of "twenty-one engine" circa 1930. William is second from left, in the hat. *(Courtesy Catherine Cole)*

At just over five foot two, Father Jim could barely see over the steering wheel of his 1929 Plymouth. *(Courtesy Catherine Cole)*

William in dress uniform, with one-year-old Bill, circa 1930. *(Courtesy Catherine Cole)*

The Irish Riviera: Catherine, Bill, and William on the beach in Rockaway, circa 1933. *(Courtesy Catherine Cole)*

Catherine with sons Jim and Bill, outside Aunt Nennie's first house in Jackson Heights, circa 1937. *(Courtesy Catherine Cole)*

Three-year-old Bill on his first fire run. Long Island City, Queens, circa 1932. *(Courtesy Catherine Cole)*

A teenage Bill doing his best James Dean. Jackson Heights, Queens, circa 1944. *(Courtesy Feehan Family)*

After months fighting the Korean War, the U.S. Army rewarded Bill by sending him to Fort Dix to train recruits. 1954. *(Courtesy Feehan Family)*

Bill on the Korean peninsula, circa 1953. *(Courtesy Feehan Family)*

Betty and Bill in Rockaway, circa 1957, with K.O. the dog. Betty was a boxing fan, an interest she inherited from her father, Bernie. *(Courtesy Feehan Family)*

Betty and Bill Feehan on the front steps of St. Stanislaus Church, July 7, 1956. Jim, Bill, Betty, and Betty's sister, Vera, are flanked by Bernie and Elizabeth Keegan far left, Catherine and William Patrick Feehan far right. *(Courtesy Feehan Family)*

Happier times: Betty and baby Billy, summer of 1961, in Rockaway. *(Courtesy Feehan Family)*

Brian Davan. FDNY's proby photo, 1989. *(Courtesy FDNY)*

On September 1, 1993, New York City Mayor David N. Dinkins made Bill the acting fire commissioner. Pictured is Dinkins and Bill on the steps of City Hall. *(Courtesy FDNY)*

On November 24, 1993, Mayor Dinkins made it official by appointing Chief Feehan New York City's twenty-eighth fire commissioner. Chief of Department Anthony L. Fusco (left) and Bill flank Mayor Dinkins. *(Courtesy FDNY)*

Chief Joseph Callan took command of the evacuation of the north World Trade Center tower on September 11. He is pictured here with First Deputy Commissioner William M. Feehan outside of a Chinese restaurant fire. *(Courtesy FDNY)*

Bill, wearing his Chief of Department helmet, at a fire scene. *(Courtesy FDNY)*

This photo of Bill and grandson Connor Davan on a fireboat in New York Harbor sat on Chief Feehan's desk in FDNY headquarters. The World Trade Center can be seen in the background. *(Courtesy Feehan Family)*

Proby Connor Davan, just before he graduated from the FDNY Fire Training Academy on Randalls Island. His grandfather's photo is above him on the memorial wall at the academy. *(Courtesy Feehan Family)*

DEDICATED
TO THE MEMORY OF

1ST DEPUTY COMMISSIONER
WILLIAM M. FEEHAN

WHO MADE THE SUPREME SACRIFICE
WHILE IN THE PERFORMANCE OF DUTY
OPERATING AT MANHATTAN BOX 5-5-8087
WORLD TRADE CENTER
SEPTEMBER 11, 2001

DEDICATED
TO THE MEMORY OF

CHIEF OF DEPARTMENT
PETER J. GANCI, JR.

WHO MADE THE SUPREME SACRIFICE
WHILE IN THE PERFORMANCE OF DUTY
OPERATING AT MANHATTAN BOX 5-5-8087
WORLD TRADE CENTER
SEPTEMBER 11, 2001

The bodies of Chiefs Ganci and Feehan were found just feet from each other in the rubble of the World Trade Center's north tower. Their memorial plaques hang in the lobby of FDNY headquarters, MetroTech Center, Brooklyn. *(Author Photo)*

Line-of-duty deaths on the memorial wall at FDNY headquarters, MetroTech Center, Brooklyn. Bill walked past this wall every day on the way to his office. His name is the first of 9/11 deaths listed on the plaque. *(Author Photo)*

first-generation Italians, the level of competition there was keen. After excelling on his college team, Billy took a year off and played for a professional team in Argentina. When he'd call his father from South America, Chief Feehan would greet him with an enthusiastic "Hello, Guillermo!" But now Billy was back at Catholic University. In the meantime, Tara followed her father's footsteps and enrolled in St. John's, where she began studying education with her sights set on a teaching career. Though John then was still in high school, it was only a matter of time before he'd add another college tuition to the pile. The children all worked summer jobs and helped out paying for their school, but it was still a remarkable feat to send three, then four kids to pretty good colleges on his civil service salary. He, of course, needed the salary from the teaching job desperately.

———

When city budget cutbacks included putting a stop to hiring substitute teachers, Bill faced the possibility of a major quandary. Betty hadn't worked in a long time, and because of her health issues and depression, the thought of her working even part-time was remote. Without the second job, Bill could barely afford the mortgage on the house in Flushing, never mind the college tuitions. The truth of the matter was that no fireman could raise a family without a moonlighting gig. Throughout the department's history, the union fought for and protected its members' right to work outside jobs. The extra income was so important to Bill, he once had to put his career on the line to keep it. Soon after he was appointed commissioner, John O'Hagan asked him to be his aide, a position of substantial influence. But, because he'd have to be on call all the time, it was also a position that would prohibit Bill from moonlighting. When he discussed his dilemma with some firemen friends, they told him that if he turned O'Hagan down, he should buy a heavy winter coat because he was going to spend the rest of his career in Siberia. Still, having the commissioner angry with him was a whole lot better than having to telling Betty they had to take the kids out of Catholic schools. Bill said thanks but no thanks to O'Hagan, and as it would turn out, the commissioner didn't send Bill packing. But now he needed another job, and fast. As it happened, a friend from Flushing would provide the opportunity.

Ed Brady was a New York City police detective. The same age, both with growing families, and both card-carrying members of St. Mel's, Bill and Eddie, as he was known, had a lot in common. As in the fire department, many cops worked second jobs, and many moonlighted in private security. Traditionally, in New York and other cities, cops and retired cops have had the market cornered in security at private hospitals, private universities, and hotels, among other businesses. Brady worked a second job as hotel security for a high-profile real estate couple named Harry and Leona Helmsley. He asked his friend if he'd be interested in working with him at the hotel. Bill jumped at the chance. Had he known what he was jumping into, he might not have been so enthusiastic.

————

Long before Donald Trump, Harry Helmsley was New York City's preeminent real estate developer and property owner. His portfolio included several landmark hotels, the most famous of which was the Helmsley Palace just down the block from Trump Tower. But it was Leona, Harry's second wife, who garnered the most newsprint, and wrestled Donald Trump for the *New York Post*'s front page.

Short, heavy, and with long black eyelashes and enough makeup foundation to get a drag queen jealous, Leona was a character of the first order. The tabloid dubbed her "the Queen of Mean," and for good reason. She was so notoriously cruel to her employees that the staff at her Greenwich, Connecticut, mansion would call workers at the hotels to warn them when she'd left for the city.

It didn't take Bill long to understand how Leona had acquired her reputation. She would arrive at the hotel in the early morning hours and order him to empty the ashtrays or some other menial job. She swam laps in the hotel pool every day, and would count them with swizzle sticks. But she demanded that the drink straws be the same color. She would send Bill to collect the blue or red straws from the hotel bars and bring them up to the pool. One day, she bought an arrangement of flowers from a Korean grocery on the East Side. Back at the hotel, she decided she didn't like them. She called Bill up to her suite and told him to return them. She couldn't, however, remember where she bought the bouquet. Bill spent most of the day going from grocery to grocery to find the correct store—all for a three-dollar handful of sidewalk flowers. Leona called Bill "Feeney" instead of Feehan the entire time he worked for her. Yet he would answer each task she gave with the same polite "Yes, Mrs. Helmsley." For him, it was the price he'd have to pay for a few college educations.

For all of her fortune and notoriety, Bill would soon discover, Leona was a sad and lonely woman. Harry was much older than her, and had slipped into dementia in his later years. She had few friends. Even her son was estranged from her. One night, she threw Harry a birthday party at the Helmsley Palace. When the celebration began, the ballroom was filled with people who had come out of a sense of obligation. Soon after the dinner was served, the room emptied. Both Bill and Ed had worked the event. Like Bill, Eddie was handsome and dapper. They spent most of the evening dancing with their boss at Leona's request while a full band played.

For much of the time Bill worked for Leona he did so surreptitiously. Moonlighting had gone in and out of favor with the fire department. Fire officers, especially, were under scrutiny not to do so.

One day, the fire commissioner and the mayor walked into the lobby at the Helmsley Palace to attend a luncheon that Bill didn't know about. When he saw them, he ducked behind a lobby pillar. On another occasion, someone who held a now-forgotten grudge against Bill told the chief of operations about his second job working for Leona. The chief called Bill down to headquarters.

"I have three kids in college and a mortgage on a house," Bill explained to the chief in his office. "I need the job." The chief happened to be the father of eight children, all of whom had Catholic school educations.

"You're dismissed," the chief said.

Bill would work for Leona for twenty years. The Queen of Mean also would hire the Feehan children for summer jobs. Liz and Tara waited tables. Billy was a bellhop. When they would complain about their boss, their father would remind them the cost of a college education. When Bill finally left her employ, Leona threw him a retirement cocktail party in the hotel. The Queen of Mean's own story doesn't end nearly as happily. In large part thanks to Rudy Giuliani, then the U.S. attorney in New York's Southern District, she was convicted of tax evasion and fraud and sent to jail in 1992. She did eighteen months in a federal prison in Connecticut and was given 750 hours of community service. The judge then tacked on another 150 hours when he found out that Leona was having her employees perform her state-ordered punishment.

———

Bill's promotion to battalion chief came at the beginning of the end of the war years. On October 5, 1977, President Jimmy Carter went to the South Bronx to see for himself the devastation of the fires that had consumed the borough. It's hard to imagine what went through the president's mind as he looked at row after row of burned-out buildings. It was an American Dresden, inhabited by mostly junkies and stray dogs. Over the coming decade, fires in New York City would decrease by nearly 30 percent simply because there was little left to burn in these neighborhoods.

Just after the department promoted Bill, Edward I. Koch was elected mayor of New York City. Tall, bald, and brash, Koch had been a city councilman in Greenwich Village and a U.S. congressman representing Manhattan's East Side before he ran for mayor. He was known for the catchphrase "How'm I doin?," which he would shout at his constituents every chance he had. His relationship with the fire department was rocky right from the start. As mayor-elect, he visited some of the busiest firehouses in the city to establish a rapport with the fire department's rank and file. Things didn't go well for "Koch the mayor," as Jimmy Breslin derisively called him. The firemen were armed with a list of complaints that included the polyester and cotton uniforms they wore that would melt near flames, and the incoming mayor's insistence on a residency requirement. Koch had campaigned on reinstituting the requirement that New York City employees, including firemen, live in the city. He was mayor for twelve years, and his relationship with the firefighters never got any warmer. At one department medal ceremony toward the end of his time as mayor, he was booed off the stage.

To close the budget shortfalls, the new mayor pared engine crews down from five to four men. When the union threatened to strike, Koch fired back saying that striking firemen would be immediately dismissed. Firehouses began falling into disrepair. Unlike other city employees, firefighters slept where they worked. Some took it upon themselves to make sure toilets and boilers worked and roofs didn't leak. Many firemen were handymen, or worked second jobs as contractors, and they used their expertise to renovate firehouses, even going as far as putting on extensions.

Meanwhile, though the number of fires decreased, the job remained as dangerous as ever. In early August 1978, city and fire union officials had to postpone contentious contract negotiations when six firemen from Brooklyn were killed when the roof of a Waldbaum's supermarket collapsed during a fire. Though the mayor was visibly shaken at the fire scene, he didn't back down from his hard stance in the negotiations. Nor would he do much over his three terms in office to make the job safer for firemen.

Firefighters had their part in the dysfunctional relationship. During contract negotiations, the union pursued aggressive, even illegal tactics to force the city into capitulating to their demands. Maybe the most egregious part of the strategy was urging its membership to abuse sick leave. The city then would have to pay firefighters for staying home (or playing golf) while paying overtime to the fireman taking the place of the one calling out sick.

Bill was all for the union, and believed all firemen deserved better pay and benefits. But he wasn't an activist. His focus was on the job in front of him, and the next rank up the ladder. An ascent that began to move very quickly.

In 1980, the fire department promoted Bill to deputy chief. His office was in Ladder Company 20, quartered on Lafayette Street, near the courthouses. At the time, Liz was in the process of starting a career as a New York State court officer. Her graduation ceremony took place on the roof of the New York County Family Court building on Lafayette Street. During the ceremony, she kept hearing someone call her name, but she couldn't figure out where the voice was coming from. That night at the dinner table that evening, Bill eyed his daughter. Both civil servants, they shared a special connection. Chief Feehan had taken Liz to buy her first gun for her new job. He would drive her to the testing sites when she later took promotional exams. They knew the sacrifice it took to study for those exams, and they shared a desire to help people.

"What's a matter?" he asked. "You become a court officer, and you're too important to answer your father?"

The graduation was a closed ceremony, and families weren't invited. Liz's father, however, did the next best thing. He got a bullhorn and stood on the sidewalk in front of the nine-story building calling her name and congratulating her.

In 1985, Bill was promoted again, this time to deputy assistant chief. Though it might sound like a step down in rank, it's actually a significant promotion. Also called a staff chief, the position meant a move to headquarters, where he would spend the rest of his career.

## TEN

# Breezy Point

The history of the beach communities in Rockaway can be traced back to the early 1900s. It was then that a bungalow craze swept parts of the United States. Prefabricated in factories, and shippable by rail, the homes were inexpensive and readily available—you could buy them from a Sears, Roebuck catalog for as little as five hundred dollars.

In 1905, a New York developer named John J. Egan bought twenty bungalows from a company in Michigan and had them shipped to Rockaway. A shrewd businessman, Egan correctly predicted that affordable summer homes would be a hit in New York City's only beachfront community. He quickly rented them for $150 for the season, and the first bungalow colony on Rockaway Beach was born.

In the context of a poker game, at least one played in a certain era in New York City, the expression "a Rockaway bungalow" indicated you were holding a full house. The phrase was apt. Beach-going families, some with a half dozen children or more, along with uncles, aunts, and grandparents, as well as the kid from the apartment down the hall, would pack into the tiny two-bedroom summer rentals. The families came mostly from the outer boroughs of New York City. They were cops, bus drivers, steamfitters, and firefighters. They would rent for the whole summer. Billy Feehan remembers coming home on the last day of school to see his father and mother packing family AMC Rambler or, later, a maroon Ford Falcon for the trip to the beach. The bungalows were furnished, which is a generous description, because you had to supply your own towels, sheets, pot, pans, and every other thing you could think of to get you through the summer months. Billy's job was to take the tray filled with silverware out of the drawer in the kitchen and put it in the car.

For the children, summer in Rockaway was a wonder world. On the boardwalk, youngsters would feast on candy cigarettes, wax lips, and little wax bottles filled with sugar syrup, while older kids would meet under the boardwalk where they'd steal kisses and, maybe if they were lucky, get to second base. The waves were big enough to bodysurf, and the children would look out on the ocean and wonder how far it was to Europe. Every Wednesday night, Playland hosted a fireworks display. Whole families would fill the beach to watch the show.

By the early 1960s, however, the rumblings of change had already arrived on the Queens peninsula. Master city planner Robert Moses began the metamorphosis of Rockaway by tearing down seaside bungalows and building a nondescript high-rise housing project. By the 1970s, the popularity of Rockaway as a summer ritual began to wane for New York's white working class. By the mid-1980s, parts of the peninsula were among the most crime-ridden in the city. But for many of the beach community's stalwarts, the Feehans included, Rockaway remained a moment frozen in time. This was especially so in the small, privately owned community tucked into Rockaway's western edge.

With its gorgeous beaches and spectacular views of the city and Atlantic Ocean, Breezy Point, known locally as Breezy, has been for generations of New York City cops and firefighters a seaside Brigadoon. With only one road in and out, and a gatehouse to monitor visitors, it is an oxymoron—an exclusive blue-collar community. It is also almost entirely white. One of the reasons it has remained homogeneous is because the twenty-eight hundred or so houses in the community are handed down from generation to generation. But there is a saying that Irish Americans have uttered since the second of them stepped off a boat in the new land—"Stick with your own kind." Though a way of protecting themselves when they were a class needing protection, the words became the ladder they pulled out of the hole after them.

———

Bill and Betty had put a down payment, 50 percent of the house's value, as per the rule of the community organization, on a bungalow in Breezy Point in the early seventies. Though the cash outlay put a huge strain on family finances, Bill saw the purchase as more of a necessity than a luxury. The sea air and relative quiet (when the kids were out of the house) were a panacea for his wife. Breezy was also a place where he could relax, at least most of the time. One day, families who lived on the narrow lane on which his bungalow sat were having a neighborhood cookout. Bill parked his car blocking the entrance to the street, which was filled with children. As a fire officer, he knew better than to block the access, but had a momentary lapse in judgment. As his luck would have it, a bungalow at the end of the block had to call the fire department, most likely because of a barbecue that got out of control. When the fire trucks arrived, they had to wait for Bill to run out and move his car. The lieutenant on the engine company, who knew Bill, gave him a withering look as he ran toward his vehicle. Chief Feehan, wearing a boxy bathing suit, hung his head and gave the lieutenant a timid salute. Still, Breezy was as much a reprise for him as it was for Betty. Workday or not, each morning would start at the coffee shop in the middle of town. There he would often run into another chief or firefighter from a family he knew. Each night after work or on his days off might end with a scotch on the bungalow's porch, cooled by the breeze from the ocean or bay. It was heaven, and in a life stretched to the limit with responsibility, a chance to exhale.

———

Breezy Point was also the place where the Feehan family of firefighters would add a significant branch. For a few generations of Rockaway's nubile youth, before the advent of dating apps, at least, the Sugar Bowl bar in Breezy was an essential meeting place for single girls and guys. A summer-only establishment, the bar filled at night with a couple of hundred flip-flop-wearing, bathing-suited hopefuls and used-to-be hopefuls as enduring summer hits such as Meatloaf's "Paradise by the Dashboard Light" or even the Shirelles' "Will You Love Me Tomorrow?" played on the sound system. Being as the bar is located in Breezy Point, the Sugar Bowl was also an excellent place to meet a young unmarried firefighter, or cop for that matter, as Tara did one night in the summer of 1987. At the time, however, Brian Davan was something of a hybrid. Although he was a police officer, and had been a member of the NYPD for six years, he had taken the fire department exam and his name had just come up for appointment. His plan was to leave the Finest for the Bravest as soon as the fire academy would have him. His father had done the same thing. Not only would a career as a firefighter complete his dream to follow in his father's path, but it would also, he thought, help his chances of meeting a pretty young lady such as Tara at the beach bar. As Brian would later recount, at the Sugar Bowl, firefighters always had a better shot with the girls than cops.

For her part, Tara wasn't overly impressed by Brian's tale of becoming a fireman. In fact, when he told her that his father was a captain in the department, she offhandedly mentioned that her dad was with the FDNY too.

"Oh really?" Brian said, genuinely interested. "Where does he work?"

Tara's father's career had gained so much momentum, she wasn't really sure. "All I know is he's a high-ranking chief," she said, shrugging, "and he has a driver."

Though his pride was momentarily deflated, Brian remained undeterred. Soon he and Tara were dating. When Tara told her father about her new boyfriend, the name Davan struck a chord.

"Is his father's first name Bob?" the chief asked. Tara said it was.

"I worked in Harlem with him."

Though they'd met only a few times, Bob Davan and Bill Feehan knew each other as only New York City firefighters of their ilk can. They'd first met at the search effort after the 23rd Street fire. They were both off that day but had spent hours together on the bucket line removing the bricks that covered their comrades' bodies. Later, when Bill was in Engine 59 and Bob in Engine 37, they'd both responded to a couple of multiple-alarm fires. In Harlem, Bill was a young captain, a rising star in the department. Bob, nine years older, and on the job twelve years longer, was a lieutenant and happy to stay right where he was. But the mutual respect they had for each other outweighed the difference in rank. In fact, Lieutenant Davan was the kind of man and firefighter Captain Feehan looked up to.

Born in 1921, Bob grew up poor during the Depression. His father, Brian's grandfather, had died of a heart attack on a Manhattan subway platform in 1929. The Davans then moved six times in one year because city landlords were offering two months' free rent to lure prospective tenants. As soon as they started charging, the Davans were on to the next apartment. At the start of World War II, Bob dropped out of high school and joined the U.S. Navy, spending the war on the battleship *Iowa* in the Pacific theater. When he returned home, like Brian would years later, he first became a cop before he went on to the fire department. In the late 1940s, he met and married Patricia Murtha, a tall and beautiful nineteen-year-old who worked in Macy's in Herald Square. She was working there on the foggy day in 1945 when the B-25 flew into the Empire State Building less than a block away. The newlyweds moved into a tenement in Inwood in upper Manhattan, a mostly Irish working-class neighborhood. Patricia worked in the rectory of Good Shepherd Church, where Bob attended Mass daily. The Davans raised six children in the small tenement apartment. One of Brian's earliest memories of growing up is watching his mother carry the family's laundry down the four flights to the washing machines in the basement and then back up again.

Bob's fire service career spanned thirty-seven years, much of it in the uncompromising Harlem inferno during the sixties and seventies. Away from the flames, however, he was a soft-spoken, humble man. In the early 1960s, long before the jogging craze took hold, he began to run regularly. He participated in New York Road Runners races and, later, when he was fifty-nine, ran a New York City Marathon. But even his rigorous physical exercise schedule could not stave off the inevitable. By the mid-1970s, his body had begun to break down—the fate of every active firefighter. Though he knew the end of his firefighting career was coming, he was still surprised at how suddenly it happened. On a hot summer day in 1976, he'd brought the crew in with a hose line into a store that contained a tremendous amount of fire. It took the team a full hour to get the blaze under control. Many New Yorkers have seen the aftermath of an intense firefight and the look of an exhausted firefighter sitting on the curb outside. Bob's helmet lay on the ground next to him, black with smoke, his eyes bloodshot, as his lungs heaved for air. Though Lieutenant Davan had been in that position more times than he could count, something was different on this day. His crew was so concerned about him that one of the senior members approached him later in the firehouse.

"It's time, Bob," was all he had to say.

Soon after those prophetic words, Bob began what he called a "semiretirement" in a firehouse in Far Rockaway. He'd been promoted to captain by then and would retire at that rank.

———

Brian says that his childhood was the best in the history of kids. If he wasn't on tar beach on the roof, he was playing Manhunt on the fire escapes. Like the Feehans, the Davans also had a bungalow in Breezy Point. During the summers, Brian practically lived in the ocean. "I didn't wear shoes for two and a half months a year," he says. When the ferry would come from Brooklyn, he and his friends would dive off Kennedy's dock for the quarters the ferry riders threw.

He was attending Brooklyn College when he joined the NYPD. His first assignment was the 66th Precinct in the Borough Park section of Brooklyn. He then spent three and a half years in the 101st Precinct in Far Rockaway, one of the busiest precincts in all of Queens during the crack cocaine epidemic. Brian would make seventy-five felony arrests in his time in the 101st. It seemed to him that he was testifying in those cases in front of grand juries or in criminal court every other day. Though he began to enjoy his time as a cop, he couldn't wait for his name to come up on the FDNY's appointment list. It's difficult to quantify the difference in the pull of the two civil service jobs. Certainly, there are many men and women who desire to become police officers, but the allure of the fire department is somehow different, more powerful. For some, especially those who have had relatives on the job, the decision to become a firefighter is instinctual, almost as if not taking the job goes against their very nature.

———

Tara and Brian married on September 23, 1989, at St. Andrew's Church in Flushing. They held the reception at the Silver Gull beach club and hall in Breezy Point. When they decided to wed, Brian went to see Chief Feehan at the Breezy bungalow to ask for his daughter's hand. He'd expected Tara to be there when he did, but when he knocked on the door she was nowhere to be seen. A cappella, Brian launched into his rehearsed speech. Many of the Rockaway bungalows were built with interior walls that didn't reach all the way to the ceiling, ostensibly for air circulation in the stuffy structures. The design, however, allowed conversations to be heard in adjoining rooms with little difficulty. As it happened, that day Betty was in the next room. When she heard Brian asking Bill for Tara's hand, she came storming through the doorway. After hugging and congratulating him, she came to the point.

"So, when are you going to start studying?" she asked with urgency.

Brian hadn't even entered the fire academy yet. But as far as Betty was concerned, if he was going to marry Tara, he had better not stay at the rank of firefighter for long.

By the time they were married, Brian had just finished up two hot summer months on "the rock," the fire academy on Randalls Island, and the department had assigned him to Engine 231 in Brownsville, Brooklyn. He was about to start a very active career as a firefighter.

————

By the mid-1980s, crack cocaine had begun to lay waste to what was left of the poorer neighborhoods in New York. The murder rate skyrocketed as the illegal drug epidemic grew. In 1988, a young cop named Edward Byrne was shot and killed as he sat in his patrol car guarding a witness in a drug trial. In 1989, there were nearly two thousand murders in New York City. By 1993, the *New York Post* was calling the neighborhood Brian's company covered "A Killing Ground." Mothers living in crack-ridden areas used bathtubs as cribs to protect their babies from stray bullets.

One night soon after he arrived in Brownsville, dispatch sent Brian's company to a nearby housing project. When a call came in for a fire in a housing project, cynical old-timers would immediately think he had to be on the top floor. The ticket they received from dispatch that night, however, was like hitting the jackpot—a first-floor fire. But the location of the fire was only the first surprise of the evening. When they arrived at the scene, two men were lying in the lobby in pools of blood. Both had been shot. One was dead. The other was alive, but barely. In order to get the hose into the seat of the fire, Brian had to step over him. Later, they would find out that the raging fire in the apartment and the two guys lying in the lobby were not separate events. The victims had been involved in some aspect of an illegal drug operation and had left the apartment's back window open a crack. A rival gang member had lit a newspaper on fire and pushed it through the crack and into the bedroom. When the two guys inside realized the apartment was on fire, they ran out into the lobby. That's where the gunman was waiting.

"They must have seen it in a John Wayne movie," Brian said. "They smoked 'em out of the apartment just like you'd see in cowboys and Indians."

———

Brian owned a small condo in Rockaway, which served as his and Tara's first home. Three years later, when Tara became pregnant, they started looking for a bigger place on the peninsula. They found a home in a section called Belle Harbor, where they would live for the next twenty-five years. Connor Davan was born in June 1993, followed three years later by Virginia, whom they called Ginna, and two years later by Kelly, the youngest. By then, life in the Davan family was like a ladder company outside a burning building—controlled chaos. One of the significant evolutions in the fire department was the role of the firefighter's spouse. Chief Feehan came from a generation in the department where all firefighters worked second jobs while their wives took care of the kids. In the Davan house, and many others like it, the daily schedule revolved around Tara's job as much as Brian's. By then, Tara was teaching full-time. She had graduated from St. John's the year before she and Brian started dating, and had taken a temporary teaching position at Resurrection Ascension School in Rego Park, Queens. At least she thought it was temporary. The teacher she was filling in for was on maternity leave and would never come back to work. So instead of using his mutuals to moonlight, Brian spent his time off watching the kids while Tara was teaching. Though they had made it clear they wouldn't be full-time babysitters, Brian's parents helped out.

When Brian worked night tours, he wouldn't be home until after Tara left for school. Patricia and Bob would stop by, make the kids waffles, and stay until Brian walked in the door.

———

Meanwhile, five miles down the peninsula, Betty's health conditions worsened. One night in the Breezy Point bungalow, she had a severe bout with her chronic anemia and had to be rushed to the Peninsula Hospital in Rockaway. Bill was working that night, and by the time he got to the hospital, Betty had gone into shock. The doctor who had treated her when she was admitted called him on the phone in the hospital room and had the tact of a bedpan. He told him that Betty would probably not live through the night. Bill hung up the phone and stared absently down the hospital hallway. Just then, the elevator doors opened and John Grant walked out.

"What are you doing here?" Bill asked Yappo in wonderment.

"I tried you at your office, they told me Betty was sick," he said.

Yappo stayed with Bill until the morning. Betty would fight through the night, and the next day doctors were more hopeful. When she left the hospital, she moved in with her parents so they could take care of her when Bill was at work. Betty was so weak she could barely stand on her own. Liz remembers once when her parents tried to visit a local Barnes & Noble bookstore. Betty collapsed on the way to the store and Bill had to carry her back to the car. That day he happened to have been using his chief's car, and an onlooker saw him carrying his wife and thought she was drunk.

"This is where my tax dollars are going?" the man sneered.

If Betty wasn't in his arms, he would have punched the man right in the nose.

# ELEVEN

# Chief Feehan

On March 25, 1990, a jilted lover poured gasoline down the steps of an illegal social club in the Bronx called Happy Land and then threw a lit match after it. The front door was the only way out of the club. Windows in the room had been filled with cinder-block and covered with bars. The back door had been welded shut. Eighty-seven people died in the fire that night. Another twenty-seven were injured. What made the tragedy even worse was that it could have easily been prevented.

Two years before, in August 1988, a fire in an illegal club in the Bronx killed seven people and injured twelve firefighters. Mayor Koch ordered a task force led by cops trained in building and fire codes to inspect illegal social clubs. The police department was supposed to work in tandem and share information with the fire department, but it's doubtful that much of the data was relayed. The fire department had cited the Happy Land club several times before the fire. But the fire department has no law enforcement power. The owners ran the club with impunity.

Chief Feehan knew firsthand about the failure of communica-tion between the police task force and the fire department. From November 1986 to December 1988, he ran the Bureau of Fire

Prevention, the same unit where his father's career ended. It was not a position that he actively sought, however. The job, he thought, was far from the front lines of fire service, consisting mostly of inspections and administrative work. In the department, the unit was colloquially known as "Lourdes." Firefighters assigned there on light duty would hate it so much, they would miraculously recover from their injuries. Bill was sent to the unit because he outsmarted himself. At the time of the transfer, he was working as staff chief in operations in headquarters. One day, the chief of the department called him into his office.

"Do you like operations?" the chief asked.

"Yes," Bill said. "I like it a lot."

"Does that mean you would refuse to go anywhere else?"

The question took him by surprise. He wanted to stay in operations, but he didn't want to sound insubordinate.

"I'll go anywhere you'd like," he said.

"Good, report to fire prevention Monday."

Though far from one, the transfer at first felt to Bill like a demotion. But Chief Feehan would later say his time in fire prevention was one of the most interesting in his career. Like most firefighters, he believed the fire department existed in a kind of ideological bubble. Though its membership might not be perfect, its role in society was unimpeachable. In fire prevention, however, he got to see his beloved FDNY through the eyes of the outside world. For the first time, he had to contend with the business community and other governmental departments. He was a quick study. One day he received a call from a Colorado lawyer who represented a five-and-dime discount store chain. The lawyer wanted to know why the fire department had shut down one of their stores in downtown Manhattan. Bill tracked down the fire officer who'd made the decision.

The officer told Bill that the store didn't have a proper second means of egress and that he hadn't shut the store down, he had vacated it. An order to vacate prevents anyone, with one or two exceptions, from entering the store. The officer didn't understand the semantics of the terms.

"What do you think they do?" Bill asked the officer on the phone. "They sell stuff. If you vacate them, you shut them down."

For the first time, he also oversaw nondepartment personnel, such as engineers who made complex inspections of major pipelines, chemical plants, laboratories, oil and sewage plants, all prime places where a fire could pose a danger to a large percentage of New York City's population.

"You went from crisis to crisis," he would later say.

———

By the time he left fire prevention, Chief Feehan was well on his way to becoming the most broadly experienced fire officer in the department. At home, however, he had few answers to his wife's health situation. Physically, Betty's immune system wasn't strong enough to fight off infections. She constantly battled pneumonia, infective colitis, and other infections and became weaker each time she experienced an illness, leaving herself open to even more sickness. But her illnesses were at least something tangible, something Bill could understand. Trying to make sense of her depression was like trying to grab a handful of dark smoke. One time, when all the children were still living at home, she'd had a reaction to the medication they'd given her for depression and became violent. One of the children had done something they shouldn't have and Betty lashed out in a scary incident that might have been much worse had not Bill been there. As the angry incidents became more frequent,

Bill worried about his children. "I don't want her to hurt you any-more," he'd confided to Liz at one point. When he wasn't home, the only answer was to separate Betty from them.

When his wife was at her parents', Bill would sit home at night in the house in Flushing, the squirrels scampering through the attic, a book about the Civil War in his hand, trying to keep the thoughts of a dark future from enveloping him. Though he would never talk about it, deep down he must have known his wife would never get better. He adored Betty, and coming to terms with her condition was hard on him. His job became his escape hatch from a situation that became more and more unresolvable. Every single ounce of his being that was not dedicated to Betty and the children was poured into the fire department. Undoubtedly it was because of that focus that his career path was so extraordinary. By 1991, there was only one rung left on the ladder in the uniformed department for Bill, and that was a job of his dreams.

———

The highest uniformed rank in the FDNY, chief of department, is a position of enormous responsibility and pressure. Department chief is the senior fire officer, and takes command of all major incidents such as multiple-alarm fires, building collapses, airline crashes, ter-rorist attacks, and more. He oversees all bureaus, programs, and activities within the uniformed force of the department. According to the civil service description of the job, the department chief is given "the widest latitude for the exercise of independent judgement and actions." It is also a position that has produced men of histori-cal significance. The first of these was John Decker, who in 1865 bridged the gap between the volunteer departments and the paid professional force. During the 1863 Draft Riots, Decker engaged in hand-to-hand combat to keep rioters from torching buildings and businesses. Just before the federal troops arrived, the rioters threatened to hang him.

Another of the early hero chiefs was Edward F. Croker, the nephew of a powerful Tammany Hall boss, and whose rise in the FDNY made Bill's look like it was in slow motion. He was promoted to lieutenant (called assistant foreman then) just forty-seven days after joining the department. He became a captain two months later. Although one has to imagine his uncle, Richard Croker, then known as "the Master of the City," played a role in the promotions, Edward would go on to prove himself as a courageous and an intelligent fire chief. As chief of department, he once ran into the basement of a raging building fire to drag the nozzleman out to safety.*

He was also an indefatigable advocate for fire prevention. Testifying in front of the Tenement House Committee in 1894, he blasted "the combustible nature"† of tenement construction. In another hearing, he used a fatal sweatshop fire in New Jersey to sound a warning that the same thing would happen in New York City if fire safety changes weren't made. Four months later, the Triangle Shirtwaist factory fire killed 146. Croker would retire right after the Shirtwaist fire, and dedicate the rest of his life to fire prevention.

Bill knew the history of the department as well as anyone. He knew the lasting mark that department chiefs like Decker, Croker, and O'Hagan had left on the FDNY. He knew the weight and responsibility he would have to carry. He also quietly believed he could do it as well as any who'd come before.

---

* The "nozzleman" was actually legendary battalion chief "Smoky" Joe Martin, for whom "Smokey the Bear" was supposedly named.

† Paul Hashagen, from his *Salty Dog* blog.

Mayor David Dinkins promoted Bill to chief of department on August 19, 1991, the twenty-fourth man to hold the position. In accepting the promotion, Chief Feehan wrote:

The New York City Fire Department has a worldwide reputation of excellence. Our officers and firefighters daily perform acts of incredible courage. Their unselfish devotion to duty, often at a terrible personal price, has always been an inspiration to me. I will serve the Department with the same intensity our officers and firefighters serve the people of this city.

Though he was eminently qualified for it, Bill's new job was one for which few could be completely prepared. A little less than a month into his time as chief of department, Engine 236 in Brooklyn responded to an arson fire in a tenement building. It was the third arson call in less than two weeks at the same address. A probationary firefighter named Kevin Kane was part of a team searching for squatters in the building. He was on the fourth floor when the ceiling collapsed on him. The proby was burned on over 80 percent of his body. Along with the mayor, Chief Feehan stood with Kane's father, a retired assistant fire chief, mother, and fiancée in the burn center where the rookie firefighter would suffer for over twenty-four hours before he died of his wounds. Later that morning, Chief Feehan went to Kane's firehouse and met with the crew of his engine company, who, as he remembered, "were going through the agony of self-doubt," asking themselves what they could have done differently.

When he returned to headquarters, emotionally drained, an official from the New York State Department of Labor was waiting for him. The state's investigation into the firefighter's death had already started. Next came a call from the department's deputy commissioner of public information. The firefighters' union had released a statement that Mayor Dinkins's cutbacks to the number of firefighters on a rig was a reason for Kane's death, and the press wanted a comment. Bill closed the door to his office and asked the secretary to hold his calls. He had felt grief from many firefighters' deaths, but the feeling from Kevin Kane's seemed different, somehow more painful. As chief of the department, he now owned a daunting responsibility for the safety of the 11,588 uniformed firefighters under him. As he sat behind his desk, however, he realized that his was far from a solitary endeavor. He picked up his pen and began to write a message to his troops that would be published in the fire department magazine:

> Today's young firefighters cannot remember a department without tower ladders, without handie-talkies, without power saws, and self-contained breathing apparatus. Terms that today are first heard in Proby school "Hazmat, scuba, 800 mega-hertz"—would have had senior officers scratching their head not so many years ago. Yes, the job is very different.
>
> Or is it? Our mission today is the same as it was when the department was founded 127 years ago. Despite all the advances in technology, we still have the same mission: to save lives and protect property. The goal is indeed simple and uncomplicated; achieving it is ever more difficult dangerous complex and challenging.
>
> Today's fire officers and firefighters face danger we never dreamed of: HIV exposure, blood borne pathogens, new

and virulent forms of TB, more toxic and lethal products of combustion.

The years ahead will see even more dramatic changes. We must always be receptive to change, always recognize that only through change can the department grow and prosper.

Our mission though will not change; to save lives and protect property. And each of us must make sure that something else remains unchanged: the dedication and commitment which were hallmarks of the generations of firefighters who preceded them. Their creativity, open mindedness, devotion to duty and love of the "job" have made this Department great. It is up to us to ensure their traditions of pride honor courage and duty will live on, for our best days are yet to come.

———

Traditionally, on St. Patrick's Day, the chief of department leads the FDNY's marching contingent up Fifth Avenue. That first time Bill did, Betty and Liz watched him go by from the steps of St. Patrick's Cathedral. As he waved to them, Betty turned to her daughter and said, "If only his father could see him now." But Betty was just as proud as Bill's father ever could be. Throughout her husband's career, she'd been overjoyed at each of his promotions. She'd arrange a family party at the house for each one. She boasted about him to parents and other family. She was also protective of his career as he rose through the ranks. Though she disliked it when he'd be called away from a dinner or some affair they were attending to respond to a fire, she defended the fire department against all detractors. One time, she was watching a news report of a fire on television and the reporter referred to the firefighters on scene as "boys." The reporter didn't mean to be derogatory; he was just being informal.

But Betty didn't see it that way. She called up the television station and demanded to speak to the producer of the news program. She refused to take no for an answer, and when the producer finally got on the line, she told him in no uncertain terms that firefighters were men, not boys. As she watched Bill walk by on Fifth Avenue that cold March day, her heart burst with love and admiration for her husband.

For Bill, the only downside to his new job was that it came with an expiration date. He turned sixty-three the first year he was chief of department. Mandatory retirement at sixty-five applied even at the highest uniform level. The clock was ticking not only on his time as chief, but on his career in the FDNY. He knew exactly how his father felt when Cavanaugh's requirements closed in on him. He couldn't imagine a life without the fire department. It was an image, however, that would never become reality.

———

As it happened, the day of Bill's promotion to department chief was also the date of one of the ugliest episodes in New York City history. The Crown Heights riots were deadly, vile, and the police response was horribly botched. They would also prove to be a mortal wound to David Dinkins's political future. For Bill, however, the riots in Crown Heights would put in motion a series of events that would catapult him into the history books.

On the evening of August 19, 1991, a Mercury Grand Marquis station wagon with wood paneling on the side sped through an intersection in Crown Heights and was broadsided by another car. The station wagon careened out of control, jumped a sidewalk, and slammed into two youngsters, cousins, who had been putting a chain on a bicycle. One of the children, Gavin Cato, was killed instantly. His cousin, Angela Cato, was severely injured. The driver of the wagon was a Hasidic Jew named Yosef Lifsh. The Cato cousins were Black.

Lifsh had been part of a police-escorted motorcade for Rebbe Menachem Mendel Schneerson, the Lubavitcher Hasidic sect's influential leader. Anger quickly swelled in the Black community. One common belief at the time held that the Jewish community was taken by surprise at the hatred exhibited toward them after the accident. One writer, who had written a book about the Lubavitcher published just before the riots, proclaimed that Crown Heights was a place "where black and Jewish homeowners co-exist as next-door neighbors, each determined to maintain the safety and viability of their community as a place for families to live peacefully."* That wasn't really the case. Twelve years earlier, a young Black man had shot and killed a rabbi in Crown Heights. The Hasidics subsequently formed private security patrols. In 1978, members of a Hasidic anti-crime patrol beat a young Black man into a coma. Around the same time, Blacks charged Hasidics with using strong-arm tactics to buy them out of their homes to provide for the growing religious sect. In the years that followed, the two communities had lived in a kind of simmering coexistence. Black leaders believed that the Lubavitcher received preferential treatment by city agencies, including the police and fire departments. They saw the motorcades the police gave the rabbi, as well as street closures on the Sabbath that caused rerouting of city buses and other inconveniences, as proof of the special treatment. They railed against the Hasidic sect's wielding far more

---

* Edward Hoffman, *Despite All Odds: The Story of the Lubavich* (New York: Simon & Schuster, 1991).

political power than they did, this despite the fact that the Hasidic made up only 20 percent of the community. They had a point.

Abe Beame was the New York City mayor who bridged the period between John Lindsay and Ed Koch from 1974 to 1977. A diminutive man, so short that aides placed a briefcase for him to stand on when he spoke publicly, Beame was an unremarkable leader during a remarkable city fiscal crisis. Perhaps the biggest moment during his mayoralty was when he went to Washington looking for a ninety-day federal bailout for the city's financial woes. A now-famous *New York Daily News* headline captured the tenor of the mayor's meeting with the president. "Ford to City: Drop Dead," it read. But it was Beame's administration that helped to redraw the community board districts in Crown Heights, concentrating the Lubavitcher's political might. Black leaders challenged the redistricting in federal court, but the case was dismissed. The Hasidic sect used that power to help open senior centers, private schools, and an ambulance force. Meanwhile, the Black sections of the neighborhood saw housing fall into disrepair and an increase in poverty and crime. Many historians today look back at the Crown Heights riots as a pure example of antisemitism, and certainly that kind of hatred was a major element. But blaming it solely on antisemitism dismisses the oppression and second-class status forced on Blacks for hundreds of years in this country and for a generation or more in Crown Heights. Anger in the Caribbean community there had been building for decades. By August 1991, it was a powder keg in search of a match.

Hatzalah, the Jewish volunteer emergency medical service, arrived soon after the accident as an angry crowd gathered. Police put Lifsh in the ambulance and directed the driver to take him to safety while Gavin Cato lay dead on the sidewalk.

The following morning a gang of Black kids attacked doctoral student Yankel Rosenbaum, stabbing and beating him. Rosenbaum, who had nothing to do with the incident the day before, bled to death in a city hospital after doctors failed to detect a four-inch stab wound. For the next three days, Crown Heights was besieged by rioting mobs from the Black community. By the time the riots ended, more than 150 police officers and 38 civilians were injured.

———

David N. Dinkins, the first African American mayor of the city of New York, was a tennis buff, dressed stylishly, and was a talented orator. But he inherited a city that was as dangerous as it was racially polarized. Crack cocaine had blown crime statistics to unheard-of levels. In Dinkins's first year in office, the city suffered 2,245 murders, a record that stood until September 11, 2001. Thirty-five cab drivers alone were robbed and killed, or killed and then robbed. Seventy-five children under the age of sixteen died of gunshot wounds. On September 2, 1990, a gang of teenagers stabbed and killed a twenty-two-year-old tourist from Utah. Brian Watkins was murdered in front of his mother and father, who were also injured in the attack. The next day, the *New York Post* ran a banner headline that read "Dave, Do Something!"

In response, Dinkins would expand the police force, but it would take years for the cops to stem the tide of crime in the city, and many believed the force was woefully mismanaged during his administration. One thing is for certain: Mayor Dinkins and his police commissioner, Lee Brown, had severely underestimated the severity of the situation in Crown Heights. At first, the mayor and police commissioner held back on sending resources into the riot. Less than six months earlier, Rodney King had been severely beaten during an arrest by Los Angeles police officers, igniting five days of riots, and Dinkins believed a show of force would inflame the situation. As for the police commissioner, Brown seemed strangely detached from the riot, delegating the responsibility for containing it to police commanders. The police commissioner's disappearing act was nothing new. Cops took to calling him "Out of town Brown," because of a propensity, they believed, for his being unreachable at the most inopportune times. The first cops on scene were tremendously outnumbered and overwhelmed. When the NYPD finally did send in resources, they did so without any kind of a real strategy. Many of those cops ended up standing around looking at each other, or forming useless human barriers. Finally, days into the riot, a few police commanders, including future police commissioner Ray Kelly, initiated a coordinated approach that included fifty police officers on horseback and multiple arrests that dampened the furor. A state investigation released two years after the riots called the response by Brown and other top-ranking members of the NYPD a "collective failure." For the law-and-order mayoral candidate Rudy Giuliani, who had run against and lost to Dinkins in 1989, and was gearing up to run against him again in 1993, the riot was blood in the water.

————

In addition to the riots, Dinkins had a host of other political problems. One of them came unexpectedly from his own ranks. The position of New York City fire commissioner has traditionally played second fiddle to its counterpart in the police department. It is the top cop, and his relationship with the mayor, that usually garners the most newsprint and scrutiny. As far as political capital is concerned, the appointment of police commissioner can appease constituents or serve as an outreach to communities that are not necessarily politically aligned with the administration. A mayor's pick for fire commissioner, on the other hand, rarely moves the political needle. There are exceptions. Lindsay's appointment of Robert O. Lowery shook the foundation of New York City politics, and solidified his progressive bona fides.

Although not quite as earthshaking as Lowery's appointment, Dinkins's choice for his first fire commissioner had a considerable political component. Dinkins had campaigned on the promise that his administration would represent the "gorgeous mosaic" of diversity in New York City. To that end, he chose Carlos M. Rivera to run the fire department, the first Hispanic person to hold the post. Initially, Charlie, as he was known, was the best of both worlds for Dinkins. He was a decorated firefighter who had a sterling career as a fire officer and, like Bill, had risen quickly through the department's ranks. But Dinkins also saw the appointment as an outreach to the Hispanic community.

When it came to how to run the fire department, however, Mayor Dinkins and his new top fire officer often disagreed. When Dinkins turned to Rivera to make some drastic cuts in the department budget, the fire commissioner balked. News articles of the day hinted that Rivera had been in secret talks with the firefighters' union, in a sense negotiating against his boss. When the city moved to reduce again the fire crews from five to four, Rivera told Dinkins he wouldn't do it. The tension between the two men was further strained when Dinkins found out that his fire commissioner had instituted a trial of "bunker" pants made out of fire-retardant material without the mayor's knowledge. You can't blame Rivera for revolting against his mayor to keep his firefighters safe. But many of the safety problems in the FDNY went far beyond Dinkins's control. By 1993, the fire department suffered from a seriously overaged fleet of firefighting vehicles, crumbling firehouses, and scarce resources for training and development.

Historically, about 97 percent of the fire department's budget was allocated to supporting field operations. The remaining 3 percent supported everything else, including paychecks, diesel fuel, firehouse maintenance, tools, safety equipment, vehicle maintenance, fire safety and fire prevention programs, health services, training programs, and personnel development, which had all fallen victim to years of relentless budget reductions. The department had reached a state of institutional stagnation that any mayor would be powerless against. Still, Rivera would continue defying the mayor and the rift would escalate into a stunning public betrayal during the final stretch of Dinkins's reelection campaign.

————

Publicly, Bill had no role in the discord between his commissioner and mayor. Chief of department is supposed to be an apolitical role, and Chief Feehan adhered to that supposition. His job was to fight the fires with what he had, and to lead the people who fought them. Privately, however, he was strongly on his commissioner's side. He wanted to keep his troops as safe as possible. The relationship between Chief Feehan and Commissioner Rivera was friendly but not particularly close. But Rivera leaned on his chief of department for his counsel. The respect that Commissioner Rivera had for Bill would play a major role in not only extending Chief Feehan's career in the FDNY but also in bringing him a step closer to a historic accomplishment.

At the very upper reaches of the FDNY's organizational chart are the deputy commissioners, positions that are appointed by the fire commissioner. Deputy commissioners are civilian posts and not regulated by city civil service rules. Some commissioners rise from the ranks of the department, but others do not. Deputy commissioners of legal affairs and public information, the press office, for instance, often come from media outlets, other agencies, or law firms. The top-ranking deputy commissioner is called the first deputy commissioner, who reports directly to the fire commissioner. Though the first dep, as it's known, is an enormously important position within the fire department, it is an administrative post and is apart from the uniform chain of command. In fact, it's often occupied by someone with little or no fire service experience. When Bill was first transferred to headquarters as a staff chief, the first dep was a man named Peter Madonia, who was a baker. He ran a family-owned bakery in the Bronx that had been there for generations. Although not the best analogy, in baseball terms the first dep would work in the front office while the chief of department is the team's manager. The chief wears the uniform, the GM wears a suit (or an apron, in Madonia's case).

During Bill's time as department chief, Marlene Gold was the first dep. Gold grew up in Brooklyn, and had a law degree from Boston College Law School. She'd been the New York Sanitation Department's deputy commissioner of legal affairs when she was offered the lofty position with the fire department, the first woman to hold the post. But in the fall of 1992, a deputy commissioner post opened up in City Hall in labor relations, a very prestigious position in city government. Gold weighed her options and seized the new opportunity.

To hear him tell the story, in his trademark self-deprecating manner, you would think Bill snuck in the back door of the first deputy commissioner's office under the cover of darkness. In fact, in the version he liked to tell he got the job because the mayor didn't think he could do the one he had. The story goes like this: One day a cold storage warehouse on the Lower West Side of Manhattan caught fire and quickly burned out of control. In a matter of an hour or so it had reached a fifth alarm. Chief Feehan took charge of the scene until ten o'clock that night and then handed it over to a staff chief in charge of operations. By then, Bill was sure that firefighters would soon have it under control. They wouldn't. At five o'clock the next evening the building was still a blazing incinerator bellowing thick black smoke that reached all the way to the park outside the mayor's office. According to Bill, Dinkins looked out the window of his office and called his fire commissioner.

"Charlie, City Hall Park is filled with smoke," he said. "Who's in charge?"

"Chief of department," Rivera said.

"You better get him another job," the mayor answered.

The truth was, Bill's appointment as first deputy strengthened the upper echelon of the department immeasurably. Instead of a baker or lawyer, Bill's appointment to first deputy brought to the position one of the most experienced fire officers in the history of the FDNY.

Still, it would take him a while to get used to the civilian aspect of his new job.

For the first time in his career, Chief Feehan didn't wear a uniform at work. Instead, he'd put on one of the tailored suits that hung in his closet. Bill looked great in a suit, a talent he honed on those nights out on the town. The suit he could get used to, but being out of the uniformed chain of command was another matter. One night, soon after he was promoted, he was in the first dep's Crown Vic heading home from Manhattan when an alarm came over the car's radio. By the time he reached the Brooklyn side of the

Williamsburg Bridge the fire had increased to three alarms. Every instinct from thirty-two years of uniformed firefighting experience informed his next decision. He turned the car around and headed back into the city.

The fire had started in a two-story wooden structure that had been a horse stable in the early 1900s and had been turned into a storage facility for veterinary medicines. Not only was the stable made of wood but so were the buildings that surrounded it. When Bill approached the scene, five houses were wholly consumed with fire. On the scanner, dispatch was trying to reach the city-wide commander to ask if he wanted to transmit the fourth alarm. When the chief didn't respond to the dispatcher, Bill grabbed the scanner's handset.

"By order of car two," he said, "transmit the fourth alarm." Car two was the designation of the first dep's car.

As Bill pulled up to the scene, the city-wide commander pulled in right next to him. The commander jumped from the car and marched right over to the deputy commissioner.

"*I* transmit fourth alarms," he said in a steely voice. "*You* don't."

Chief Feehan might have had the second-highest rank in the department, but at a fire scene he no longer made the decisions.

———

His new role also opened his eyes to the fire department's place in city government. For twenty-nine of his thirty-four years in the FDNY, Bill had acted in a supervisory role. He'd worked every conceivable kind of city fire, from tenements in poor sections to luxury high-rise buildings. During all of that time, his focus was fighting fire, saving citizens, and protecting firefighters in every way possible. When the city denied a request for apparatus, cut back personnel, or closed firehouses, Bill was indignant. How dare they, he would say. Don't they know the risks firefighters face? As the first deputy, however, he began to realize that the department had to operate within the bounds of a budget that was never large enough. He now had to make decisions despite his personal feelings and allegiances. Cold, hard dollars-and-cents decisions that oftentimes put fiscal concerns ahead of everything else. Ultimately, however, the fire commissioner made the final decisions and took all the heat for them, which was just fine for Bill. In March 1992, five thousand firefighters, angry over budget cuts and contract disputes, marched around City Hall chanting, "Rivera must go!" Two weeks earlier, the commissioner had been relegated to the last pew in a church holding the funeral for a fire lieutenant killed in the line of duty. Happily out of the glare of the press, Bill joked one day during this time, "They don't shoot arrows at the second in command."

Still, as first dep, Bill was intimately involved in the administrative decision-making process. Though he quickly became skillful at walking the tightrope between the city, the unions, and the fire department, it took him a while to be comfortable in the role. He was especially adept in his relationship with the firefighters' union. Now, as management, he was on the opposite side of the bargaining table from the union. Cool under pressure, voluminously knowledgeable about the department, and with an English professor's command of the language, he was a formidable negotiator to say the least. But what made it impossible to argue with him was that everyone in the room knew his heart was with the firefighters. He also remained a staunch advocate for fire safety. After the 1 New York Plaza fire, O'Hagan had championed what would come to be called Local Law 5, which mandated construction in buildings that would keep fire from jumping floor to floor. It also required sprinkler systems in both new and older buildings. Over the years, lawyers from developers and the real estate industry began chipping away at the law to save money for the builders. But Bill made it his cause to reinforce the law to its original language. He testified often in front of the city council, and successfully pushed back to keep the law intact.

The most consequential event during Bill's first tenure as first dep (he held the position twice), however, did not concern an ordinance but a terrorist attack on February 23, 1993.

On that cold, late-winter day, two Jordanian nationals drove a rental truck filled with thirteen hundred pounds of urea nitrate into a sub-basement garage of the north tower of the World Trade Center and blew a six-story crater into the foundation of the building. The intent, experts believe, was to topple the north tower so that it would act like a 110-story domino and take down the south one. Had the plan worked, the attack might have killed a hundred thousand people and destroyed perhaps the most famous symbol of America's financial might. Those who helped design the World Trade Center, however, believed that nothing short of a monumental natural disaster or a nuclear-sized explosion could bring the buildings down. In fact, the buildings drew praise for their sturdy foundations and massive support beams that didn't give way during that first attack.

The basement might have been able to stand a nuke, but the same couldn't be said for the top floors of the building. Typically, skyscrapers are built with cement on a skeleton grid of steel columns. The World Trade Center towers, however, were supported by exterior, hollow steel load-bearing walls. Simply put, the building's cores were attached to the exterior walls by steel trusses that supported the floors like a suspension bridge. This type of support, much lighter than traditional methods, allowed for the developers to build to soaring heights. If any experts then knew such a design would leave the towers vulnerable to the impact of a jet airliner, their fears went unheeded. After the first terrorist attack on the World Trade Center most believed the buildings were practically indestructible. Bill was one of them. Brian Davan was with his father-in-law at the site a few days after the attack. He remembered the chief, still astonished, shaking his head at the size of hole the blast blew.

"These buildings can never come down," he said.

# TWELVE

# Commissioner Feehan

In 1989, Rudy Giuliani lost to David Dinkins by just two percentage points, one of the closest mayoral races in New York City history. Had the election been held even a week or so later, it might have been Rudy who moved into Gracie Mansion, the mayor's home. Giuliani was closing fast, narrowing to a whisper what had been Dinkins's roaring twenty-three-point lead in the polls just a few months earlier. Rudy had his eye on the 1993 race as soon as the 1989 one was official. He was sure he would win in his next try.

In '89, Rudy had fashioned himself as the new sheriff in town, a man with a reputation burnished as the U.S. attorney for the Southern District of New York. While a prosecutor, he specialized in charging and trying organized crime figures, using the RICO statute's wide net to snag high-profile mob bosses. Without question he put a lot of bad guys away, though the scales of justice, with RICO, were clearly tipped in his favor. It might come as little surprise, but Giuliani basked in the spotlight his crimefighting career drew. As the crime rate in New York rose, so did his star. With the scourge of crack cocaine one of the major reasons, the crime rate only got worse during the Dinkins administration. For many white voters the Crown Heights riot was the final straw.

In the 1993 election Giuliani campaigned on quality-of-life crimes, like ridding the streets of the "squeegee men," who would rush to clean your windshield with a dirty rag as you waited at stoplights. The idea was that once you stopped minor crimes like graffiti and panhandling, major crimes would decrease. Rudy didn't come up with the plan. The credit for the "broken windows" theory goes to two criminologists, James Q. Wilson and George Kelling, who introduced it in an *Atlantic* article in 1992. Whether or not the broken windows theory can actually make cities safer is still debated, but it did solidify Rudy's hold on the white vote in New York.

Still, right up to election day, the polls had the 1993 mayoral race razor tight once again. If there was an edge left to be found, it was in the Hispanic community. It was here that the last of the tumblers of fate would fall into place and provide Chief Feehan an opportunity to write his name in the history books.

———

On September 1, 1993, a little more than two months before election day, Charlie Rivera resigned his post as fire commissioner and signed on as an advisor to Rudy Giuliani's campaign. He told the press that he had quit because he thought the city, helmed by Mayor Dinkins, was treating the fire department as second-class citizens when it came to funding. He wasn't wrong. After the Brian Watkins murder, Dinkins added thousands of cops to the NYPD while cutting the FDNY's budget. What blazed across the front pages or the city's newspapers, however, was the fire commissioner's accusation that the Dinkins administration treated him with "disdain and disrespect" because of his Hispanic heritage. He said that they had failed to punish an administration official who called him an ethnic slur. Though the allegations might have been true, the timing of them was certainly suspect. The day Rivera resigned, the Dinkins campaign had sent out a campaign mailer to one hundred thousand Hispanic households touting the number of Hispanics, including Rivera, whom Dinkins had hired. Rivera was media-savvy enough to know that his resignation would be both an embarrassment and a campaign nightmare for Dinkins. It was. The mayor was roasted in the tabloids. His aides quickly assembled a photo op and press conference that included every Hispanic person they could find in City Hall to try and contain the fallout. With his race for reelection in full damage control mode, Dinkins called a meeting with the then chief of department, Anthony Fusco, and the head of the Uniformed Fire Officers Association, Richard Brower. Dinkins asked them who they thought could take Rivera's place and plug the political hole he had caused by his resignation. Brower didn't hesitate. Bill Feehan, he said.

"You mean Chief Feehan?" the mayor asked.

"Yep," Brower answered. "That's the guy."

———

Bill's phone in Flushing rang at five in the morning. What Dinkins wanted to know first was if Bill knew about Rivera's resignation. He did, of course—he was the commissioner's first deputy—but he didn't know about it beforehand. Why Rivera had kept Chief Feehan in the dark about his plan we don't fully know. The relationship between them was respectful and friendly. Their lives and careers were nearly mirror images of one another. Rivera grew up in the Bronx and went to Catholic schools. He served in the U.S. Navy during the Korean War and became a firefighter in 1958. By 1964, he made lieutenant, then captain in 1970, and battalion chief in 1977. Perhaps Rivera didn't tell him because he wanted Bill to have plausible deniability so he wouldn't end up as collateral damage. He'd already given Chief Feehan's career a second life by backing him for the first dep job.

The deputy mayor told Bill to be in City Hall at 8 a.m. He almost didn't make it. Riding in the back of car two, with lights flashing and the siren wailing, he headed out of Brooklyn toward Manhattan. Just before the first dep's car reached the Brooklyn Bridge, a tractor-trailer took a wide turn, smashing into it and forcing it into a streetlight. The Crown Vic was demolished, and the driver, a firefighter named Sal Lupino, was slightly injured. Chief Feehan, unhurt and as cool as ever, radioed for an ambulance and a ride to City Hall.

He spent the rest of the day in the basement of the domed building being grilled by deputy mayors. By the end of the day, Dinkins's deputies were convinced that he knew nothing of Rivera's plans. That evening the mayor announced Chief Bill Feehan as acting fire commissioner.

Later, Bill would shrug off the moment, saying that he was only a placeholder. He wouldn't even move into the commissioner's office and continued to insist that he be called Chief Feehan. Not too long after he'd assumed the top post, he and Betty were having dinner at a Queens restaurant with friends. As they walked from the restaurant, one of the friends looked at the license plates on the company Crown Vic, which read FD-1.

"Pretty fancy plates," the friend remarked.

Bill reminded him that thirty years earlier they were having dinner together at a restaurant nearby, and that night Bill was driving the Rambler. "Yeah," the new commissioner said, "and we don't have to push the car to start it."

———

Bill's appointment mitigated some of the political damage of Rivera's desertion—the press lauded the pick. And though the polls indicated that Rivera's defection had helped Giuliani in the short run, by election day it mattered little. In fact, Dinkins would end up doing better with the Hispanic vote than he did the first time he ran. Again, the race was close, but once the votes were counted, Bill found himself in a losing administration. Not only were his days as fire commissioner numbered, but the end of his fire service career was fast approaching. Undoubtedly, he thought, a new broom in City Hall would sweep him out the door. One of Father Mychal Judge's favorite prayers contained the line "Lord, take me where You want me to go." No other holy words were more appropriate for Bill's journey. Soon after the election, but before he stepped down as mayor, Dinkins called Chief Feehan and told him he was going to remove the word "acting" in front of his title. In one of his last acts as mayor, Dinkins officially made Bill Feehan the city's twenty-eighth fire commissioner.

At least you'll be remembered in the history books, the outgoing mayor told him. Though Chief Feehan remained humble, his accomplishment was anything but. His appointment to fire commissioner was the crowning achievement of a unique fire service career. No other person has held every rank in the fire department, and perhaps no one else could. In the official letter, dated November 24, 1993, Dinkins wrote in part:

> Anyone can guide a ship when the waters are calm and the weather's fair. The work of the finest skippers is marked by how they navigate rough waters. And these last four years have been difficult ones for this city and the Fire Department. Your presence there has made a significant and

beneficial difference to the members of the Fire Department,
to me, and to all the people of our city.

*David Dinkins 106th Mayor of the City of New York*

———

Though Bill might have been on the losing side, with the election of
Rudolph W. Giuliani as the 107th mayor of New York City, the fire
department would be a big winner. Not only did firefighters vote
for Giuliani en masse, but they waged an aggressive get-out-the-
vote campaign. They were an obvious presence in turnout coats in
polling places throughout the city. Many were certified poll watch-
ers. During the transition, Randy Mastro, Rudy's chief of staff and
hatchet man deputy mayor, took firefighter union president Tom
Von Essen to lunch to thank him for the union's help.

"We're going to do something nice for you," Mastro said. "We're
going make Charlie Rivera fire commissioner."

The last thing Von Essen wanted was Rivera returning to the
commissioner's office. He had thought Rivera's high-profile defection was self-promotional and put the department in a bad light.
One union boss called Rivera's actions "a sidewalk act."

"Oh God," Von Essen responded. "He's a nice man and a good
fire chief, but he sucked as commissioner."

Mastro shrugged and then asked whom he wanted instead.

"Just get somebody who's close to Giuliani and who thinks big,"
the union president said.

Von Essen got his wish.

———

On the day he took office, January 1, 1994, Mayor Giuliani tapped
Howard Safir as fire commissioner. Safir's appointment was

unexpected, to say the least. His last job was as an associate director for the U.S. Marshals Service. Before that, he ran the marshals' witness protection program. Without any experience in fire service, he might as well have been in the witness protection program himself as far as firefighters were concerned. No one knew who he was. For Von Essen, however, the new commissioner checked all the boxes: He was the mayor's pal and thought big. Really big.

The post of fire commissioner was a kind of consolation prize for Safir. He wanted to run the city's police department and later would. But his friend Giuliani had passed him over for William Bratton, the chief of the New York City Transit Police. Two years later, Bratton would wear out his welcome with his boss, and Safir would get the job he really wanted. But during his short time as fire commissioner, from 1994 to 1996, the fire department would have a champion in City Hall like they'd never had before.

As far as Bill was concerned, Safir's appointment as fire commissioner meant it was time to start packing up his career with the FDNY. Why would Rudy want to keep Dinkins's fire commissioner around, even in some other role? But Bill's career would find new life. The new mayor had a close campaign advisor named Tom Regan, who'd been a firefighter in Brooklyn. When the topic of choosing a fire commissioner first arose, the mayor-elect asked Regan for a suggestion. "Appoint whomever you want," Regan said. "Just keep Bill Feehan as first deputy, and let him run the department."

———

Rudy would take Regan's advice, and Chief Feehan would go on to build a strong working relationship with the new mayor and his fire commissioner. It was common knowledge that Rudy was a fire buff. Bill knew he had an uncle who'd been a fire captain (and four police officer uncles). Chief Feehan made sure word of any fire over two alarms got to Gracie Mansion right away. As an aside, being a buff might not have been the only reason Rudy was eager to answer fire calls. It was no secret that the mayor was unhappy in his marriage to Donna Hanover, his second wife. Bill also knew he would use any excuse to get out of Gracie Mansion. According to news reports, Rudy had plenty of alternative places to find comfort. One of his more publicized affairs was allegedly with his press secretary. A reporter from one of the tabloids spied him in a lingerie store, buying a scanty negligee that was purportedly a gift for her. Bill could care less about Rudy's peccadillos. He just wanted to be on the mayor's good side, and that meant giving him notice of every flame bigger than a church candle. His plan worked. When the idea of recommissioning engine companies shut during previous administrations was aired, Bill, among others, was a Rudy whisperer, urging the mayor to push ahead with the plan. Not only would Rudy bring back the fire companies, but he allowed them to be turned into elite squads, which was mostly Chief Feehan's idea. "Bill's fingerprints were all over that," Tom Fitzpatrick remembered.

―――――

Chief Feehan's knowledge of the department was invaluable to the new fire commissioner, who might have been lost at the helm of an agency and culture he knew little about. In maritime law there's a saying: Master's orders; pilot's advice. Though Safir was seen as making all the decisions, it was Bill, and other chiefs, who were pointing him in the right direction. One story that captures Safir's reluctance to be involved in the department's primary function is told by Henry McDonald, Chief Feehan's executive officer. One of the hats Henry wore was as operations liaison to the commissioner.

It was his job to notify Safir about fires above a second alarm, the ones that Rudy would surely show up at. Safir wasn't a warm and fuzzy guy under the best of circumstances. He never really went out of his way to build relationships with anyone under his command in the FDNY, perhaps because he had his eyes on a bigger prize. Sometimes Henry would have to call him in the middle of the night. When he did, he'd be greeted with a frosty silence. Henry would relay the information, and Safir would hang up without saying a word.

Still, the new commissioner turned out to be a godsend for the department. Coming from the federal government, he was used to the fat federal wallet. For instance, when the city issued him a Chevrolet Caprice, the new fire commissioner sent it back and bought two brand-new Mercury Marquis at a price tag of $44,000, a considerable sum back then, for himself and Chief Feehan. Once the press got hold of the story, Rudy had him cancel the order. As it would turn out, the cars were nickels and dimes compared to the city money he was about to spend on his fire department.

On March 28, 1994, a flashover in an apartment fire in SoHo killed Firefighters James Young and Christopher Seidenburg and Captain John Drennan. A flashover is an explosion that happens when gases from a fire combust. The fire started in a first-floor apartment. The resident had left a bag of used food containers on the stove, and a pilot light ignited it. The engine company ran a line into the building. Later, investigators would discover that all the windows in the apartment were shut tight. There was a fireplace, with a working flue, but it did little to vent the fire. When the engine company opened the door, a large flame shot through the doorway like a giant flamethrower and up the stairs where Drennan and the others were. One of the primary rules in firefighting is to protect the guys above you, as they are in one of the most vulnerable positions during a fire. Drennan spent forty days at the burn center in New York-Presbyterian Hospital. Giuliani and his fire commissioner went to meet Drennan's family in the hospital. After the emotional get-together, Safir took the mayor aside.

"This could've been different," Safir said.

"What do you mean?" the mayor asked.

At the time, New York City firemen wore thigh-high boots and long fire-resistant Nomex coats, but the upper thighs and groin area had little protection. Neither did the back of the neck. The firefighters' union had pushed the previous administration for the gear that would shield these areas without success. At one point, it looked as though Dinkins was going to release the funds, but his number crunchers nixed the plan. Giuliani wasn't aware of the bunker gear drama until Safir told him. Within months, the city was shipping the protective gear to firehouses around the city.

Safir's biggest contribution to the fire department was not in the area of safety equipment, however, but in self-esteem. For more years than anyone wanted to remember, FDNY headquarters had been located in a city-owned building that had once been a Macy's warehouse on Livingston Street in downtown Brooklyn. During budget cuts in the sixties and seventies, many of the city's municipal buildings fell into abject disrepair and few were in worse shape than fire department headquarters. Plaster fell from the walls. Toilets, if you could find one, didn't work. Fluorescent lights buzzed and blinked. The plastic coverings were filled with prehistoric bugs. The offices were tiny, the furniture worn out. The rat infestation was so bad, workers took to putting traps under their desks. The elevators were covered in graffiti, and were out of service for as much time as they worked. Headquarters didn't even have a conference room.

The chiefs in operations put up plastic partitions in an elevator lobby and held meetings with local architects and developers while separated from civilians who waited for elevators by the see-through sheets. For any city agency, let alone one as important as the New York City Fire Department, headquarters was an embarrassment. After Giuliani appointed Safir, the new commissioner was given a tour of the building. Afterward, he stormed right into Chief Feehan's office.

"We're out of here," was all he said.

The new fire commissioner wasn't blowing hot air. Soon after he marched into Bill's office, he walked into his friend Rudy Giuliani's and told him pretty much the same thing. And just like that, the machinery of city government began to churn, funds magically became available, and a move to new headquarters went from a heated promise to a planned reality.

# THIRTEEN

# The Squirrels

On June 14, 1996, Bill stood in the kitchen of the house in Flushing with the rotary phone in his hand. His eyes shone with tears. Outside the kitchen window, the first light of the day began to filter through the leaves of the oak tree that stood next to the house. For months, Betty had been in and out of the hospital progressively getting worse. By then, the kids were out of the house and on with their lives, and aside from the squirrels, Bill spent much of his time there alone. He clicked the cradle on the phone and dialed Henry McDonald's number.

"Betty's gone," he said into the receiver.

———

Bill's wife had spent her last days in St. Clare's Hospital, in the Hell's Kitchen section of Manhattan. He'd fussed over Betty so many times when she was hospitalized, making sure she had what she needed and that her room was tidy. Sometimes he'd go to see her alone, and other times with the children. Afterward, he'd take the kids to the Woodside steakhouse in Queens where the Irish waitresses fussed over them. Right to the end, Bill was crazy about Betty, and she was crazy about him. Ultimately, there was nothing he could do to save her. Betty was sixty-two when she died.

McDonald wanted to drive to Flushing, but Bill told him not to. Over the years, Betty's illnesses and the psychological effects had brought incredible stress to the whole Feehan family. But Bill had it the worst. The migraines he'd get from pressure at home were so bad he'd throw up in the wastepaper basket in his office. Henry would tell him to pull the shades and lie on the couch and wouldn't let anyone in to see him.

"No, don't come in," the chief said to Henry on the phone. "I have to call the kids." He dialed Billy's number. It took him a moment or two to realize the phone had gone dead. He'd forgotten to pay Ma Bell, and the telephone company had shut off the landline in his house. His absentmindedness at home bewildered those who knew him at work, where he was considered a fire department savant. He grabbed his cell phone and walked out the door. He made a dozen calls sitting in car two in the driveway. Then he called Henry back and asked if he knew someone at the phone company.

Though expected, the bad news still rocked him to his core. As a defense mechanism, as Billy had done when he looked down at his father's dead body, he forced his thoughts to the things he needed to take care of. He called the funeral home in Flushing, scheduled the wake, and arranged with St. Mel's for the funeral Mass. But he hadn't planned a burial plot, perhaps because, on some level, he refused to believe the inevitability of his wife's condition. Calvary Cemetery, where his parents were buried, didn't have any plots available. He dialed his friend Jim Marron, who now lived on Long Island, and asked him for help. They buried Betty, with Bill's commissioner's badge in the casket, in St. Charles Cemetery in Farmingdale, thirty miles east of Queens. When they lowered her into the ground, Bill looked at his oldest daughter and shook his head. After a lifetime of holding on to Queens with both hands, in death Betty found herself in the suburbs.

"She'd rather be buried under the Brooklyn-Queens Expressway," he said.

On the day of Betty's funeral, the new neighbors, a couple in the real estate business, put a note in his mailbox asking if he was thinking of moving.

"I'll burn the house to the ground before I'll let those people sell it for me," he said to Liz.

———

There were those who worked with him who say that the years after Betty's death were the best of Bill's life. In one way, they were. He'd worried so much about his wife. There was always a medical emergency around the corner. He hated to see her suffer. But to say he didn't feel a bottomless loss was to dismiss a lifetime love affair. It had always been Betty and Bill or Bill and Betty, and her death for him was a grievous loss.

His children and grandchildren helped heal the wound, the grandchildren especially. Siobhan and Kelsey called Bill Pop-pop, and in his house in Flushing they'd eat brown sugar instant oatmeal and watch the movie *Grease* over and over again in the small converted TV room. Sometimes, Pop-pop would take them to the park down the block to feed the ducks. Still, even the girls could feel the shadow that surrounded their grandfather. Siobhan would go on to study art in college. Years later, her visits to the 9/11 reflecting pools inspired her to pursue her career in landscape architecture. Being an artist, most of her recollections of visits to her grandparents are sensory. The darkness of the house in Flushing is what she remembers most. The oak tree and the overgrowth of other vegetation blocked the physical light, but there was also a kind of gloom there. Neither Siobhan or Kelsey has many memories of Betty, though Kelsey remembers climbing into her grandmother's bed and eating the hard candies she kept in a dish on the nightstand.

When it came to the fire department, however, it was his son John who filled his firefighter heart with the most pride. As his dad did, John also went to St. John's University, but there he studied nursing. He rightly believed that medical experience would help him in a career as a firefighter. Like his dad, he joined the Fire Patrol while he waited for the fire department entrance exam to be given. Later, in an interview, Chief Feehan said he nudged his son to join the Fire Patrol to get him out of the house and Betty's hair. "I didn't want a murder on my hands," he joked. When John finally took the test for the FDNY, he aced it, and then graduated on January 17, 1995, valedictorian of his class at the academy. First Deputy Commissioner Feehan handed him the award.

Right from the start of his career, John was an active firefighter. He had his dad to thank for some of that activity in the beginning. Chief Feehan would pore over the charts compiled by the department's computerized dispatching system, trying to figure out ways to route more fires to his firehouse in Brooklyn. He knew the best way to keep his son safe was to get him as much experience as possible. Like his father and grandfather before him, John chased fire. And like them, he also shuns the spotlight, a commendable trait that is in a way more illustrative of a firefighter's mindset than hours of interviews could ever capture. Part humility and part disdain for those who practice self-promotion, this reticence is a heroes' code passed down in the Feehan family and throughout the history of the department.

Though John doesn't seek attention, we do know, from some who worked with him and other sources, that his devotion to the fire department and family is every bit as deep as his father's and grandfather's. At this writing, John is still a member of the FDNY as a battalion chief. According to the website of NY Fire Consultants, an outside agency that prepares building owners and managers for fire safety certificate exams, John worked in the department's Special Operations Command as a firefighter. There he was trained by FEMA in the recognition and mitigation of hazardous material. He also taught new recruits at the academy in both firefighting and hazardous material operations. He obtained a master's degree from John Jay College in protective management, a course of study that specializes in emergency management. Without question, his father would be enormously proud of how his fire career has progressed.

———

Even with the love of his family, Bill's routine became one of a lonely man. He would leave for work at six each morning, stop for the same breakfast every day at the North Shore Diner—eggs over easy and bacon. He would sit in the same booth and read the *Daily News*, known simply as "the paper" in Queens. His car was always the first in the parking lot at headquarters and nearly always the last to leave. Friends invited him to family functions, weddings, and anniversaries, but he would rarely attend. Sometimes he would get as far as driving to the event, but then he'd turn the car around and head for home. His favorite excuse was that he couldn't find a parking space. Even at his own family gatherings, he eschewed the limelight. Instead, he would wind up talking to one of his grandchildren.

It is true, however, that he filled much of the emptiness he felt with his work. There he assembled and drew close a circle of firefighter purists. Like Henry McDonald, some were "off the line" men who'd spent years in the trenches facing down the red devil before coming to headquarters. Ray Goldbach was one of these. He'd been an active firefighter in the Bronx. He found his way to headquarters right after passing the captain's test. At the time, Commissioner Safir had begun an initiative for new captains to gain management skills, and as part of that program they would spend six months in the commissioner's office. Goldbach thought he was going to hate it. You take an active firefighter out of a busy firehouse and put them behind a desk and you can bet they'll be unhappy. But he'd worked in the Bronx with Tom Fitzpatrick, then Safir's executive assistant. One day, Fitzpatrick took Goldbach to the side. "Why don't you come and work with me in the commissioner's office?" Fitzpatrick said. "We have a lot of good things going on here."

"I want to do my penance and get out of there," Ray answered.

"Well, you're going to have to stay for six months anyway," he said. "You might as well give it a try."

When he met Henry and, later, Mike Regan, his opinion about headquarters began to change. Goldbach liked being exposed to the brain trust that ran the department, especially Chief Feehan, and he would end up staying at headquarters for the rest of his career.

Outspoken and hilarious, Goldbach would over time become the counterweight to Chief Feehan's quiet personality and subtle humor. By his own admission, Goldbach wore his feelings on his sleeve. When Bill hosted a morning coffee gathering in his office, Goldbach would burst into the room already on fire, animatedly describing the argument du jour with his wife or a complaint about one of his daughters. He thought nothing of having a heated discussion over the phone in front of the rest of the crew. The gang would joke that they would take his BlackBerry from him or break his fingers so he couldn't dial it. Ray coached his daughter's softball team and did so with an NFL defensive coordinator's seriousness and intensity. According to his own stories, he gave them little sympathy and yelled at them for everything. The truth was, all of Ray's histrionics were for show, and Chief Feehan and the gang knew it. He would do anything for his family.

————

Mike Regan was another of the chief's inner circle. Though he hadn't come from the ranks of the department, Regan was from FDNY stock. Both his father and his uncle were New York City firemen. His uncle was the Tom Regan who was part of Giuliani's political team and advised the incoming mayor to keep Chief Feehan as first deputy. Before joining the fire department in 1995, Mike headed the communications office at the Port Authority of New York and New Jersey. He held that position in 1993 when terrorists set off a bomb in the sub-basement of the north tower. With all the elevators out, Regan had walked up sixty-three floors and broken into a cabinet with a fireman's ax to retrieve work profiles of the people killed in the attack. He assumed the deputy commissioner of public information post at FDNY headquarters in stride. Still, there were one or two things for which he had to familiarize himself. Soon after he arrived, he rushed to a multi-alarm fire. Chief Feehan was on the scene and took him to the side.

"Where's your car?" the chief asked.

"Right there," a bewildered Regan answered.

"Next time you might want to park about four blocks away," Bill said calmly. "In about two minutes there are going to be big red trucks parked all around it, and you might not be able to go home for a couple of days."

Chief Feehan saw the value of the press office. He had worked to make it a twenty-four-hour-a-day operation. Before Bill directed his attention toward it, the press office was run like a neighborhood weekly newspaper. It would close shop at night, so if a major fire happened at midnight, say, the media would have little or no sourcing from the FDNY. Bill protected the reputation of the department like he protected his family, and he believed the department's public information office was an integral part of that protection. When Regan took the job, Bill gave him only one bit of advice. The heroic, lifesaving tradition of the New York City Fire Department had gone on unabated for over 130 years, he told his new deputy commissioner.

"What do you say we don't mess that up?"

———

Though Bill's hours were long, he worked a regular Monday-to-Friday workweek with weekends off, unless, of course, there was a fire or other emergency to which he needed to respond. The department radio scanner in the car always had the last word. When Betty was alive, she would bristle when they were on their way out to dinner or had some other plans and the radio would blare to life. If it was a major fire, the plans would be canceled. But on those occasions when the radio was quiet, Bill loved visiting his daughters and son and his grandchildren. With Betty gone, he leaned on Liz and Tara. At work, too, he found female friendships that helped fill the hole in his life from Betty's death.

Lynn Tierney had worked for Mike Regan as the media relations officer for the Port Authority Police before she joined the fire department. She likened her time with the cops in the Port Authority to the old police sitcom *Barney Miller* and a popular Jack

Lemmon–Walter Matthau comedy. "I called them the Grumpy Old Men," she remembers. Though experienced in male-dominated work situations, she had trepidation the first day she showed up at fire department headquarters. A colleague of Tierney's had made the same transition from Port Authority to the fire department a few weeks earlier.

"The day starts in Commissioner Feehan's office," he said. "Break into that group like you own the place."

At the time, headquarters was still located on Livingston Street in Brooklyn. Tierney remembers walking in that first day and looking out the chief's office's large windows to the grimy Brooklyn street scene below. There were only two available seats, one near the back wall of the office, and one right in front of Chief Feehan's desk. She took her friend's advice and sat directly in front of her new boss. It was the right move.

"Welcome, Lynnie," the chief said with a welcoming smile.

Tierney and Bill shared a love of Irish music, especially Irish tenors such as Ronan Tynan. At the end of the day, Bill would slip in a cassette and play Tynan's arias, or the songs of other Irish singers. Often the group would join him in his office, where a scotch on the rocks or two would be had. One day, Tierney admitted to Bill that her attraction to Tynan went further than admiration for his prodigious diaphragm. Tierney thought the substantially sized singer would be a good fit as a husband. One night in December 2000, Bill's children took him to a Tynan concert at Madison Square Garden. Coincidentally, Tierney happened to be at the same show. The next morning at the coffee klatch, Bill was enthusiastic about the marriage idea.

"I think you're right, Lynnie," Bill said. "I think he's the guy for you."

Several months later, she would get a chance to meet with the tenor, but under the saddest of circumstances. He sang at the funerals for the fighters who died fighting a blaze on Father's Day. Lynn drove Tynan back to Manhattan, and though a marriage wasn't in the offing, a close friendship would develop.

In a way, the chief's relationship with Tierney was out of the *Mad Men* era. If she showed up late to a fire, say, he might joke that she'd been busy shopping for pocketbooks in Macy's. But though he kidded Tierney at every chance, he also supported her as she helped try to open the department to women.

————

In 1996, Commissioner Von Essen had initiated a cadet program to entice minorities and women into the FDNY. Tierney devoted much of her time to that initiative. As Commissioner Lowery had done, partly the idea was for Black and Latino firefighters to recruit prospects from poorer neighborhoods. Tierney met with representatives from the U.S. Army and Navy. She called on city universities and canvassed businesses that employed young men and women. Once enrolled, a cadet received a small stipend for a six-month work-study program. The fire department then trained and hired them as EMTs. Once they were members of the FDNY, they were then eligible to take a separate written entrance exam to become firefighters.

Though innovative, the program ultimately had limited success. One of the reasons was because it hadn't been confined to minorities. While inner-city recruits struggled with a system and culture of which they had no knowledge, young men from firefighter families thrived in the program. Many of them came from Long Island and Rockland County north of the city. Some of them were fire chiefs' sons. For minorities, it wasn't a fair fight. Few of them had driver's licenses, a distinct disadvantage when the job required you to drive an ambulance. Tierney remembers instructors giving driving lessons, and helping recruits get prepared for the driver's test. But even if they got as far as getting a license, imagine being a new driver behind the wheel of an ambulance in New York City traffic? From 1996 to 2002 (the program ended in the wake of 9/11), the fire department hired only forty-five nonwhite men and only three women from the cadet program. Though an admirable idea, the cadet program had little chance to crack an unyielding institution like the FDNY.

———

Tierney wasn't the only woman in the chief's inner circle at headquarters. In 1992, Lai-Sun Yee was hired to work in the department's Bureau of Investigations and Trials. A Cornell-educated attorney, and a self-admitted workaholic, she forged a friendship with the chief late in the evenings in headquarters when nearly everyone else had gone home. At first their interaction was relegated to a quick nod and hello from Bill. But in time, as he would pass Lai-Sun's office and see her, hard at work under a lamp, a kinship developed. He began calling her "pal." Yee's hard work paid off. She was promoted to assistant commissioner and then deputy commissioner. With the promotion to deputy commissioner, the department issued her a Crown Vic. Since she was only five foot one, the car felt to her as big as a yacht; she could barely reach the pedals. One night, she mentioned her dilemma to Chief Feehan.

"Let me see what I can do," the chief said.

A few weeks later, the department changed the vehicle to a more manageable Ford Taurus. One time, Lai-Sun's parents came from Ohio to visit. Chief Feehan treated the Yees like royalty at MetroTech.

————

The women of his inner circle, Lai-Sun, Lynn, and also Dr. Kelly, the chief medical officer, would mother Bill. Tierney had a house in Maine, and on the way back to New York, she'd pick up a raspberry pie from Moody's, a diner on Route 1 famous for them. Bill would keep the pies in his office and cut a slice in the afternoon for himself.

The men at headquarters, too, watched over him. Many nights they would take him out to dinner. Someone would ask, "Chief, you feel like a bowl of spaghetti?"

"I would love a bowl of spaghetti," he'd answer.

————

Despite all the family support and friendship, the loneliness Bill felt after Betty's death remained and was exacerbated by the tragedy that came with cold regularity in the fire department. By this time in his career, Chief Feehan had been to a battalion of firefighter funerals. He'd written and delivered scores of eulogies. "He could sit down and write something right off the top of his head that was beautiful and pure, and perfectly appropriate," Lynn Tierney remembered. Tierney herself wrote eulogies for firefighters, but when she did she would always let Chief Feehan see her first draft. "He would add the history, grace, beauty, and the gravitas that was necessary for burying a New York City fireman," she said.

In one, he wrote, "The truest kind of love is to lay down your life for another, but the purest form of love is to cherish each other every day. Never leave a moment's doubt that you love with your whole heart and soul."

At headquarters, Feehan had become part father confessor, part history professor, and part fire department Yoda. He was a wellspring of information, advice, and solace. His civilian wardrobe had not lost a single stitch. He must have been on a first-name basis with his dry cleaner. He wore immaculate suits, crisp dress shirts, and an array of striped ties. He kept his office just as tidy. His desk was clutter-free, the drawers neatly lined with files and operations manuals. Fronting a pull-out couch was a heavy oak coffee table on which sat thick photograph books of fire departments from around the world. In his office, everything had its place, and Chief Feehan was in complete control. He thrived in the orderliness at work, a place where he was in command. Betty's illnesses were beyond his control at home, and the memory of losing her made him feel helpless. The march of time made him feel helpless too. But the department still provided the ballast in his life. Without it he'd be set adrift.

# FOURTEEN

# Union Boss

After a photo of Bill Bratton in a crimefighting trench coat found its way onto a *Time* magazine cover, a vacancy opened up in the New York City Police Department's commissioner office. Like his friend Donald Trump, Mayor Giuliani didn't take kindly to anyone drawing the spotlight away from him. When word emerged that the police commissioner was on his way out, rumors followed that the fire commissioner would take Bratton's job, the position he'd always coveted.

As those rumors found their way to FDNY headquarters on Livingston Street, Henry McDonald walked into Bill's office and asked if he thought they were true.

"Let's find out," Chief Feehan said.

Along with Henry and several others of his inner circle, Bill walked into Safir's office and asked him point-blank if he was leaving for the police department.

"You're my guys," Safir said. "If I'm leaving, you'll be the first to know."

An hour later, Commissioner Safir was on television with the mayor announcing his new post as the top cop.

Although he didn't talk about his feelings until much later, there was a part of Bill that was deeply disappointed by the news. Safir's appointment as PC meant Bill had been passed over, once again, for the commissioner post. Giuliani wouldn't have made the announcement about giving Safir the police commissioner's job unless he'd already chosen his successor. What stung even more was whom Giuliani had picked to fill the role.

Tom Von Essen grew up in Ozone Park, a working-class section of Queens, and attended Bishop Loughlin High School in Brooklyn, the same school that Giuliani attended (Von Essen was three years behind Giuliani there and didn't know him then). After serving in the U.S. Navy, he joined the fire department in 1970. For the next thirteen years, he was a firefighter in Ladder 42 in the South Bronx. Still, he found time to go back to college and then obtain an advanced degree. He started substitute teaching, thinking he could build a second career in education. However, his experience in front of a classroom in South Ozone Park convinced him that he didn't have the patience to be a teacher. In 1984, he left teaching and entered firefighter union politics. Over the next seven years, he rose in the UFA from Bronx trustee to union secretary and vice president. Von Essen took the lieutenant's test twice but never really studied for it and failed the exam both times.

In 1990, with twenty years on the job, he decided to retire at the rank of firefighter. For a short time, he worked for a building management company in Manhattan. He liked the job well enough but soon realized he'd made a mistake leaving the department he loved. When you retire from a civil service job in New York City, you're given a short grace period in which you can change your mind and be reinstated as if you never left. By the time Von Essen decided to go back to the department, however, his grace period had lapsed. At the time, Bill was in his initial tenure as the first deputy commissioner. Bill and Von Essen knew each other from union interactions. Chief Feehan had helped Von Essen's younger brother, Roddy, get assigned to a good firehouse in Brooklyn. He knew Von Essen was no hairbag, a derogatory term for firefighters who just mark time until retirement.

"Don't worry about it, Tom," Bill said to him. "We'll get you back in."

Soon after, Von Essen happily returned to his old firehouse. He also decided to reenter union politics. He did, and in a big way. In 1991, he ran for union president and won.

Chief Feehan and Von Essen liked and respected each other. Still, it was hard for Bill to understand the mayor's reasoning in choosing the firefighters' union president as fire commissioner, which was a little like wearing a Yankee hat at a Red Sox game—it just wasn't done. Also, having never risen above the rank of firefighter, the new commissioner knew little of the inner workings of headquarters. Von Essen would later say that was exactly the reason why Rudy, always a contrarian, gave him the job. Bill was a humble man. *Too* humble, some of his friends would say. But despite his good soldier act, in his heart, Bill at first believed that the mayor had picked the wrong person. Chief Feehan didn't hold a grudge, however, and soon he and Von Essen would become a productive team. On Von Essen's part, his respect of Bill Feehan never wavered. "I can't imagine a fire department without him," he once said.

———

Giuliani's reasoning behind his choice of fire commissioner might have been more than just going against convention. At the time, the mayor had begun plans to merge the Emergency Medical Service, the city's Health and Hospitals Corporation's ambulances and medical technicians, into the FDNY. Giuliani had already combined the transit police with the NYPD. The idea of merging fire with EMS was not a new one, nor was it particular to New York City. Across the country, larger fire departments had done the same thing, primarily as a cost-cutting measure. Some data also supported the idea that it reduced response times for medical emergencies. The thinking went, big city fire departments already had sophisticated emergency response networks. On paper, the merger had only a plus side for Giuliani and the city and had plenty of outside support. However, getting the rank and file of the FDNY on board with it was a different matter. Having the former union president on his team, Rudy believed, might help mitigate some of the backlash that was sure to come from union membership who thought the merger was just a way to get more work out of them.

Chief Feehan at first was firmly against the idea. He thought a merger would come at the expense of the fire department's culture by bringing into the department a significant number of people who didn't share the same calling as the firefighters. It would mean training twelve thousand firefighters in nonessential medical attention, which would be a logistical nightmare, and would draw the ire of the unions despite the ex–union president commissioner. Though he might have voiced his displeasure to Von Essen and some of the staff chiefs at headquarters, there was nothing he could do to stop the merger. The city officially joined the two agencies on March 17, 1996. Whether or not Rudy purposely finalized the deal on St. Patrick's Day we have no way of knowing. For Bill it was the final insult of the episode. In fact, he might have held on to those hard feelings about the merger if not for a fresh new EMS addition to headquarters.

In June 1998, after a Medal Day celebration, a group of firemen went to an outdoor bar and restaurant in Bryant Park behind the New York Public Library. There, as the Irish might say, drinks were taken. As it happened, several off-duty police officers were also imbibing there.

Jim Dwyer, the late great columnist for the *New York Times*, called the rivalry between city cops and firemen "laddish." It's undoubtedly one that can quickly end up in the backyard trading punches. The history of the bad blood between the agencies dates back perhaps to the volunteer fire regiments' days. The disputes nearly always occur over who's in charge of an emergency scene. Ed Koch, in the last years of his mayoralty, gave the police department total dominion over large emergencies. In 1986, cops blocked firefighters from accessing a building that had collapsed. Books have been written about the communications failure between agencies after the attack on the World Trade Center. Some of the disputes, however, are just plain ridiculous. For example, in 1988 the department commissioners publicly fought over who had the better scuba team.

The dispute in Bryant Park began with heated words and quickly escalated into a brawl. Diners sat horrified, watching the fight. One of the cops found himself headfirst in a planter, according to reports. Those reports ran prominently in the next day's newspapers. For the most part, the departments ignore such altercations. But when blood from split lips becomes newsprint, chances are an internal investigation will follow. Early evidence was not helpful to the firefighters involved. All indications pointed toward them as the instigators. Then, out of the blue, fire marshals informed Regan that a videotape existed that could exonerate the firemen. The amateur filmmaker with the recording, however, had gone back home to Rhode Island. Regan and Chief Feehan wanted that tape, and they had the perfect person to go retrieve it.

———

Cookie McCarton got his nickname on his first day on the job as an emergency medical service worker. During roll call, he announced himself as Frank McCarton. "That's not your name," one of the old-timers in the room intoned, as a way of initiation. "You're Cookie the Rookie from cupcake town."

The veteran EMS worker then told him he would be known as Cookie the Rookie until he went on his third gunshot victim call. Since it was the last years of the crack cocaine epidemic, it didn't take much time for him to do so. True to his word, the old-timer stopped addressing McCarton as a rookie. But the name Cookie has remained until this day.

Mike Regan hired Cookie to work in the public information office. After the merger, the fire department needed people who knew the EMS's inner workings, and Cookie certainly did. For McCarton, becoming a member of the fire department was a dream come true. He'd been a volunteer firefighter on Long Island and was a fire buff his whole life. The day he put on the shirt with an FDNY patch, he says, was one of the proudest in his life. With the assignment to FDNY headquarters, he didn't think life couldn't get any better.

Chief Feehan took notice of Cookie almost right away. It was hard to miss him. He showed up early for work each day with his uniform clean and creased, his shoes shined to a luster. He always seemed to be around. One day, Von Essen was going over payroll with Mike Regan looking for places to cut back overtime. He came upon a timesheet with so many extra hours it made him blow his top.

"Who the hell is Frank McCarton?" he bellowed.

"That's Cookie, boss," Regan said.

"Oh, it's Cookie." Von Essen shrugged. "Okay, then."

Basically, McCarton's job was to answer inquiries from the press, but he quickly became the jack-of-all-trades for the chiefs in headquarters

Regan got Cookie on the phone. As it was his day off, McCarton showed up in Chief Feehan's office wearing a T-shirt and shorts. Regan handed him the keys to his brand-new company Crown Vic.

"We want you to go to Newport, Rhode Island," Chief Feehan told him. "And get there as fast as you can." The interdepartmental hearing was to start later that day.

Cookie did eighty all the way up Route 95. Regan called him every fifteen minutes to check his location. Each time he did, in the background, Cookie could hear Chief Feehan ask his ETA. Two and a half hours later, McCarton stopped at a Dunkin' Donuts outside Newport to use the bathroom. When Cookie got back to the car, he called Regan.

"Get back here as soon as you can," the deputy commissioner said.

"What?" Cookie asked, nonplussed. "What about the tape?"

"Never mind the tape," Regan ordered. "Just return to headquarters."

It had turned out, there was never a videotape. Someone had started the rumor, and like most rumors in the fire department, it had found its way to headquarters before the truth pulled on its boots.*

In the background, Cookie could hear Chief Feehan ask Regan to tell him his ETA.

---

* With apologies to Mark Twain, or Jonathan Swift, or whoever you believe came up with the quote.

———

Chief Feehan had no time for people who didn't share the same pride in the FDNY. Bill knew that for every hero firefighter, there was at least one hairbag looking to game the system. The holy grail of grifts was to get out on a three-quarter, tax-free medical pension and still be able to play golf. In his eyes, the greatest sin a firefighter could commit was to denigrate the name or take advantage of the fire department. He took disciplining transgressors himself. Each morning, he would go through the list of firefighters out sick, looking for goldbrickers using made-up excuses for their absence. One night, he and Betty had been out for dinner in a restaurant named Harbor Light in Rockaway. At a nearby table, a fireman, who had had more than his share to drink, was bragging about being out on sick leave while enjoying himself at the beach. The next day, Bill pulled the files on the company that the firefighter had mentioned he belonged to. He identified the loquacious fireman by his proby photo. Tapping the picture with his finger, Bill looked up at his executive assistant.

"I want this guy to report to my office first thing tomorrow morning."

Partly what fueled Bill's anger was a spate of criticism in the press about fraudulent disability claims by firefighters. An ex-fireman named Gary Muhrcke won a 102-story race up the Empire State Building staircase while collecting a disability pension from the fire department. The department's pension board opened a review. They would ultimately decide that though he was a world-class marathon runner, Muhrcke couldn't perform the physical duties required to do his job. "I proved that the ability to run is different than the ability to pull a 200-pound person out of a burning building," Muhrcke would later say.

The firefighter whom Bill overheard at the restaurant showed up at headquarters the next day without a clue as to why he'd been called there. Chief Feehan had left instructions to make him sit in the hall and wait. Lunchtime came and went, and still he sat there. At the end of the day, he was instructed to come back the next morning. When he asked Henry what he'd done, he received only a shrug in return. He went through the same ordeal the following day. Finally, Bill had him sent into his office at the end of the second day.

"My wife and I were at the Harbor Light for dinner the other night," the chief said.

The blood drained from the firefighter's face. When Bill recounted what he'd heard, the man hung his head, sure he was going to get fired.

But Bill saw something in the firefighter, perhaps his contriteness, that made him think he was worth another chance. He was returned to his company that day and almost immediately went on a fire call. On the way to the fire, his rig hit a pothole, which caused the fireman to hit his head on the truck's ceiling so hard the impact opened a gash that bled down his face. A fellow firefighter suggested he get some medical attention.

"Not a chance," he said. "I'm going to this fire."

———

Another time, the chief called a young firefighter to his office with every intention of firing him. The firefighter had been disciplined several times for his behavior outside of the department. Bill was behind the office's closed door with the young man for so long, Henry McDonald went in to see what was going on. He walked into the office to find both his boss and the firefighter in tears. The young man had told Bill about his difficult family situation and home life.

"He's a good kid," Chief Feehan would say later to Henry. "He's going to be a good fireman."

Though something of a pushover, especially with people with personal hardships, Chief Feehan knew when someone was trying to put one over on him. During the Bryant Park brawl hearing, the department brought in a firefighter named John Ceriello to testify. Though only peripherally involved in the fight, Ceriello ended up with blood on his shirt from a proby who was one of the main combatants. He had told the rookie to leave the scene posthaste. Chief Feehan attended the hearing. A department lawyer asked Ceriello to assess the firefighters' demeanor at the Bryant Park bar that night.

"They were wonderful," he said with a shrug. "Everybody was well behaved and having a wonderful time."

Chief Feehan met Ceriello in the hallway afterward.

"Wonderful?" Bill asked drolly. "Really?"

# FIFTEEN

# Father's Day

On October 9, 1997, the New York City Fire Department officially moved its headquarters into a brand-new building at 9 MetroTech Center in downtown Brooklyn. Part of the large-scale urban development that had begun to transform parts of the borough, the complex was designed to be Brooklyn's version of Silicon Valley. When the developer, Bruce Ratner of Forest City Ratner, promised the fire department he would finish the building in fourteen months, the staff chiefs at headquarters snickered. Well versed in New York City's bureaucratic red tape, they thought it was just another worthless promise. Fourteen months later, however, eight stories of brand-new brick and glimmering glass stood ready for them to move into. Not since the Romanesque Revival–style headquarters of the Brooklyn Fire Department graced Jay Street had they enjoyed such luxury. Howard Safir had more than his share of detractors in the FDNY. The feeling among the chiefs was that he would never possess the same love of the fire department that they did. But Safir was a transformative figure, and being the driving force behind MetroTech alone is enough to place him as one of the FDNY's most influential commissioners.

For some of the old guard, however, the new digs were going

to take a little getting used to. The move to MetroTech was literally a jump from analog to digital. Tom Fitzpatrick, who was Commissioner Safir's executive officer at the time, tells a story that best illustrates the dark ages from which the fire department was about to emerge. As the building started to near completion, the architects wanted an accounting of the existing computer network service the fire department had so they could configure it for the new building. Specifically, they asked for the appropriate IT people to advise them about the transfer of the computer terminals. They were under the impression that the old building had a few hundred "computers" that needed to be networked or reconfigured. Fitzpatrick told them he would be happy to assign someone, except for one small problem.

"What's that?" they asked.

"We don't have any networked computers," he said.

The terminals they believed were computers and part of a computer network were actually early-version word processors and weren't connected to the internet or any internal network, for that matter. The department didn't use email. They used fax machines to get information out to the battalion offices and firehouses. All they had was a handful of personal computers that were used exclusively by fire marshals for investigative purposes. Meanwhile, the NYPD had initiated "Comstat," an innovative, up-to-the-moment computerized crime data collection net that put it on the cutting edge of crimefighting while the fire department was still waiting for the fax to arrive.

The new headquarters would instantly make the FDNY one of the most modern fire departments in the world. They went from no network to eight hundred fully networked computers. Technicians installed a state-of-the-art telephone system with a dedicated "999" exchange, and an electronic communications and records management system. The building included a command center to monitor city-wide fire operations, and a modern health services facility and rehabilitation center. It had auditorium space, air-conditioning, working elevators, and vastly improved public access to fire prevention meeting rooms and permitting services. The department's library, which occupied a dark, damp storage room at the old building, was relocated to its own new building at Randalls Island.

For many staff chiefs and civilians alike, most of whom could clearly remember the prehistoric days of the rotary phone as the primary interdepartmental mode of communication, working the "information highway" at the new headquarters was a culture shock. Only the ones who had Windows 95 on computers at home had any idea of the size of the tech upgrade at headquarters. Leave it to Bill to bring the heady, ultramodern surroundings down to earth. At Metrotech's ribbon-cutting ceremony he noticed the Latin phrase *Requiescat in Pace* (Rest in Peace) above the fallen firefighters' names on the colossal bronze plaque in the lobby. Chief Feehan, the Latin scholar, elbowed the chief standing next to him.

"They conjugated the verb wrong," he said.

———

Brian Davan took the lieutenant's test in Murry Bergtraum High School in Manhattan. It was common practice for the city to use public high schools for testing sites. Brian studied hard for at least a year for the exam. He'd taken it once before as a young firefighter and hadn't prepared sufficiently for such a difficult exam. But now, with a growing family, he hit the books hard. He set two alarm clocks so he wouldn't oversleep. The doors to the school opened at eight in the morning, and if you were late for the test they would turn you away. The night before the exam, Brian drove to the school so he'd know the route the next morning. He checked out parking options. He wanted to leave nothing to chance. He arrived early the morning of the exam. He wasn't the only one. There were a couple hundred firefighters waiting outside the school, some of them still studying preparation books. Some drank containers of coffee and smoked cigarettes. Others were so nervous it looked to Brian like they might get sick. For some reason, there was a delay, and at twenty after eight the doors were still locked. As Brian waited in the anxious crowd, nearby an especially nervous firefighter turned to another. "When is this test going to start?" he asked plaintively.

"For you, it already has," his friend answered.

Brian's preparation paid off and he passed the test. Now all he had to do was wait to be appointed.

Meanwhile, Brian's career at the rank of firefighter went through a dramatic change. About the same time as he'd taken the lieutenant's test, he was transferred "across the floor" to the ladder company. In double firehouses like Watkins Street, it wasn't unusual for a firefighter to start in the engine company and then after a few years be assigned to the ladder truck under the same roof. Both of Brian's firefighter brothers had taken that journey. Though a common practice, it doesn't always happen that way. William Patrick Feehan and Bob Davan worked in an engine company most of their active careers.

For Brian, becoming a "truckie," as firefighters in the ladder company are known, opened a whole new world of fire service. A successful engine company relies on synchronized teamwork, with each firefighter dependent on the firefighter next to him to charge the line and get it to the seat of the fire. Truckies, on the other hand, are given separate tasks. Firefighters are dispatched inside the building, to the roof, or to the back of the structure. The OV (outside vent) firefighter reports conditions in the back of the building to the incident commander or chief out front. Based on those reports, the commander might change entire strategies to fight the fire. Brian had plenty of experience on the radio from his time in the police department. But all those years playing "Manhunt" growing up in Inwood had imbued him with a natural aptitude as an OV man. Fire escapes on the rear sides of H-types (buildings with front court-yards) and tenements are not easy to figure out. A non-city kid might find it challenging to know which fire escape to climb. Brian could tell in a glance, and he could also go up them like a gymnast and without incident. At least most of the time.

But more important, he also had the considerable collective experience owned by the guys in Ladder 120 from which to learn. One of those pros was a firefighter named Michael Cummings who became something of a mentor to Brian. Cummings had a heroic and colorful fire service history. One of his more courageous feats came on the morning of July 31, 2000. The fire occurred in an apartment on the thirteenth floor of the S.J. Tilden Houses, a hous-ing project just a few blocks from the firehouse. By the time Ladder 120 arrived, flames and heavy, dark smoke engulfed the dwelling, trapping people inside. Complicating matters further, a standpipe on the floor had been painted over so many times that the engine company had difficulty opening it. Without water, the fire burned unabated.

Along with his lieutenant, Dennis Gordon, Cummings crawled under the smoke and flames to a bedroom. There they found two adults and three young children huddled on a mattress under a win-dow gasping for air. The youngest, just three years old, was obvi-ously struggling to breathe. For the next seventeen minutes, the entire duration of the air supply in their Scotts Air-Paks, Gordon and Cummings administered oxygen to the adults and children while taking a gulp for themselves every now and then. Brian, and a few other firefighters, happened to be in the apartment directly above the fire and could hear over the radio the dire situation below. They began to initiate a rope rescue with a firefighter in a harness. Meanwhile, the engine company worked feverishly to get a charged hose line into the room. By the time the water began to flow and firefighters were able to beat back the flames to clear a path, Gordon's and Cummings's Scott Air-Paks were nearly emptied. Because of their heroism, all five of the civilians and both firefighters survived.

But perhaps the event that solidified Cummings's lore in the firehouse came a few years before, during a fire in the top floor of a three-story tenement building that was known for illegal drug use and squatters. One-twenty's rig was "tower ladder," that is, a telescoping seventy-five-foot ladder with a basket or bucket that carried firefighters. Cummings flew in the bucket up to the third floor, smashed the window with his tool, and climbed into the smoke-filled room. There he found a man that was mentally out of it, either from the fire smoke, crack-cocaine smoke, or both, and pulled him out to the safety of the bucket. Mike then tried to get the man to tell him if there was anyone else in the building. Realizing, however, that a crowd had gathered on the sidewalk, the man, who had gained some cognizance, decided to take advantage of his moment of neighborhood celebrity. He ignored Mike, and began play to the crowd below. Mike shook the man by the shirt and pulled him close. "Is there anyone else in there?" the firefighter screamed. The man blathered an incoherent response, then turned back to the crowd. Meanwhile, behind them, conditions in the apartment had severely deteriorated. Mike had to make the decision whether or not to reenter a life-threatening fire scene to search for possible victims.

Firefighters call this a "risk/reward" moment. Mike turned and climbed back through the window. As he did, a huge ball of fire blew right over his head. He dove back into the bucket and on top of the man he saved who was no longer playing to the crowd but in a fetal position as the flames roared above him.

———

That particular fire was also the scene of one of the most embarrassing moments in Brian's career, and not in the most flattering way. While Cummings was in the bucket in the front of the building, Firefighter Davan was the outside vent firefighter in the rear. Orange flames shot from the windows. The blaze had fully involved the top floor, and there was a significant chance it was trying to jump to the buildings next door. There is common space in row houses called a cockloft that runs between the ceiling of the top floor and the roof of the structure. Often in such fires, the cockloft becomes a conduit for the flames. Brian used his hook to free the drop ladder on the fire escape, and then, in full gear, including the bulky air pack, began to climb the back of the adjacent building. Zigzagging up a fire escape and squeezing through tight openings onto wrought-iron balconies is not an easy proposition. By the time Brian got to the top he was just about out of breath. The window wasn't locked, so he opened the bottom half of it from the outside. As he crawled through, however, the top sash of the window knocked off his helmet, which bounced on the balcony railing and fell to the ground below. A firefighter without a helmet, he liked to say, is practically useless.

But it wasn't only the danger of being helmetless that bothered him. Before the advent of radio communications at fires, a fireman in trouble would throw his helmet out the window of a fire as a mayday signal. Although the practice had been off the books for years, most firemen with any time, or who had fathers on the job, were keenly aware of it. Brian certainly was. Meanwhile, the fire had gone to three alarms, and because of all the air traffic, he couldn't get through on the radio to tell someone to disregard the wayward helmet and that he was okay. For a moment he thought about climbing down to retrieve it, but he could feel the radiant heat from the building next door and knew he had to do his job. He began using his hook to poke holes in the ceiling to check for fire in the cockloft. Then he heard the incident commander's voice comes over the radio, and felt his heart in his throat. "Mayday, Mayday. Four-four battalion Mayday, I have a one-twenty helmet in the rear yard!"

When a Mayday is issued, all other radio communication ceases. The sound of the silence of a hundred firefighters pulsed in Brian's brain. He opened a communication to the chief out front and told him the helmet was his.

"One-twenty OV, report to the incident commander immediately," the chief responded.

The incident commander that day was Chief Thomas Galvin. Three weeks earlier, Chief Galvin had been the commander at a fire on Atlantic Avenue in Brooklyn that killed two firefighters. Believing an elderly woman was trapped inside, a report that turned out to be erroneous, two fire companies climbed to the second story of a burning building. As they did, the stairway beneath them collapsed, dropping them into a first-floor inferno. A lieutenant named James Blackmore died at the scene. Captain Scott LaPiedra held on for four weeks in unfathomable pain at the Cornell Burn Center before he died. Twelve others firefighters were injured, including Timmy Stackpole, who'd been trapped under burning embers. Firefighters dug for thirty-five minutes before they found him. By then, however, his legs had suffered catastrophic burns. He was put on a respirator in his first week in the hospital, and would spend sixty-six days in the burn unit. Stackpole's recovery and eventual return to his firehouse was nothing short of miraculous. He had multiple operations and three long years of rehabilitation. Chief Feehan spent hours in the hospital with him, and when he returned to the front lines he did so against Bill's advice. Chief Feehan even suggested that he come to headquarters and work for him. But Timmy would have none of it. He returned to duty in March 2001.

Later, it was determined that a homeless squatter had set the Atlantic Avenue fire on purpose.

———

Chief Galvin waited at the command post with Brian's helmet in his hand. By then, radio communications had resumed. Around them were the sounds of a hundred firemen and dozens of rigs in full firefight posture. For Brian, however, it was as though he and the chief were the only people in the entire world.

He looked the chief right in the eye.

"No excuses," he said.

For his part, Chief Galvin, who would later become a four-star chief and an incident commander on 9/11, knew Brian was an active firefighter with good fire sense. He handed him his helmet without saying a word.

———

By the summer of 2001, Brian was still on the list for appointment to lieutenant. Because of the limited number of positions and slow turnover, such a wait was not unusual. But for Brian it seemed interminable. Not even having a first deputy commissioner as a father-in-law could hasten the process for him. One day, Bill asked Brian where he hoped be assigned once he was made lieutenant. Though he couldn't help improve his son-in-law's position on the appointment list, First Deputy Commissioner Feehan could certainly have some influence over where he would be sent. Brian had given the possibility plenty of thought. He knew he didn't want to be sent to a middle-class neighborhood in Queens like Hollis, Jamaica, or Springfield Gardens. Going from Brownsville to a single-family-dwelling neighborhood would be like going from a NASCAR race to a riding lawn mower. One day, when he mentioned to Tara that he wanted to go to Harlem, his wife played the devil's advocate.

"You sure?" she said. "It's a pretty long trip." In fact, it would double her husband's commute. But Brian was adamant.

"It's where your father was a captain, and where my father was lieutenant," he said. "That's where they met, and where I want to work."

Later, Bill would tell his son Billy that he was never prouder of Brian than when he heard where he wanted to be assigned.

————

By then, however, the writing was on the wall for Bill. The next mayoral election was only months away, and a new mayor undoubtedly would install a new commissioner and first dep. By then, Bill had outlasted nearly everyone with whom he'd come on the job. Even his coterie of disciples had begun to leave. Henry McDonald retired in 2001. Mike Regan left to take a job in City Hall. Even Cookie the Rookie had moved on to the city's Office of Emergency Management.

In an interview he gave in April 2001, Chief Feehan told of a conversation he'd had with one of his heroes on the job, a borough commander named Matty Farrell. He asked Chief Farrell how he would know when it was time for him to retire. Farrell told him he would wake up one morning and just know.

"It does not require an extraordinary intellect to understand that no matter who we are we are all bound by the same laws of nature," Bill once wrote. "Time, for all of us, marches forward. And nowhere does time pass more quickly than in this department. Nowhere.

"As a young firefighter, I smiled at the old-timers who spoke of how quickly their 20, 25, or 30 years had gone by, me wondering how such a long time could seem to anyone like 'only yesterday.'"

But Bill also knew that his future with the FDNY would stretch further than his own career. Son John had taken the lieutenant's test, and was waiting to be appointed. Brian Davan, too, had years and years of fire service ahead of him. Bill knew through his relationship with his dad that as long as John and Brian wore the uniform, part of his firefighter soul would stay very much alive. And it might even outlive son's and son-in-law's careers.

A couple of times a year, the chief would take his grandchildren to the Marine Unit on the Lower West Side of Manhattan. The department ran weekend harbor cruises for firefighters' widows and children, but there was often room on the boat for others. The day would start with donuts in the boathouse, and then Sunday Mass, celebrated by Mychal Judge. Out in the harbor, Connor Davan remembers standing on the stern watching the water churn into a wake. The pilot would also let him have a few moments on the wheel. The photo that sat on Chief Feehan's desk in MetroTech was taken on one of those trips. In the frame, a smiling Bill has an arm around Connor. In the background, rising above the churning harbor water, are the World Trade Center's twin towers. Bill, of course, had no way of knowing the darkness that would befall him and those looming towers. Nor would he know that his grandson would also take the Feehan family's well-worn path to the FDNY. And yet, perhaps as seen through the prism of what was to follow, the photo now seems to foretell Connor's future.

———

As usual, Bill planned to spend the summer of 2001 in the bungalow in Breezy Point. As many firefighters with houses on the peninsula did, he would commute to his job from there. Early in the morning, he'd stop at "the breakfast place," a diner in a small strip of stores that locals euphemistically refer to as "downtown Breezy." There, he might run into another chief or the son in a firefighter family that he knew and spend a few minutes catching up on the local doings. In June 2001, the summer stretched out in front of him like the blue expanse of the Atlantic Ocean. That idyllic view, however, would be fleeting. The months ahead would bring the most tragic events in the history of any fire department.

The first of those events happened on Father's Day. On Saturday, June 17, 2001, Tara and Brian were hosting a barbecue at their house in Belle Harbor. Liz was living in Park Slope, Brooklyn, at the time, and Bill drove the company Crown Vic to give her a lift to the party. On the way to Tara's, they stopped at Coney Island to pick up tickets for the Cyclones, a minor-league team that played in a small stadium right next to the amusement park. Bill took his grandchildren to see the Cyclones, which are part of the New York Mets organization—the kids grew up in Flushing rooting for the Mets. Bill was a lifelong Yankee fan. After they picked up the tickets, Bill asked Liz if she wanted to get a couple of hot dogs at the famous Nathan's on the Coney Island boardwalk.

"We're going to a barbecue!" Liz protested.

"How many chances do you have to get an original Coney Island Nathan's?" Bill answered with a shrug.

They were on the Cross Bay Bridge headed toward Tara's when the Mayday came over the fire department scanner Bill had in the car. The fire was in a warehouse-sized hardware store in Queens. It had already gone to multiple alarms. By the time they got to Tara's, firefighters were reported missing.

Chief Feehan dropped Liz off and raced toward Astoria. When he arrived, things were worse than he'd imagined.

———

For Harry Ford, Brian Fahey, and John Downing, it was a fire not unlike hundreds they'd fought before. All three were elite firefighters. In 1994, a photograph of Downing on the wing of an airliner that had aborted takeoff at LaGuardia Airport and slid into Flushing Bay ran on the front page of the *New York Daily News*. Both Fahey and Ford worked at Rescue 4, William Patrick Feehan's old squad. Ford played for the FDNY's football team and had calves the size of oak stumps. He once carried a baby from a building fire in a scene that looked as though it was shot on a movie studio's backlot. Fahey was so good at what he did, he taught his techniques at the fire academy.

The blaze had been started by two young teenagers who were spraying graffiti on the back of the General Supply Company hardware store on Astoria Boulevard. Inadvertently, the kids had knocked over a can of gasoline, which streamed into the store's basement and was ignited by a pilot light on a boiler. The first firefighters on scene saw that the flames in the basement were blue and green, an indication that some kind of accelerant was burning. Not a good sign. The incident commander was about to call for a second alarm when his world, literally, turned upside down.

A small explosion came first, but the one that followed was so powerful it propelled a fireman right through the front window, and blew the incident commander and the chief of special operations from the sidewalk into the street. According to witnesses who talked to newspaper reporters, every imaginable household item, from shower curtain rods to vacuum cleaners, rained from the sky. The building's side wall collapsed on Ford and Downing. The floor beneath Fahey had given way, sending him to the cellar and covering him in brick, wood, and other debris.

By the time Bill arrived, they'd found Harry Ford and John Downing under the bricks and had taken them to nearby Elmhurst Hospital. The rescue attempt for Fahey was ongoing. The last contact with him was a plea by a man running out of hope. "I'm trapped under the stairs," he'd said. "Please come get me."

At Tara's, Bob Davan had a fire department scanner on, and the family was gathered around it listening to reports. Then Brian's phone rang. As the expression on the young firefighter's face fell, the gathering became silent. Brian didn't have to say a word. In firefighter families like the Davans and Feehans, bad news is conveyed with a subtle shake of the head. Though only eight, even Connor realized that something was terribly wrong. Liz remembers holding the boy. As it happened, the news couldn't have been much worse. Ford and Downing had died of blunt force trauma from the collapse. It took firefighters four hours to reach Fahey. By the time they did, he had run out of air.

———

Hours after the fire was out, Bill, wearing a navy blue windbreaker with FIRE N.Y.C. emblazed across the back, walked into the remains

233

of the store. After a lifetime of fighting fire, he saw in the charred wood and smoldering rubble the events that had unfolded in the chaotic, horrible moments that stole three firefighters' lives. Afterward, he went back to headquarters. There, on a whiteboard, he re-created the scene and began to dissect the response to find where the system had failed the three dead and fifty injured firefighters. Chief Feehan had the ability to look back at even the most devastating fire with the cold, focused eye of a research scientist. He found plenty of blame to go around. Investigators discovered that the owner of the hardware store had kept an illegal quantity of flammable liquids in the basement. But Bill was as angry with fire officers as with the owner. A routine inspection might have saved the lives of Fahey, Downing, and Ford. After the Father's Day fire, building inspection safety systems and sharing information between city agencies became the chief's crusade. The move to MetroTech, and new computers, had markedly increased the department's ability to get building information to fire officers on the way to fires. But Bill wanted the fire department to be able to share with other city agencies. Eventually, the agencies did share data. The upgrades in the system, however, would not come until long after the attack on the World Trade Center.

Harry Ford left behind his wife, Denise, and three children. Brian Fahey's wife was Mary and they had three sons, including three-year-old twins. Anne Downing, John's wife, was from County Down, Ireland. They had two children; the younger was three at the time. The loss to the department was staggering. A few months after the Father's Day fire, the names of Harry Ford, Brian Fahey, and John Downing were added to the list of heroes on the bronze plaque in headquarters, which the chief passed every day.

In an interview, he once said, "No matter what we do, no matter how well we train, no matter how good our equipment is, no matter how hard we try, no matter what, the time will come when we will lose another firefighter."

It didn't take long for time to prove him right. On August 28, 2001, a twenty-seven-year-old proby firefighter named Michael Gorumba would die of a heart attack during a fire in an auto repair shop on Staten Island.

Firefighter Gorumba's would be the last line-of-duty death before 9/11.

# SIXTEEN

# The White Helmet

B ill was in Flushing that Tuesday morning and began his day at the crack of dawn at the North Shore Diner. He had eggs over easy with bacon and a cup of coffee for breakfast. He read the *Daily News* at the table. The night before in Denver, the Broncos handed the New York Giants a loss in the first Monday night game of the year. However, his beloved Yankees had pounded the Red Sox over the weekend. Led by the pitching of Orlando "El Duque" Hernandez, they'd leaped to a thirteen-game lead in the American League East. In the front of the paper, there were news stories about the election primaries that day. The paper had endorsed Mike Bloomberg for mayor on the Republican side, and Peter Vallone on the Democratic. Mike Regan had signed on with Vallone's campaign and was probably, Bill guessed, on his way to a polling place somewhere in Queens. The chief didn't linger over the political stories, however. The thought of the impending mayoral election made him uneasy. Although he'd escaped possible endings before, he would need one worthy of Houdini to extend his career under a new administration. Once he finished breakfast, he paid the check, left the *News* on the counter, and headed to work.

As usual, Chief was one of the first into headquarters that morning. Soon after he arrived, Deputy Commissioner Fitzpatrick and Tom McDonald, Henry's brother and the assistant commissioner of fleet and tech, had a regularly scheduled 6 a.m. Tuesday meeting. Under a new fleet modernization program, the department was adding an unprecedented number of new trucks, ambulances, and support vehicles. In one of his last initiatives, Chief Feehan fought hard to get specialty squads, a sort of all-purpose fire response team trained in hazardous material and chemical operations, into service. In addition, construction workers had begun laying the foundation for the $50 million expansion of the Randalls Island training facilities, and the department was in the process of upgrading facilities at Fort Totten in Queens, a U.S. Army post that dated back to the Civil War, for additional classroom space for recruits. Originally the department was going to move the entire fire academy to "the Fort" in Queens. Giuliani had released the money, and the deal was all but done. When architects first unveiled their plans to the FDNY, however, the drawings included a shaded round disc that sat in between buildings that housed high-end condos and the Long Island Sound. When Fitzpatrick saw the blueprint, he asked what the disc signified. Architects told him it was a soaring water tower for the facility. The deputy commissioner shook his head. Blocking upscale residents' view of a harbor in New York City would cause a blowback of epic proportions and a *New York Post* story in an instant. The chiefs went back to the mayor and persuaded him to repurpose the funds for a complete renovation to the Randalls Island facility instead, and upgrade Fort Totten for expanded EMS and firefighter classroom training.

But what Bill was looking forward to that day had nothing to do with upgrading facilities or adding trucks to the fleet. Henry was meeting him at headquarters and they were going out for lunch. Bill, sitting at his desk, was looking forward to hearing about his former chief executive officer's hunting trips and retirement. But then he heard Ray Goldbach calling his name from down the hall.

———

Goldbach's office abutted the commissioner's and faced the downtown Manhattan skyline, including the twin towers of the World Trade Center, a sight at which he often marveled. That morning, the azure sky was especially appealing. Just as he was turning away from the view, he saw something out of the corner of his eye, an explosion on a high floor of the WTC's north tower. In an instant, a plume of black smoke sprouted from the skyscraper. Goldbach ran into the hall and called for Chief Feehan. Fitzpatrick and McDonald joined them in Ray's office. Like countless others, Goldbach at first thought it was a small plane that hit the tower. Fitzpatrick knew right off that wasn't the case.

"Look at the size of the hole," he said. "It was commercial."

Specifically, it was a Boeing 767 traveling at 500 mph and carrying eighty-seven people and fifteen thousand gallons of high-octane jet fuel. The impact and explosion registered 0.9 on the Columbia University Lamont-Doherty seismograph twenty-two miles north of the city. According to one report, the windows in FDNY headquarters bowed when American Airlines Flight 11 smashed into the north tower. It would have taken the airborne shock waves less than ten seconds to reach the MetroTech complex.

Goldbach's phone rang while the group was still in his office. Dispatch had issued a 10-60, the battle alarm for major disasters.

———

For Battalion Chief Joseph Pfeifer, the day began, now famously, with the report of a possible gas leak fourteen blocks north of the World Trade Center. As it happened, a young French filmmaker named Jules Naudet was riding along with Chief Pfeifer. Along with his brother Gédéon, Jules was shooting a documentary about probationary firefighter Tony Benetatos of Engine 7, Ladder 1. The original idea of the film was to capture the day-in, day-out, sometimes mundane experience of a rookie firefighter during their nine-month probationary period. The filmmakers also hoped to document the life and hierarchy within a firehouse. That morning Gédéon had shadowed the proby while his brother accompanied the battalion chief on the run.

They were on the sidewalk at the corner of Church and Lispenard Streets, less than a mile north of the Trade Center, when American Airlines Flight 11 roared over their heads. Instinctively, Naudet swung his camera skyward and captured the moment the jet slammed into the building. Chief Pfeifer's eyes, too, had followed the roar of the engines. Pfeifer, Jules, and Pfeifer's aide that day, Firefighter Edward Fahey, jumped into their red Chevy Suburban and raced toward the Trade Center. On his way, he issued a second, then third alarm, and, a few minutes later, the 10-60, the major event notification. Pfeifer was the first member of the fire department to realize that the crash wasn't an accident. The documentary footage captures him moments after the impact. "It looks like the plane was aiming toward the building," he said on the radio to dispatch. He was also the first FDNY chief through the doors of the north tower lobby that morning. In his book *Ordinary Heroes: A Memoir of 9/11*, Pfeifer described the lobby looking as though it had been hit by a bomb. A fireball from the explosion ninety-three floors above had descended in the elevator shafts and had blown out the lobby's floor-to-ceiling glass windows. Two people lay on the floor severely burned from the explosion, their clothing still on fire. Others walked around dazed, bleeding and burned. Ceiling tile and chunks of the marble-paneled walls covered the floor. Meanwhile, Jules stayed at Pfeifer's side, and would remain there for most of the rest of that morning. The footage he shot would become part one of the most remarkable documentaries ever made. Firefighters from the two ladder trucks and two engine companies, the complement that had accompanied Pfeifer to the gas leak report, raced into the lobby of the World Trade Center's north tower. Some of them carried Halligan tools and axes, while others had folds of hose over their shoulders. The FDNY's response to the largest fire in the history of New York City had begun.

————

Chief Feehan's Crown Victoria raced over the Brooklyn Bridge, which the cops had already closed to non-essential traffic. When Bill first saw the wounded tower clearly, the site stunned him. Even with an encyclopedic fire service knowledge, it was hard for him to grasp the magnitude of the sight before him. The lessons from the 1 New York Plaza fire thirty-one years earlier and all he'd learned about high-rise fires seemed inadequate. Perhaps he even thought about the B-25 bomber that had crashed into the Empire State Building on the foggy morning in 1945. The pilot had yanked back the yoke when the famous building appeared from the low-hanging clouds. But his last-minute evasive maneuver came too late. This was a much different event. For one thing, the morning of September 11 was crystal clear in New York City, a visibility bounded only by the human eye's limitations. Pilots call conditions like this "severe clear." For another, there had to be thousands of people in the building.

Tom McDonald and Tom Fitzpatrick and the chief's driver, Pete Guidetti, were in the car with Feehan. As they sped down Broadway, Guidetti pulled in behind an NYPD Emergency Service truck and, like a NASCAR driver, drafted it all the way to the corner of Cortlandt Street, just a few blocks from the towers. On Broadway, the first wave of what would become a sea of civilians streamed from the wounded tower.

Guidetti parked the chief's car just a short distance from the Trade Center plaza and the huge bronze sculpture *The Sphere*. Bill was putting on his helmet when the deafening roar of Boeing 767 engines thundered above his head. As the jet exploded into the southeast-facing side of the south tower, Chief Feehan and the others dove for cover. Goldbach would later joke that McDonald tried to climb into a manhole. He had good reason. A wheel housing from the jet crashed to the street just yards away. Pieces of the fuselage and other aircraft parts fell from the sky. Then came body parts. A horror movie scene, one that was impossible to comprehend. Bits of the building, cement dust, and office paper continued to fall as they got up and ran toward 5 World Trade Center, a nine-story building that sat north and east of the north tower. To get to the command post in the north tower lobby, they needed to either go around the building or through it. As they began to head around the building, they heard the first body hit the pavement. Frank Gribbon would later say the noise the bodies made when they hit the ground sounded like shotgun blasts. He witnessed at least twenty of the two hundred who would make the inconceivable decision to jump. Daniel Suhr, the first firefighter killed that morning, was in the plaza just after

Bill and the others had passed by. A jumper fell right on top of him. Dr. Kelly, the department's chief medical officer, was nearby. She directed the firefighters to get him into an ambulance and to begin resuscitation. But his head wound was too severe to save him. Chiefs stationed a firefighter outside the lobby to warn those approaching to watch for people jumping to their deaths.

————

By the time Chief Feehan and the others entered the north tower, the lobby was filled with seventy-five to a hundred firefighters and fire officers. The accumulated fire service knowledge in the room was staggering and included Deputy Chief Peter Hayden, who had jurisdiction over the World Trade Center. Hayden had grown up in Rockaway and was from a firefighter family. He'd fought the "war years" in busy houses in Brooklyn, and had been a fire officer in lower Manhattan for years. He knew every inch of the World Trade Center. Fire Commissioner Von Essen was already there. He was in his car heading toward headquarters when he received word about the first jet hitting the north tower. Along with the brass, the fire companies had begun to arrive, one right after the other. Radios crackled with distress calls relayed from dispatch. Victims in the towers had suffered severe burns, others were trapped in elevators, and some needed wheelchairs. There was one woman who was blind and alone. As those calls came in, Hayden and Pfeifer sent firefighters up the stairs on rescue missions. One of the first to go up the stairs was a lieutenant from Engine 33 named Kevin Pfeifer, Chief Pfeifer's brother. The brothers had a brief conversation before Kevin disappeared into the stairwell. It would be the last time they would see each other.

———

The initial command post in the lobby of the north tower below the plaza on West Street was a predesignated location for FDNY and the Port Authority to coordinate their emergency operations at the Trade Center. Escalators connected the lobby on West Street to a mezzanine floor. As the firefighters went up, a steady exodus of people rode the escalators down to the entrance hall. At first, they did so in an orderly fashion. But as the minutes ticked by and the level of emergency response in the lobby increased, the evacuees' distress heightened. People were crying; a few came over to Bill to ask what they should do. In the uncertainty, his white helmet and sagacious appearance was a beacon of hope. Still, each time a jumper would crash through the glass canopy and hit the pavement outside, his reflex was to flinch. Though a natural reaction under the circumstance, some in the lobby, like Goldbach and Von Essen, were worried about Bill.

———

Twenty years later, the former commissioner tells the story of how he asked Chief Feehan to leave the north tower lobby that morning and report to the Office of Emergency Management in 7 World Trade Center. There, the commissioner reasoned, he could help on a macro level, dealing with the city-wide and interdepartmental issues. But the real reason he wanted him to go was to get him out of the lobby and keep him safe. "This is no place for a seventy-one-year-old," he'd confided to a nearby chief. Asking Chief Feehan to leave the incident command post, however, was like asking a general to leave his troops on the battlefield. To add insult to injury, Von

Essen told him to give his helmet to Tom Fitzpatrick. Rushing to get into Chief Feehan's car at headquarters, Fitzpatrick didn't have time to get his helmet out of his own car. In thinking of that moment twenty years later, Von Essen shakes his head. The last image he has of Bill Feehan is the "You gotta be fucking joking" expression on the chief's face. Bill wasn't going anywhere, and he'd sooner have given Fitzpatrick his pants than his helmet.

———

By 9:30 a.m. there was no indication of a collapse. The lobby was crowded but not chaotic. It was overcrowded and chaotic. Chiefs continued sending fire companies into the tower's staircases while the companies in front of them climbed higher. The staircases were wide enough for only two people abreast. Firefighters, carrying sixty pounds of gear and equipment, rose single file as civilians evacuated single file down past them. Simultaneous communications between the command post in the lobby, and between the north and south towers, were spotty at best. During the 1993 response to the terrorist bombing at the World Trade Center, fire department radios had performed horribly. In the aftermath of the event, the city installed a repeater in 5 World Trade Center. The repeater channels were supposed to boost radio signals within the towers, but they proved nearly useless when they were needed most.

———

Father Mychal Judge had begun the day of September 11 leading morning prayer at his home, St. Francis of Assisi Church and Friary on West 31st Street. After prayers, he went to his room to take a rest on his pull-out sofa. It was then that a fellow friar named Brian Carroll rushed in the door. "Mychal, get up," Carroll said. "A jet just hit the World Trade Center." Directly across the street from the priory sits the Engine 1, Ladder 24 firehouse. He ran there and met Captain Danny Brethel and Firefighter Michael Weinberg, both of whom were off duty. Together the three sped down Seventh Avenue. Below 14th Street the sound of sirens was deafening. It seemed every emergency vehicle and worker in the city was converging on the towers, including just about every off-duty firefighter. Just the day before the attack, Father Judge had offered the benediction at a ceremony commemorating renovations to the firehouse in the South Bronx that quartered Ladder 42, Commissioner Von Essen's old firehouse.

"You have no idea when you get on that rig," Father Judge had said. "No matter how big the call. No matter how small. You have no idea what God is calling you to do. But he needs you. He needs me. He needs all of us," he'd said.

Over the years, at hundreds of fires, he'd been a ballast of faith even in the most dangerous of situations. In the lobby that morning, however, Father Judge, in his chief's white helmet and turnout coat with FDNY CHAPLAIN M. JUDGE stenciled across the back, could offer them no solace. His face seemed frozen in horror. People who saw him said he watched the jumpers with a stunned disbelief. Some said his lips moved in prayer. At one point, he left the lobby for a short period to administer the sacrament of Last Rites to Firefighter Suhr. When he returned, his prayers went from silent to a loud plea. "Jesus, please end this now!" he cried out. "God, please end this."

———

For many, the idea of a collapse was inconceivable. "We were taught from our earliest exposure to the Trade Center that they could withstand a plane," Mike Regan remembered from his time at working for Port Authority. Much later an architect for Leslie Robertson, the firm that designed the towers, was even more forceful in his defense of the building's integrity.

"We don't build anything to fall down," he told a battalion chief.

Perhaps the first in the fire department to articulate the unthinkable was a battalion chief named Ray Downey, the head of Rescue Operations and the commanding officer of the Special Operations Command. Downey had led FDNY's response to the 1993 terrorist bombing of the World Trade Center in 1993. He'd also headed the rescue teams for the Federal Emergency Management Agency and oversaw search-and-rescue operations in the devastating aftermaths of Hurricanes Hugo and Andrew, and the Oklahoma City bombing. He'd been to more building collapses than he could count. The firefighters who worked in SOC called him the "master of disaster," or just "God."

"These buildings can come down," he said matter-of-factly to Von Essen. But not even Downey believed the collapses would occur as quickly as they did.

———

Moments after Downey's warning, Deputy Chief Joseph Callan felt the north tower move. At 9:32, he ordered firefighters back down to the lobby, according to a department interview he later gave. For the most part, his command went unheard or unheeded. Because of the damaged and faulty building communication system, chiefs in the lobby had little or no situational awareness about what was happening ninety-nine floors above them, or around them for that matter. The only communication systems within the building that withstood the exploding jet fuel were intercoms to a few elevators. What made matters infinitely worse was the lack of communications between other city agencies, like the police department. An engineer in the Office of Emergency Management in World Trade Center 7 warned that the towers were "near imminent collapse." But officials couldn't reach the chiefs in the command post by radio. Instead, they sent a messenger on foot from the office to Ganci with the information. By the time he got there, the south tower had already started to implode.

———

By the time Callan ordered the evacuation, Tom McDonald, Tom Fitzpatrick, and Chief Feehan had left the lobby to look for a suitable location to move the lobby command post. The World Financial Center is a cluster of office, hotel, and retail space across West Street toward the Hudson River. Two pedestrian bridges over West Street connected the World Trade and World Financial Centers. Along with McDonald and Fitzpatrick, Lynn Tierney joined the group, and together they crossed the north bridge and came upon the Winter Garden, a 150-foot glass atrium filled with soaring palm trees and other vegetation. The space that day had been set for some type of event. Large round tables filled the tiled floor. Fitzpatrick thought it was adequate for command post support. A security guard told him he could get a communication system set up in the room. Tierney, however, thought the glass enclosure was dangerous.

After about ten minutes in the atrium, they headed to a secondary command post that had already been set up on West Street in a loading dock to the Merrill Lynch building. Establishing the primary command post in the north tower's lobby might have been protocol, but it proved far from ideal for this scale of operations. From the West Street command post, however, chiefs could see the entire World Trade Center for the first time that morning. Both towers' top floors were fully engulfed in flame, with plumes of dark smoke billowing from the open wounds in the buildings. They could see the people jumping from the floors above the fire.

In the loading dock driveway, the command personnel had set up magnetic command boards, which kept track of unit locations as best they could. They used multiple handy-talkie channels for communication with the units, again, as best they could. In normal times, West Street, a thoroughfare that fed the West Side Highway, would be bumper-to-bumper with traffic. But this day it was crammed with fire department apparatus and emergency vehicles from all parts of the city. Chief Feehan realized that ambulances wouldn't be able to access the World Trade Center, or at least would have to navigate the fire department's rigs to do so. He gave an order to have the trucks moved to the side of the road. He wanted to clear a path so ambulances would have access in and out of the area.

Then, at one minute to ten, something caught Bill's eye on the south tower, a glitter-like effect that seemed to ring the upper floors. "Fitz, what's that?" he asked Tom Fitzpatrick.

———

John Ceriello, the same firefighter who had testified at the department hearing where he called the mood at the bar fight behind the public library "wonderful," had begun that day in his home in Brooklyn. When he learned of the attack, he rode his mountain bike across the Brooklyn Bridge. He was on the bridge when United Airlines Flight 175 flew into the south tower. He didn't see the jet crash into the building, but he felt the air pressure from the blast. On the Manhattan side of the bridge, he headed toward Ladder 20 on Lafayette Street. He worked in Squad 18 in Greenwich Village, but repairs were being done on his firehouse, so the squad was temporarily quartered in SoHo with the ladder company. Along with a firefighter named Howie Scott, Ceriello jumped in a car with some fire marshals. Lights flashing and sirens blaring, they raced to a staging area on West Street. There, Chief Downey directed him to join a makeshift Special Operations Command company that was a combination of Rescue 4 and Squad 288. Lieutenant Ronald Kerwin from the 288 squad wrote Scott's and Ceriello's names on the Battalion Form 4, a roster of firefighters in the company. Neither Scott nor Ceriello had air masks or cylinders. Kerwin told them to find some and get back as quickly as they could. "If we're not here," the lieutenant said, "we're in the building."

Although there were dozens of rigs on West Street, firefighters had stripped them clean of the self-contained breathing apparatus. After searching several rigs without success, Ceriello saw a hazmat truck parked near Vesey Street. He and Scott jogged to the truck. While they did, Ceriello looked back and saw the men of Rescue 4 and Squad 288 walking in single file across one of the West Street bridges toward the south tower. A resource man on the hazmat truck, a firefighter named Tony Casagna, pulled out two half-hour air cylinders for them from a hidden compartment. But just as Ceriello and Scott were strapping them on, Casagna told them he had one-hour cylinders too. The decision to change out the cylinders couldn't have taken more than two minutes. By then, Ceriello had lost sight of the company. They had already entered the Marriott hotel on the way to the south tower. With Scott, he ran down West Street to catch up with them. As they reached the north walkway, however, a thunderous rumble from above stopped them in their tracks.

———

According to recorded radio communications, at about the same time, Battalion Chief Orio Palmer and Fire Marshal Ronald Bucca were directing civilians down from the seventy-eighth floor of the south tower. Palmer and Bucca, followed by several members of Ladder 15, were the only firefighters to make it all the way up to the point of impact. Palmer had taken the one working elevator in the south tower to the fortieth floor and then, carrying full gear, climbed the stairs the rest of the way. The battalion chief had run New York City marathons. He'd won the department's fitness medal, an award that later would be named after him, so he was better suited than most for the climb. Palmer also had an associate's degree in electrical technology, and wrote articles about radio equipment for a fire department newsletter. Some of the communications failures inside the towers came simply because firefighters didn't know how to properly use the equipment. Palmer knew his radio down to its circuits, and was in communication with command in the lobby the whole time he was in the building. On the seventy-fourth floor, the stairwell was so damaged he had to look for another way up. He climbed the last four floors in the tower's south stairwell.

In the 2009 documentary *9/11: Phone Calls from the Towers*, Jim Dwyer called the seventy-eighth floor in the south tower "the bridge point between the living and the dead." It was a transfer floor for the elevator banks to the lobby. After the hijacked airliner hit the north tower, people who worked in the upper floors of the south tower had massed on the seventy-eighth floor hoping to evacuate. When United 175 crashed into the south tower, the tip of a wing of the jet sliced though the seventy-eighth floor like a scythe, killing and injuring scores of people. According the recording, Chief Palmer had radioed that he encountered a number of 10-45 Code Ones, the department radio designation for civilian fatalities. He also reported two "pockets of fires" on the floor and asked for engine companies to put them out. The last communication from Palmer came at approximately 9:52 a.m. Seven minutes later the building began to collapse into itself. Later, Orio's wife, Debbie, would be one of the first to hear her husband's calls after the fire department released the tapes to the public. She wasn't surprised her husband had climbed to the point of impact. "He left a story behind," she said. "My kids will have it and their kids will have it." Chief Palmer's teenaged daughter Dana, the oldest of his three children, would write this letter to her dead father:

Dear Dad,

A friend gave me the idea of writing to you. She said it might help. Oh, how I wish you could write back, or I could hear your voice again, or see you—even if it's just a quick glimpse. I hate knowing that you're really not coming home this time, and all I remember about when I saw you last was that I was doing my homework when I got up and kissed you goodbye. I didn't know it would be forever, though.

When I was listening to all your favorite music the other day, I thought I would feel sad and I'd miss you. But instead, I felt closer to you, and it was quite comforting because there's not one time that I can remember when you didn't have the radio on. You were the music man.

Always know that you're my hero. I could never compare any man to you because that would be unfair to him. For, like Keith said, you're one of a kind—the very best there is out there.

My birthday is coming up, but I'm sure you already knew that. It won't be the same without you, and I'm not really looking forward to it. I feel that way about a lot of things, though. I would do anything to have you back.

Love always,

Dana

Chief Feehan and Tom Fitzpatrick stood at the top of the driveway to the loading dock and looked almost straight up at the south tower. Later, Fitzpatrick would realize the "glitter" they saw was in fact the tall tempered glass windows in the tower being pulverized and expelled outward as the outer support columns buckled inward. At least from a distance, the building came down in an orderly fashion—think of one of those orchestrated construction demolitions you see on TV. However, this one featured a dense, dark cloud that reminded Fitzpatrick of the seventh plague depiction in the movie *The Ten Commandments*.

Though the tower came down at a rate of 120 mph, it seemed to some eyewitnesses as if it were happening in slow motion. As the cloud descended to ground level, it grew bigger and began to spread outward in all directions. The fifty people or so in the secondary command post across West Street ran toward the loading dock. The wall of choking, debris-laden smoke hit the command post with the force of a Cat 4 hurricane wind. It knocked some people off their feet. To Tom Fitzpatrick, it felt like someone had put a pair of hands on his back and shoved him forward. He was able to make it to the bottom of the driveway and then, with others, blindly into the building's bowels.

The collapse caused chunks of cement and steel to fire like cannonballs through the wall of cement dust. The lobby of the north tower shook violently. Those still inside scattered for their lives. In his book *The Book of Mychal: The Surprising Life and Heroic Death of Father*

*Mychal Judge*, the journalist Michael Daly recounts the last moments of the fire department chaplain's life. Perhaps the last person to see Father Judge alive was the department's photographer, Lieutenant Richard Smiouskas. As the priest headed out of the lobby to what Daly describes as a "field of burned and splattered bodies," Smiouskas yelled after him, "Don't go out!" Though he had already made it through the door to the plaza, he quickly turned and headed back into the lobby. Through the wall of dust, Father Judge made it to the interior escalators. It was then that he stood and called upon Jesus to end the horror. It was then he was consumed by the stone and dust of the south tower.

———

For John Ceriello, it was as if night fell in an instant, a pitch-black void that enveloped him. He didn't have his mask on and couldn't breathe. One of the first things a proby learns is to hold your breath if the smoke overwhelms you. He did long enough to shake out his facepiece and press it to his mouth. The air he gulped was filled with the cloud material. As a nozzleman would under smoke, he crawled under the dust until it settled enough for him to see. Chiefs Feehan and Downey were the first images that came into view. They stood some twenty-five yards south of the loading dock, and looked to him like statues, covered from head to toe with pulverized cement. Downey didn't have his helmet, and the dust on his uniform matched his grey hair and mustache.

———

Like the others, Bill had found shelter from the wall of debris and dust hurtling toward him deep into the loading dock. But unlike Fitzpatrick, whose pathway took him into the building, Chief

Feehan, along with Chief of Department Pete Ganci, followed the retaining wall on the south side of the loading dock and made their way toward the dull light coming from the street. Bill was limping. Chief Ganci's aide, Steven Mosiello, took hold of his elbow to help him, but Bill pulled his arm away. "I don't need your help, Steve," he said. "Thank you."

When the oatmeal-thick cloud began to settle, some of the handy-talkies blared to life. Fire officers with bullhorns, loudspeakers on rigs, implored people to run north on West Street. The Marriott hotel that fronted the south tower had partially collapsed, trapping firefighters. Downey and Feehan began to direct rescues in the hotel. Ganci's radio had been damaged. He told Mosiello to find a couple of rescue trucks to help with the search. Downey directed John Ceriello to head north to Chambers Street where they were going to re-form the command post. "From there we'll have at it," Ceriello remembers him saying. But just then, Chief Feehan lowered his handheld radio.

"There's a fireman at Liberty and West," he said to Ceriello. "Go get him." Ceriello turned and headed south, a change in direction that would save his life.

In the sky above Ganci and Feehan, three NYPD helicopters circled the remaining tower of the World Trade Center. From their vantage they could see that the center of the north tower was glowing red. "I don't think this has too much longer to go," the aviation cop radioed. "I would evacuate all people within the area of that second building." The warning, however, was transmitted to the police command post at the corner of Vesey and Church and was never relayed to the fire department.

As Jim Dwyer and Kevin Flynn reported so forcefully in their book *102 Minutes*, as the building's supports began to fail, firefighters went about their trained duty and followed their instincts to help. They kept moving up, kept carrying rollups of hose, kept checking floors, disregarding warnings from cops and even some of their own to retreat. One of these firefighters was William Francis "Billy" Burke, the captain of Engine 21. Captain Burke and his men had climbed to the twenty-seventh floor of the north tower. There they came upon several civilians, including Ed Beyea and Abe Zelmanowitz. Beyea was a quadriplegic, and a big man, weighing about three hundred pounds. Abe was his best friend. They both worked for Blue Cross Blue Shield insurance. Getting Beyea down the stairs presented a monumental challenge for the captain. Captain Burke also realized that they had perhaps limited time to do so. He was one of the few in the north tower who'd witnessed the south tower's collapse. He'd watched the building implode from a twenty-seventh-floor window. When the Mayday came over his radio for his company to evacuate, he undoubtedly sensed that the north tower was about to fall also. Still, he had a job to do. Burke's father was a retired deputy chief in the department. He'd always told his son that the first order of business for a firefighter was to save the civilians. When he received the Mayday to evacuate the tower, Captain Burke sent his men down the stairs. He stayed with Ed and Abe.

At forty-six and single, Burke still had movie-star good looks. He worked a second job as a lifeguard at Robert Moses State Park on Long Island. He liked to write and was a talented amateur photographer. Like Bill Feehan, he was also a Civil War history buff and often visited battlefields such as Gettysburg. The story goes that on one first date, he took a girlfriend to Grant's Tomb, on Manhattan's West Side.

Perhaps Captain Burke thought he could find a working elevator. But he had to have known that jet fuel from the airliner had turned most of the elevator banks into Roman candles. More likely, he stayed with the civilians because he believed in his father's words. He stayed because it was his duty. He wasn't going to leave the civilians behind. Investigators identified Abe's and Ed's remains in August 2002. Captain Burke's were never found.

———

John Ceriello climbed through the Marriott's rubble, looking for the firefighter Chief Feehan had directed him to find. Buried beneath the pile of cement and steel lay the bodies of six members of Rescue 4 and eight from Squad 288, including Lieutenant Kerwin. Had he not waited to change to the one-hour air cylinder, Ceriello would have been with them. As he searched, he saw firefighters nearby walking around in a daze—the realization that they had just lived through the collapse of a 110-story building had not yet formed in their minds. And then, like the worst possible recurring nightmare, the horror began again.

Ceriello didn't need to look at the building to know what was happening. The successive booms sounding like the footsteps of a massive giant was all the information he needed. He saw an ambulance parked with its doors open and dove into the back of it. A wall of cement dust and debris slammed the doors shut behind him. He prayed as the earth shook beneath him. Behind the dust came something even more lethal.

Like the south tower did, as the north collapsed it spewed chunks of cement and steel outward. Imagine slamming a ripe tomato with an open palm, and you have some idea of the dynamics. The distance from the west side of West Street to where the tower stood is at least a couple of football fields. Yet the entire area around the command post filled with splintered steel girders and huge jagged shards of cement from the building's facade. Most of the rigs parked near or on West Street were completely destroyed. The front of the Merrill Lynch building was shorn off. Scores of car gas tanks exploded, setting the vehicles afire like funeral pyres. Frank Gribbon remembers seeing at least forty of them in a nearby parking lot. When the destruction was complete, noxious smoke from the fires and cement particles from the tower filled the air.

Though Gribbon headed the fire department's public information office then, he'd had a long career as an active firefighter in the Bronx, holding the rank of lieutenant when he moved to headquarters. On 9/11, those active instincts kicked in. There was no water pressure in the fire hydrants since the integrity of the connecting infrastructure had been severely damaged or destroyed when the buildings came down. But fireboats had reached the North Cove in the Hudson behind what was left of the Winter Garden. One was the *John J. Harvey*, first launched in 1931 and reactivated during the attack. Along with two other fireboats, the *Harvey* pumped water to the World Trade Center site for eighty straight hours. Gribbon commandeered an ambulance and used it to run a five-and-a-half-inch hose line from the boat to the parking lot to extinguish the scattered fires. Around him, dust-covered firefighters began to form rescue teams. Some of them tried to climb over the mountains of debris where the command post once operated. Others went into the Merrill Lynch building and came out through the loading dock.

––––––––

It took some time for the first search teams to climb the remains of the north tower piled on West Street. When they finally reached where the command center had been, a firefighter saw something glimmering in the six-inch-deep layer of dust. It was a white helmet with a gold-colored front piece emblazoned with 1ST DEPUTY COMMISSIONER.

Within his knowledge of military history, Chief Feehan had a special fondness for George S. Patton's poetry. In *Through a Glass, Darkly*, the general wrote:

> *So forever in the future,*
> *Shall I battle as of yore,*
> *Dying to be born a fighter,*
> *But to die again, once more.*

The end of a towering fire service career came to rest in the jagged remnants of the towering building, but the kind of heroism owned by Chief Feehan, and all firefighters who sacrifice their lives on the fire field, cannot die. It must live on, from generation to generation, in those brave enough to answer the siren's call.

# SEVENTEEN

# The Aftermath

Henry climbed in the back of the fire department ambulance that held the body bags containing Pete Ganci and Bill Feehan. In looking back, Henry can't tell you if the ride took five minutes or five hours. To him, it felt like a lifetime. He's shared a friendship with Chief Feehan that was as close as either of them had in the fire department.

In the confusion that ensued after the north tower fell, it's difficult to recount the exact details of Chief Feehan's death. Frank Gribbon, who'd been near the command post, remembers Bill directing the rescue operations for firefighters trapped in the Marriott hotel. "He was a chief first that day," Gribbon said. "And he was committed to doing everything he could, including laying his life on the line to help rescue and save members of the department."

Some of those firefighters were saved. Some were not. One of the last people to see Chief Feehan alive was one of the ones saved from the collapse of the hotel. At the time, John Citarella was a lieutenant from hazmat operations at the fire academy. According to an interview he gave to the department after the attack, he'd been in the Marriott on his way to the south tower when it came down on him and the other firefighters. The south tower's collapse had split the twenty-two-story hotel in two. Buried under a pile of cement and iron, he was encased by the debris for twenty minutes before firefighters even knew he was there and alive. With the help of his rescuers, Citarella limped out onto West Street. There he saw Chief Downey and a battalion chief named Lawrence Stack helping an injured civilian. By then, the perimeter columns that supported the north tower had begun to fail. Downey ordered Citarella north toward Chiefs Feehan and Ganci, who were several yards away on the street just south of the command center. As he approached the chiefs, Citarella remembers Ganci asking him for his handy-talkie, but the radio had been damaged when the hotel came down on him. He also remembers Bill wearing an expression of disbelief that a firefighter had survived the damage to the Marriott.

Ganci directed Citarella to keep moving north. For Ganci, Downey, and Chief Feehan, and every other fire officer in the area, the priority then was to evacuate civilians and firefighters from the carnage of the south tower collapse. And none of them would leave until they got everybody they could to safety.

When Lieutenant Citarella reached the north footbridge over West Street the world began to violently shake again. Downey and Stack reportedly ran into what was left of the Marriott for cover when the north tower started to come down. Chief Ganci and Feehan had also run toward the Marriott when parts of the building began raining from above. It wouldn't have mattered had they reached what was left of the hotel, which they didn't. Stack and Downey did make it but were killed by the avalanche of steel and cement. Ganci and Feehan had no chance to escape. It would take firefighters nearly three hours to find their bodies.

———

In the months after the terrorist attack on the World Trade Center, the dark shadow of 9/11 hung over the fire department and its members. Each day brought more sorrow and pain. Nine days after the attack, Captain Timmy Stackpole's body was unearthed not too far from where they found Chief Feehan's and Ganci's. Stackpole was a devoted husband and a father of five children. His fellow firefighters called him "the bishop" because of his devout faith. Father Judge had ridden with him in the back of the ambulance after the Atlantic Avenue fire where he was so severely burned. As the priest began to pray over the firefighter writhing in pain, Stackpole asked him to stop. "I have to pray in my own way," the hero firefighter said to the department chaplain. He then began to pray aloud, asking God to help the others. The morning of September 11 he was supposed to teach Confirmation classes at his parish church, Good Shepherd in Brooklyn.

Tragedies similar to Stackpole's were duplicated scores of times during the recovery effort at the World Trade Center site. Along with Stackpole, some sixty other off-duty firefighters died that day after responding to the full recall the department had issued. Hundreds of firefighter families were left without a body to bury.

The recovery effort at the World Trade Center site officially ended on May 30, 2002. At 10:28 a.m., the time of the north tower's collapse, the uniformed members of the department carried an empty stretcher draped with an American flag from the pit. A drummer from the FDNY's bagpipe band provided a mournful cadence to the solemn ceremony. Over the department radio, a bell sounded four sets of five tolls, the signal issued when a firefighter dies in the line of duty. In *Strong of Heart*, Von Essen writes about the feelings he experienced that day. "The emptiness in my heart will never be filled," he wrote.

From September 12, 2001, to January 1, 2002, when the Bloomberg administration installed Nicholas Scoppetta as fire commissioner, Von Essen oversaw the herculean effort to begin to rebuild. According to the *New York Times*, 4,400 collective years of firefighting experience died when the twin towers came down. In the wake of September 11, the retirement rate in the FDNY skyrocketed. Some retired because their spouses and families, fearing for their safety, pressured them to. And still others, who perhaps would have stayed long after the twenty-year retirement eligibility, were so emotionally scarred that it was just impossible to go back to work. Meanwhile, the number of applicants taking the entrance exam plummeted for many of the same reasons.

The department held a promotion ceremony on the Sunday following the attack in the plaza in front of MetroTech headquarters. The fire commissioner promoted seventy firefighters to lieutenant and ninety-eight officers to higher ranks. Daniel A. Nigro, who'd been chief of operations, became chief of the department. Mayor Giuliani and Von Essen appointed Michael Regan to Chief Feehan's post of first deputy commissioner. Regan will tell you those shoes were impossible to fill. Ray Goldbach said the department lost Bill Feehan "just when we needed him most."

———

Connor was only eight years old when his grandfather died in the attack on the World Trade Center. At the wake, a grizzled old fire eater approached him.

"I worked with Chief Feehan in fifty-nine engine," the old-timer said. "Do you know where that is?"

Connor nodded resolutely.

"Five floors up, and five rooms in," he said, quoting the company's creed.

Connor knew the difference between a ladder and an engine company about the same time he learned the frog's name on *Sesame Street*. He grew up in Belle Harbor, a beach community on the Rockaway peninsula. Cops and firemen have called Belle Harbor home or a summer residence since before the invention of the flip-flop. His maternal great-grandfather, both grandfathers, his father, three uncles, and a handful of his cousins have all worn the New York City Fire Department's shoulder patch. The firefighters in Connor's family tree could fill a firehouse.

He attended St. Francis de Sales Academy, a Catholic grammar school just down the block from the Davans' house in Belle Harbor. St. Francis de Sales Church held six funerals for firefighters killed on 9/11. As if that wasn't enough grief to witness, two months later the gymnasium in his school was used as a makeshift morgue and held scores of bodies from one of the worst air disasters in U.S. history.

It was Veterans Day, November 12, 2001, just two months and a day after the terrorist attack on the World Trade Center, and Rockaway was still an open wound. Not only had the community lost many firefighters and police officers who had called the community home, but it had also lost a large number of Wall Street traders, most of whom worked for Cantor Fitzgerald. Breezy Point alone lost thirty-two people on 9/11. Tara was home alone that Veterans Day. Brian was working and the Davan children were staying with Brian's sister. Brian and Tara were having an extension built on the house and there were workers on the roof. Tara heard the sound of the jet engines overhead. At first she thought it was the Concorde. The supersonic jet flew over the house in Belle Harbor on landing and takeoffs from JFK across Jamaica Bay. But then she heard the men on the roof yelling about a plane coming down. The tailfin of an American Airlines Airbus had broken off and landed in the bay. Both engines detached from the wings in midair. One of the engines crashed into a gas station called Bullock's two blocks away. The other sailed directly over the Davan house, so close that the workers jumped off the roof, one breaking his ankle from the fall. The engine slammed into the ground just across the street and set a garage on fire. The jet itself crashed four blocks away, killing five people on the ground and all 260 souls on board. Tara called Brian at work. He remembers her at first being calm. "I think a plane just crashed across the street," she said. But then Tara's voice started to shake. "I'm on the front porch and all I can see is smoke and flames," she said. Someone in Brian's firehouse changed the fire dispatch channel to the Queens scanner, which announced a fire involving multiple houses in the Davans' neighborhood. Brian jumped in his car. As he did, a firefighter ran out with his turnout gear and helmet. He then raced home. Two months earlier, he had headed to Manhattan on the same route he was now traveling in the opposite direction. Near a section of Queens called Howard Beach he could see the column of smoke from the World Trade Center; now he could see a column of smoke coming from his neighborhood.

Most of the passengers on the plane were Dominican. The crash devastated the Dominican community in New York City, and families in the Dominican Republic. For Belle Harbor, numb from 9/11, it was as though a cruel biblical god had it in for them. There had been just too many funerals, too many memorials, and the wail of too many bagpipes. There had been too much personal torment, too much drinking to cope. Over the next three years, the department's employee assistance program saw a 50 percent increase in substance abuse problems. Behind the walls of the neatly kept homes in Belle Harbor and other firefighter communities, families tried to process emotions that could not be processed. In a way, Brian and Tara were lucky. They had small children at the time, and making sure the kids were okay crowded out the emotional pain. At least for the most part.

By the time Brian got to his house, an engine company had the fire in the garage across the street under control. He went inside to check on Tara, then pulled on his gear and helmet and headed to the primary crash site four blocks away. When Brian had walked on "the surface of the moon," as he called Ground Zero, he didn't see any bodies. He heard the PASS alarms, and knew what was buried under the rubble of the towers, but he saw victims. Now charred bodies and wreckage lay strewn all over his neighborhood. People on the block brought him blankets and sheets, and Brian helped cover the corpses. Off-duty and retired firefighters dressed in shorts and flip-flops helped stretch hoses. The fires would go out, but the trauma would remain.

———

During the twelve months following the attack on the World Trade Center, the department made 671 promotions, including 48 chiefs, 71 battalion chiefs, 179 captains, and 331 new lieutenants, of which Brian Davan was one.

Brian's promotion ceremony was held in the MetroTech headquarters' lobby. Traditionally, FDNY holds promotion ceremonies in large halls. Following 9/11, however, instead of one big ceremony, the department held a series of smaller promotional events. Brian was one of only twenty firefighters promoted to lieutenant the day of his ceremony.

Because of the large number of retirements and the loss of life during the attack, assignments for new lieutenants were fast-tracked.

Brian had to wait only a year for his assignment to come through. When it did, he would get his wish. The department sent him to Ladder 28 in Harlem, affectionately known as "the Harlem Hilton." Like Engine 37 where his father worked as a lieutenant, and Engine 59 where Bill Feehan was captain, twenty-seven truck was a busy Harlem company. It was also a legendary firehouse. Over the years, five firefighters from Brian's new firehouse won the department's highest award for bravery, and one, Thomas Neary, won the medal twice. Brian embraced the history of his new unit. As a lieutenant he now sat in the cab of the truck with the chauffeur, and when he would climb into the rig he was both proud and felt the responsibility of occupying the same seat that Neary once did.

As a lieutenant, Brian's role changed again. Most of the time, the lieutenant in a ladder company is the first through the door at a fire in a building. His job is to find the seat of the fire. Today, inside teams are equipped with thermal imaging cameras, but not so in Brian's time. Instead, he'd stop breathing through his mask so he could listen for a crackle, or feel for the heat on the walls and doors with his hands. Then if they had to force the apartment door they would. The object was to get to the origin of the fire as quickly as possible. He would then communicate the fire's location to the engine company. There are times when entry into the apartment or room is impossible, however, when fire "meets the fire officer at the door," as the expression goes. In those instances, they have to wait for the engine company to beat back the flames.

One night in Harlem, Brian's company responded to one such fire, where the flames had reached the doorway. But on this occasion, Brian already had a good idea of how the fire had started, and even had a rough plan to evacuate the occupants of the building. A week earlier, the engine company in his firehouse had responded to an EMS call in the same building. Often the fire department goes on serious medical calls—someone in cardiac arrest, for instance— because their response time is quicker than EMS. The person in distress was in an apartment that caught the attention of the lieutenant from engine company. With ten people crammed together in the same living space, without heat or electricity, it was obvious to him that the occupants were squatters. Candles burned all over the apartment. After the medical run, when the engine company returned to the firehouse, the lieutenant wrote a memo about the dangerous situation in the apartment and passed it out to all the other companies. When Brian read it, he took a ride to the building and familiarized himself with the interior. The following week, on Super Bowl Sunday night, a call came in for a fire at the very same apartment. When Ladder 28 turned onto the block, Brian could see flames shooting from at least three windows on the fourth floor. Though there was no way he could enter the apartment, he knew the layout inside the building and was able to help facilitate the rescue operation. The fire would grow to three alarms and extend to three floors. The squatters had left as soon as the fire started. But Ladder 28, and Ladder 30 that also responded, were able to safely remove the occupants from adjacent apartments and the apartments above the fire. The department awarded citations to two ladder companies and an engine company for the heroic work they did that night.

Brian liked being a lieutenant. He was a natural leader and had a great rapport with the men in his company. Three times a week they would conduct building inspections in their first due response area. Not only would they check the buildings for hazards, but they would go over strategy in case they had to respond to a fire at the location.

One day, they were out on a building inspection run near St.

Nicholas Park, not too far from the firehouse. In our country's formative years, Harlem was mostly farmland, and a house built just after the Revolutionary War still stood in the park. Though now a museum and National Monument, the house, called Hamilton Grange, was the summer residence of Alexander Hamilton. In front of the famous structure, Brian asked the firefighters if they knew anything about Hamilton. "He's the guy on the ten-dollar bill," came the lone, uninterested response. Now, in all fairness, this was years before Lin-Manuel Miranda and the popularity of *Hamilton* the musical. And some of the guys knew more about Hamilton than they were letting on, but they didn't seem too enthused about the subject. Brian, on the other hand, is an American history enthusiast, and had just finished reading Ron Chernow's Hamilton biography. He began to deliver an impromptu lecture about the American statesman to his company. He told them how Hamilton was George Washington's right-hand man during the Revolution, that he had founded the national bank and secured the nation's finances after the costly war against Britain. He told them that he was the first secretary of the treasury and the father of the Coast Guard. But it was only when he told them that Hamilton died in a duel with Aaron Burr, the sitting vice president of the United States, that he had their full attention. They wanted to know every detail about the gun fight, which Brian was happy to relay. He was so involved in his presentation that he didn't notice the tour guide of the museum standing behind him.

"You should have my job," the man told him.

———

Lieutenant Davan would spend five years in the busy house in Harlem, all the while studying for the captain's exam. In 2007, he was promoted and would carry the bag at that rank of captain for six long years, covering assignments while he waited for a permanent spot. "I was like Aaron Burr," he says, "a man without a country." Finally, he found a home in Ladder Company 147, "Da Pride of Flatbush," one of Brooklyn's busiest companies. While waiting for the assignment, he also studied for and took the battalion chief test and was on the list for appointment. All those years before, in a Rockaway bungalow, Betty had made it clear that she expected Brian to climb the ladder. No doubt she would have been thrilled with how her son-in-law's career turned out.

By then, Brian's father was in his nineties and wheelchair-bound. Each time they'd meet, Bob would ask his son if there was any news about the battalion chief list. He wanted to live to see Brian promoted. When the day finally came, Bob sat in his wheelchair in the fourth row of the Christian Cultural Center's auditorium in Brooklyn. He watched his son take the oath and salute the fire commissioner and department chief. After the ceremony, Brian went into the audience and hugged his father.

"I outrank you now," he whispered to his dad.

It was then that he noticed the tears in his father's eyes.

———

When the department promoted Brian to battalion chief, Connor was attending Siena College, a Franciscan school outside of Albany, New York. There he took courses in political science. His major at school, however, was a fallback plan at best. He will tell you that the decision to become a firefighter was solely his own, that he was drawn to the job by its noble mission. He'll say he always felt the need to help people and always admired those who committed their life's work to the service of others. All of that is undoubtedly true, but given his lineage, the job, it seems, was imprinted in his DNA. He took the written portion of the FDNY's entrance exam during spring break of his freshman year in 2012. The test that year would turn out to be a watershed moment for the FDNY.

————

The short history leading up to the groundbreaking test begins in 2002. It was then that the Vulcan Society filed a federal discrimination complaint against the fire department's hiring practices. The Vulcan's complaint alleged the department's bias was decades old and went deeper than just the examination procedure. The Vulcans believed the department's background checks, which were sometimes performed by firefighters on "light duty" because of injuries and other reasons, were biased against Blacks. They also thought that recruitment efforts purposely excluded minorities, and that workplace discrimination complaints were dismissed unfairly. The pressure on the department grew further in 2007 when the U.S. Justice Department sued the fire department, saying that the entrance exam discriminated against Blacks and Hispanics. The Vulcans then joined the suit with the Justice Department. In 2010, a federal judge found that the exam was biased and violated civil rights, calling the FDNY a "stubborn bastion of white male privilege." The city agreed to pay $98 million to settle the suit and the test was updated.

In the months before the 2012 exam, Vulcan firefighters began a social media campaign, and canvassed inner-city shopping centers and Black churches looking for candidates. It wasn't the easiest sell to the Black community. Black people and the New York City Fire Department have shared an unamiable history since the Draft Riots.

Despite the anger toward the FDNY held by the Black community, the Vulcan outreach worked. Of the 42,000 people who took the 2012 test, nearly 20,000 were minorities, and 2,000 were women. Almost 40 percent of the 9,400 who passed were women, people of color, or both. Over 40 percent of the 294 probationary firefighters who graduated with Connor were people of color. For women, however, the numbers weren't nearly as dramatic, which was nothing new.

The first New York City Fire Department entrance exam that allowed women to participate came in 1977. But the department opened the exam to women after Title VII of the 1964 Civil Rights Act, which prevented discrimination based on race or gender, was finally enacted. The FDNY acquiesced under pressure from the federal government—they weren't about to let the feds change their culture. They altered the requirements of the physical test that year to the hardest ever given by the department. Much of the physical exam centered on upper-body strength. The contention was that a firefighter would have to be able to carry a two-hundred-pound person out of a fire, not to drag as Gary Muhrcke, the winner of the Empire State Building race, had argued. The so-called requirement was false on its face. Firefighters mostly fight fires on their knees. When they come upon someone trapped or in distress in a fire, they pull them out. With the exception of ladder rescues, and other rare situations, carrying a fire victim over the shoulder happens only in the movies. The test also overlooked assets that women possess and most men don't. Smaller bone structure means women can climb into places that men wouldn't fit. Because their lungs are smaller, women can also last longer on an oxygen tank. Ninety women, including Brenda Berkman, a third-year law student at NYU, went on to take the physical portion of the test. At the time, Berkman was a marathon runner. Still, she, and the other eighty-nine female participants, failed the physical portion. Berkman decided to sue the city and the fire department. Things became ugly when she did. She received countless death threats over the phone. Vile quotes from firemen filled local newspaper stories. When a federal judge decided the test was unfair to women, ordered a new one, and said that up to forty-five female applicants qualified for the job, Berkman's situation became markedly worse. When the judge ordered the designation "fireman" changed to "firefighter" lines were drawn.

Along with ten other pioneers, Brenda Berkman entered the department in November 1982, only to face physical, sexual, and emotional abuse. In one firehouse, an antiharassment memo was stabbed to a bulletin board with a knife. Berkman remembers firemen in her firehouse not letting her eat with them at the table. They wouldn't cook for her, or buy food for her. In the documentary *Taking the Heat: The First Women Firefighters of New York City*, one of the pioneers recalled a story of her company answering a call at large, active fire. As she approached the burning building, she switched on her oxygen supply, only to realize someone had emptied it. Because her tank was empty, she didn't go into the building, and later a superior reprimanded her for shirking her duty. In 1983, Berkman was fired for supposedly not being able to handle the physical part of the job. When she left her firehouse that day, the men she'd worked with applauded. She would sue to get her job back, and was reinstated a year later, in 1983. Not too long after, she was sexually abused by a fire department doctor. Other female firefighters came forward with the same complaint. The department eventually brought charges against the doctor, but the only penalty he paid was losing his job.

In 1994, the fire department promoted Berkman to lieutenant. Since then, she's become both a national spokesperson for female firefighters and a target of the anger and resentment that many male firefighters still hold. She was off the morning of 9/11, and five firefighters from her firehouse died in the collapse of the World Trade Center. Like thousands of other members of the FDNY, she raced to the towers that morning and would spend weeks upon weeks on the pile as part of the rescue, then recovery, effort. In some quarters, however, the fact that no female fighters were killed in the terrorist attack in New York was twisted into a lack of courage by them. Berkman once again became a lightning rod for the anger that comes from bias and small-mindedness. In 2002, the department promoted her to captain, a rank she would retire at four years later. As of this writing, she remains active in empowering women, and is on the board of Monumental Women, an organization that helps honor women and people of color in public spaces.

Though two thousand women took the 2012 test, only five would graduate in the November 2016 academy class. Many who had passed the test just couldn't wait four years to start a career. Others failed medical or background checks. The five graduates brought the total number of female fighters in the FDNY to fifty-eight in a department with over ten thousand uniformed employees, the lowest male-to-female ratio of any major fire department in the country.

———

Connor scored a 94 on the exam, and the department added a bonus of five points for his being a New York City resident. A 99 placed him high on the list for an appointment. For most prospective firefighters, taking and passing the test and becoming a firefighter can be an excruciating wait. With the exception of the period right after 9/11, attrition by retirement in the fire department totals only about fifty firefighters a year. The list for an appointment is long. For

Connor, however, who spent the time finishing up college, the wait wasn't all that bad.

Along with his studies, he played club rugby during his four years at Siena. He made a bunch of friends and experienced the usual college antics of keg parties, spring break, and summers at the beach. In the middle of his junior year, he and the Feehan family attended the christening of the *William M. Feehan*, a brand-new sixty-six-foot fireboat. The boat builders forged the fireboat's nameplates, displayed on both sides of the wheelhouse, from steel I-beams that came from the World Trade Center.

As if it were in the cards all the time, the fire department personnel office called Connor toward the end of his senior year. The official from headquarters said they were getting close to his appointment number and asked if he was still considering becoming a New York City firefighter. The question was procedural. The answer was preordained. The young man with shoulders broadened by rugby and a handsome, easy smile was about to step into the family business.

He entered the fire academy in June 2016 and spent four grueling months at the fire academy. With his head shaved and under constant berating by fire department drill instructors, it was almost like being a Marine recruit on Parris Island.

In the years after the terrorist attack on the World Trade Center, the fire department had completed the $50 million upgrade at the training facility. Some of the improvements included a "burn building," a three-story brick structure where fire simulations are conducted, a subway simulator, and an airplane hangar–sized structure complete with a full-scale city street scene. Academy training included enhanced response techniques to biological, radiological, and other events of mass destruction. Since the terrorist attack,

FDNY hazardous material companies had tripled in size. Firefighters now carry meters that detect alpha rays, gamma rays, and biological weapons. Protocols are now in place for responding terrorist attacks such as the London and Madrid subway and train bombings. Connor also trained for shooter scenes such as the recent ones in Las Vegas, the Pulse nightclub in Orlando, and Parkland, Florida. Instructors teach them to enter an active shooter situation with a police escort to administer essential life support and first aid and remove victims from harm's way. Bulletproof helmets and vests are now part of firefighters' equipment.

Some things in the department, however, remain just as they've always been. Connor was assigned to Engine 231. He knew the firehouse well. Growing up, he had gone there with his dad for fire company picnics, softball games, and the annual Christmas party. He received official word that he was going to his dad's old firehouse a few days before he graduated. The assignment wasn't exactly a surprise.

Very often, a firefighter's first firehouse dictates the direction of his or her career. If the department sends you from the academy to a camp, as Chief Feehan called a slow firehouse, you can spend years there and not learn what a proby in a busy house experiences in a month. Brian wasn't going to let that happen to his son. In that paradoxical way of thinking formed by years in the fire service, the elder Davan wanted his son as busy as possible so he could accumulate experience to use when he needed it. Brian put together a list of firehouses he thought would be suitable, and then discussed the possibilities with Connor. By then, Brian was a respected battalion chief in Battalion 19, which covers the busiest area in the Bronx, and had his own influence in the department. They decided, to no one's surprise, on Engine 231 in Brownsville.

On November 1, 2016, academy instructors sent Connor and two other recruits from his class to their new firehouse to meet with the captain, officers, and firefighters with whom they'd be working. The Watkins Street firehouse is called a "legacy house," and is known colloquially as "the House of the Rising Son." When Connor was assigned there, the Davans became the firehouse's twentieth father-and-son combination. There were firefighters in Watkins Street who'd worked there with his dad. One of them was Will Hickey. Hickey knew Brian Davan most of his life—they played softball together in Rockaway. As fate would have it, Connor's first day at the Watkins Street firehouse was Hickey's last. He'd been promoted to lieutenant and assigned elsewhere.

When Connor and the other recruits were at the firehouse for the meet-and-greet, dispatch called Engine 231 to respond to a multiple-alarm fire in Queens. Before he knew it, Connor and the other probys were on the rig headed to the fire. They wouldn't find themselves face-to-face with the red devil, but they would, still dressed in their Class A's, stretch hose lines on the Queens street. Heading back to the firehouse, Connor had to believe that fire action for him would come fast and furious. As it turned out, however, he would have to wait a while to feel the heat from a fire on his face.

————

The Brownsville neighborhood that surrounds the Watkins Street firehouse is not the Brooklyn you might have heard of or seen in movies or TV, the one filled with battery-powered scooters and oat milk lattes. In just a one-square-mile section, there are eighteen city-owned low-income housing projects in which twenty thousand people live. It's the densest concentration of public housing in the country. Good people live in the neighborhood's projects and tenements. They do so, however, in a community that has led the city in violent crime longer than most of them can remember. It's only getting worse. Deadly shootings have skyrocketed since the early days of the COVID-19 pandemic. Fire and crime are natural companions.

Connor just missed a major fire soon after he arrived at Watkins Street. It was a clear, crisp December morning when the call came in, just minutes before Connor started his tour. Fifteen minutes later, he would have been the nozzleman. Instead, it was a proby with whom he'd graduated the academy who had the nozzle that day. The fire was in a housing project just down the block from the firehouse. With some other members of the oncoming crew, Connor ran after the rig. The blaze had fully engulfed the apartment. He could see the flames blowing out the windows on the thirteenth floor. "It was like a holy crap moment," the young firefighter said. The blaze that day would kill three people, including a one-year-old baby. Ladder 120, quartered with Engine 231, won medals for saving six from the burning apartment.

Connor would go his entire probationary period, eighteen long months, without being assigned the nozzle. And it wasn't as though business in the House of the Rising Son was slow, in fact, Engine 231 was one of the most active in the city. But the luck of the draw, if you want to call it that, hadn't been with Connor. Finally, his moment came.

———

The young firefighter looped the fifty-foot fold of inch-and-three-quarter hose over his arm and headed toward the tenement building.

"Come on, come on," Lieutenant Early yelled.

The fire officer's voice was calm, but there was no doubting the urgency it contained. The fire, in a third-floor apartment in the walk-up, had started in a bedroom and was gaining intensity.

Connor stretched the line up to the third-floor landing. Down the hall, the smoke was a thick black curtain. Visibility near zero. He masked up with the facepiece of his Scott Air-Pak and followed his lieutenant. The twenty-five-year-old firefighter could feel his heart beating in his chest.

The door in the narrow hallway led directly into the bedroom, which was the first stroke of luck for Connor and his company. The ladder company had already forced the door with "the irons"—the Halligan tool—and an ax.

"Okay, let's go," the lieutenant said. The fire officer led the way into the room.

Connor couldn't see anything. The lieutenant acted as his eyes and ears. He could feel firefighters moving past him, fast, their radios crackling. The blaze in the bedroom had self-ventilated, meaning the intense heat had blown out the windowpanes. This reduced the temperature somewhat, the second stroke of luck. Still, it was hot. Real hot. Behind his mask, sweat burned his eyes. Had the room not ventilated, he would have had to duckwalk or even crawl to stay under the smoke and heat. "Lay low and let it blow" is an expression you might hear a nozzleman say. Connor made his way around a couch or a chair, he couldn't tell. Children's toys were strewn about the floor. Often with fires like this one, the nozzleman can't even see the flames.

"Deeper," the officer said. "You gotta get deeper."

When Connor was in position, the lieutenant radioed to the chauffeur on the rig to charge the line. The chauffeur set the pressure and radioed back the officer. "Okay, here comes your water," he said.

The line filled and stiffened. What had been a flat length of woven polyester with a polyurethane lining became a living, breathing 250-foot snake. The water pressure needs to be right. Too little, and the fire has the upper hand; too much, and the nozzleman becomes a Saturday morning cartoon character wrestling the hose for control. He bled the air from the line, then closed the valve. In reality, the time it takes the water to make it from the source through the line to the nozzles is a matter of seconds. For Connor, however, the flow of water through the hose traveled the better part of a century, starting back when his great-grandfather, William P. Feehan, fought his first fire.

In the apartment, Connor pointed the gushing hose where Lieutenant Early told him to. The fire went out fairly quickly, but he was so amped up, the lieutenant had to tell him to cut the water. Outside on the street, Early told him he did a good job. Firefighters are not known for gushing praise. His company knew it was his first time on the nozzle—they all knew how much the moment means to any firefighter. That silent understanding is what bonds them as brothers and sisters.

Back in the firehouse, Connor climbed the stairs to the quarters and looked, as he always did, at the 9/11 memorial on the wall of the staircase. The first photo he sees is of his grandfather William M. Feehan. Sometimes the photo reminds him of fireboat rides in the New York Harbor and Hot Wheels fire trucks in Pop-pop's rollup desk. But on this day, it reminded him of the family tradition he carries.

For ninety-five years and counting, the Feehans and Davans have fought fire and lived lives of quiet heroism.

# Epilogue

In early July 2020, some of the Davan and Feehan clan met in Breezy for dinner at Kennedy's. With COVID-19 restrictions, they sat at a table outside at the rear of the restaurant. Kennedy's is on the bay side of Breezy, with one of the most spectacular views in all of New York City. On a clear evening, which this one was, you can see the famous parachute drop across the bay in Coney Island. Farther in the distance, you can see the top of the Verrazano Bridge and the northern shoreline of Staten Island. You can even see as far as the shipping docks on New Jersey's northern coast. But the marquee attraction is the view of the Manhattan skyline. Backlit by a pastel-colored sunset, on this evening One World Trade Center gleams.

A short stroll from Kennedy's is Suffolk Walk, the block on which Bill and Betty's bungalow sat. In October 2012, Hurricane Sandy nearly destroyed the original beach house. Wind and water weren't the only agents of destruction in Breezy that night. A six-alarm fire burned blocks of Breezy Point during the storm. Seawater caused an electrical spark in one home, and hurricane-force winds blew the fire from house to house like a match lighting candles on a birthday cake. Because of flooding in the streets, the fire department apparatus couldn't get near enough to fight the blazes. The fire went to six alarms and burned for six hours. It reduced more than a hundred homes, blocks and blocks of them, to charred rubble. Firefighters who had survived the World Trade Center attack owned some of the houses. To add insult to injury, floodwaters from Sandy filled the 9/11 museum in lower Manhattan, completely covering the remains of Ladder 3's rig.

———

On December 3, 2020, Tom Von Essen looked out the window of a FEMA conference room on One World Trade Center's fifty-second floor. The replacement of the Twin Towers is a marvel of engineering, and soars 1,776 feet high. Von Essen's view of the city's harbor is spectacular. The day was clear and crisp. Ships and ferries leave long, graceful wakes that meander around a figurine-sized Statue of Liberty.

Then, Von Essen headed the New York office for FEMA Region 2, which covers New York, New Jersey, the Virgin Islands, and Puerto Rico. He spent a lot of time in the latter after Hurricane Maria. A retired fire captain named Mike Byrne offered him the FEMA job in 2017. Byrne runs the federal response and recovery support in Puerto Rico for the federal agency. When Von Essen heard that his office would be in the new World Trade Center, he recoiled. Fifty-two floors below sit the twin towers' footprints, now one-acre-sized reflecting pools and part of the 9/11 memorial. Just to the pools' right is West Street, and across the busy thoroughfare is the loading dock for the Merrill Lynch/American Express building. How could he take the job? he thought. How could he sit high above such hallowed ground? How could he endure the constant reminder of the unimaginable grief he shared with so many?

Von Essen is a likable man. It's easy to see why he was elected the firefighters' union president before Mayor Giuliani appointed him as fire commissioner. He owns a cynical, self-deprecating humor, which tries but cannot conceal a sharp intellect. Though he is seventy-five, his quick smile and a ruddy face belie his years. There is a sadness to him, though. An invisible weight he seems to carry.

Though FEMA has the whole floor, and the one above, only a handful of people sit at the hundreds of cubicles that line the open office. The second or third surge of COVID-19 has invaded the city, and just about everyone who can is working remotely. Von Essen will leave FEMA at the end of the month. Surrounded by an empty office, he seems wistful as the conclusion of his working life approaches. When he talks about the darkest day in the New York City Fire Department's history one can almost see the weight of grief on his back. That load has continued to increase in size.

———

On September 8, 2011, the FDNY unveiled the new memorial plaque in its headquarters dedicated to those firefighters who died from 9/11-related illnesses after working the rescue and recovery effort at the World Trade Center site. Unlike the original line-of-duty death plaque on the opposite wall of headquarters, this one conjugates the Latin phrase for "Rest in Peace" correctly. Fifty-five firefighters were in the inaugural class memorialized on the plaque. Two of those who died from working on the pile are Raymond and Robert Alexander. Bob Alexander was an FDNY marine engineer who helped design the *William M. Feehan*. He'd been a New York City cop at the time of the attack, but then joined the fire department. "When I was hired by the FDNY after September 11," he said at the launch of the *Feehan*, "we knew then that our probationary class was in the shadow of giants."

Across the lobby, twenty-seven names have been added to the original memorial plaque since 9/11.

———

For Chief Feehan the line-of-duty death memorial plaque on the far wall at headquarters was the most important piece of bronze in the city of New York. If not fate, it is certainly appropriate that his name would reside forever among those heroes. Though made of inanimate metal, the plaque expands in size and importance with each line-of-duty death. In a speech he gave in 1991, Bill Feehan said:

> We've had 127 years of a paid fire department in New York City, and in that 127 years we've lost 752 people. That's an awfully large number and...I think we all have the same wish that we'll never lose another. But I know, as sure as I'm sitting here, that no matter what we do, no matter how well we train, no matter how good our equipment is, no matter how hard we try...no matter what, there'll be a 753rd.

On April, 24, 2022, Firefighter Timothy Klein was killed when a ceiling collapsed during a fire in Canarsie, Brooklyn. Klein grew up in Belle Harbor. Connor went to grammar and high school with him. Brian knew his father, Patrick Klein, a retired firefighter, his whole life. Timothy Klein was the 1,157th to die in the line-of-duty. Without question, there will be a 1,158th.

———

Back at Kennedy's, Brian and Connor were wearing Breezy Point's official summer uniform—shorts and Ray-Ban sunglasses. At the table, they swapped fire stories, as the family leaned in to listen. Connor now owns the easygoing confidence of a five-year engine company veteran. He is also a young man with his whole life in front of him. After dinner, he was heading to the New Jersey shore to meet some of his friends from college. As a twenty-six-year-old and single, some fun might have awaited him there. He might as well take advantage. They'll be plenty of fires ahead to fight. For the Davans and Feehans, there always are.

# Acknowledgments

Much of the first draft of this book was written in a pandemic lock-down. In those scary, first-wave days of COVID-19 in New York City, the sound of sirens outside my window was constant, as was the ritual of banging of pots and pans each evening to thank those on COVID's frontlines. In an upside-down way, I'm grateful that this project came to me when it did, for it gave me an even deeper appreciation for those who set aside risk in the service of others.

A gratitude list for the people who helped make this book possible begins, of course, with the extended Feehan and Davan families. Thank you for trusting me with your stories. I would especially like to thank Beth Feehan's indefatigable advocacy for the Feehan family story. Others who provided me with essential help include but are not limited to Firefighter Jack Sweeney (ret.) for his invaluable insight, writer Kiley Bense for newspaper archive and genealogical research, Deputy Commissioner Thomas Fitzpatrick (ret.) for his voluminous knowledge of the FDNY (especially its operations), legendary fire expert Deputy Chief Vincent Dunn (ret.), Firefighter Donald Blaskovich (ret.), author and retired Rescue 1 firefighter Paul Hashagen, unofficial expert on Breezy Point, Mark Zunic, Brian Manning, Catherine Cole, and Kelly McLees for all her support. Thank you one and all.

The FDNY, especially Frank Dwyer, Deputy Commissioner,

## Acknowledgments

Public Information and External Affairs, and Lisa DeFazio, Assistant to the Fire Commissioner, was especially gracious.

I would like to thank Executive Editor Suzanne O'Neill, for her steady hand and practiced eye. I am also much obliged to Assistant Editor Jacqueline Young, Bob Castillo, and the rest of the crew at Grand Central Publishing. Special thanks to my agent, Richard Abate. Thank you for all your help.

Finally, this list would not be complete without a nod to the men and women, past and present, of the FDNY. We all owe you a debt of gratitude.

# Index

# About the Author

Brian McDonald is the author of six books including *My Father's Gun, Last Call at Elaine's,* and *Death Need Not Be Fatal,* which he co-wrote with Malachy McCourt. He lives in New York City.